The Home Office Book

How To Set Up And Use An Efficient Personal Workspace In The Computer Age

Mark Alvarez

Illustrations by
Vanna Prince and Mel Mathewson

Goodwood Press
1990

Copyright © 1990 by Mark Alvarez

Published by Goodwood Press, Woodbury, Connecticut

All rights reserved under International and Pan-American Copyright Conventions.

Except for brief quotations in reviews, this book, or parts thereof, must not be reproduced, stored in a retrieval system or transmitted in any form or by any means, electronic, mechanical, photocopying, recording or otherwise, without permission in writing from the publisher.

ISBN 0-9625427-9-2 (paper)
ISBN 0-9625427-8-4 (cloth)

Printed and manufactured in the United States of America

For Holly and Hilary

without whom I wouldn't have a home worth putting an office in.

Contents

CHAPTER 1: WHY DO YOU NEED THIS BOOK?   **1**

    Computers and electronic equipment have changed the way we need to look at modern home offices. Real choices for real people. The focus on efficiency, flexibility and utility.

CHAPTER 2: FINDING A SPACE   **3**

    An environment to let you use your modern electronic tools efficiently. Negotiating for privacy: it doesn't have to be spatial. Priorities: yours and those of others you live with. Boundaries: physical and symbolic. Bigger is Better. Wall spaces: basic for apartments. Nooks and crannies: some are obvious, some you have to think about. Converting rooms from other purposes. Careful, the cook may want that pantry! Bad Space: can you really be comfortable here? Big Moves: expensive remodels or additions.

CHAPTER 3: FURNITURE   **19**

    Four basic office needs. A simple definition of ergonomics. Choosing a good chair: don't go cheap. The dreaded chair mat. Computer racks, carts and cabinets. Modular desks. The wonders of adjustable tables. Think hard before building-in. Storage. Suit yourself.

viii   Contents

> *Box:* You can save a lot of workspace by tucking your computer out of the way.   37

CHAPTER 4: COMPUTER HARDWARE   47

The *real* home computer is the home *office* computer. Mac or IBM-style? Computer terminology and configurations: speed, memory, storage, ports and cables, monitors, power supplies and keyboard concerns. IBM clones, package deals and portables. From Mac Plus to Mac II. Buying your computer: retail store or mail order? Finding a guru.

> *Box:* Speed doesn't kill but it does make you crazy.   54
> *Box:* Why buy a clone?   57
> *Box:* OS/2, PS/2, MCA, EISA: what do all these initials mean?   61
> *Box:* Eight tips on buying your computer.   77

CHAPTER 5: COMPUTER SOFTWARE   84

When the choice is obvious. What to do when it isn't. Inexpensive integrated packages. Choosing individual packages. Ease of learning, ease of use. Can you get help once you've bought? Word Processing. Spreadsheets. Databases. Communications packages. Desktop Publishing. Pop-up programs. Personal information managers. Help with connections and conversions. Shells. Utilities. Backup programs. Buying software.

> *Box:* Software viruses.   88
> *Box:* Shareware: good software, cheap.   95
> *Box:* Pirating and copy protection.   102
> *Box:* On-line services.   107
> *Box: HyperCard*: nifty, hard to explain.   118
> *Box:* The importance of backing up your hard disk.   125

CHAPTER 6: COMPUTER PERIPHERALS   129

Printers. The obsolete daisywheel. The dominant dot-matrix. The amazing laser. Paper handling, noise, speed, type quality, size and weight. A few laser drawbacks. Modems: the keys to electronic communication. Scanners: "printers in reverse." Surge protectors and back-up power supplies.

Box: PostScript™: the wonderful page description language many covet but most don't need.   141

CHAPTER 7: ELECTRONIC EQUIPMENT   152

Phones, headsets, fax machines, fax boards and personal copiers. Everything you wanted to know and then some. Info and opinions on features, variations, drawbacks, integration and cost. The Principle of Obsolescent Technology: don't get sliced by the cutting edge.

Box: Should you buy special features built into your phone or order services like TotalPhone from the phone company?   155
Box: Phone strategies: ideas on setting up two- or three-line systems.   159
Box: AT&T Readyline: An 800 number that works over your current phone line.   164

CHAPTER 8: DESIGNING YOUR HOME OFFICE 185

An exercise in pleasing yourself. Analyzing your body, your habits, your work, your disabilities. Standards. Working up your "program." Basic office plans: the strip, the L, the galley, the U. Drawing scaled plans. Using cutouts. Walk-throughs.

Box: What if you have clients?   191
Box: Finding more space in your space.   197

CHAPTER 9: LIGHTING 203

Vital but often ignored. Avoiding glare: "lighting is angles." Ambient, task and natural light.

Box: Electrical concerns. Dedicated lines and wiring runs. 205

CHAPTER 10: USING YOUR SPACE 213

Discipline and the rhythms of work. Developing a ritual. Dealing with distractions. Fear and the importance of stress. Working too hard. Solitude and loneliness. Regulations concerning working at home. Taxes: get an accountant. Insurance: you're not covered. Projecting an image. Solo efficiency. Health.

Box: Here's Looking At You, Kid—A lesson in perspective and patience. 219

BUYERS' GUIDE 235

Including hundreds of listings, addresses and phone numbers for: furniture, mail order supplies, computers, replacement keyboards, expanded memory boards, tape backup drives, software, on-line services, printers, postscript boards, modems, scanners, surge suppressors, emergency power supplies, telephones, answering machines, headsets, voice mail, fax units, fax boards, personal copiers, business organizers, and organizations of interest to home workers.

Computers	235
Portable computers	238
Computer keyboards	240
Expanded memory boards	240
Tape backup systems	241
Personal copiers	242
Surge suppressors and emergency power supplies	242
Facsimile machines	244

Fax boards 245
Furniture 247
Mail order supplies 252
On-line services 254
Organizers 256
Organizations 256
Telephones and answering machines 257
Telephone headsets 258
Voice mail 259
Modems 259
Printers 261
PostScript™ boards 263
Scanners 264
Software 266

INDEX **273**

The obligatory disclaimer

Technology changes fast. This fact is the great bugaboo for anyone trying to provide accurate information on a timely topic. Luckily, I have been able to make adjustments to my manuscript much later than most authors are allowed to, so I was able to keep up with the lion's share of this evolution.

Nonetheless, some of the specific information in this book will inevitably have become inaccurate by the time you read it. Some companies will have changed their names or been bought out. Some products will have been renamed or superseded. Many prices will have risen or dropped.

Fortunately, you'll still have the information you need to make proper choices.

- In the first place, most names and numbers will still be valid in 1990-91.
- In the second place, the Buyers' Guide will give you the names and addresses you'll need to get up-to-date information from most of the major suppliers of hardware, software, other electronic equipment, furniture and supplies of all kinds.
- Most important of all, you'll have a common-sense method for putting together your home office based on keeping things simple, carefully assessing your own needs—and then pleasing yourself.

The Home Office Book

1

Why Do You Need This Book?

This is a book about the choices real people have to make when they want to set up an office of their own at home.

Check that sentence again. A few years ago, the idea of a book that began that way would have been ridiculous. I can hear myself now: "Are you kidding? Who needs a book to tell you to lay a hollow-core door across a pair of file cabinets and buy a typing stand?"

But home offices have changed.

- The personal computer and its electronic brethren have touched off a revolution that gives you or me sitting at home a range of capabilities that until recently was available only to the largest corporations with the biggest staffs. A lot of us have already taken advantage of that power, and the flexibility it grants us to work—at least part of the time—in our own homes rather than in big offices at the other end of long and unpleasant commutes. Many more of us are dreaming about following suit.
- But setting up an office centered on the special capabilities of a personal computer and equipment like advanced phone sys-

tems, answering devices, photocopiers and fax machines requires a whole new approach to personal work space.
- This doesn't mean letting our amazing new machines run us. Just the opposite, in fact. At bottom, these remarkable gizmos are really just tools. They are valuable to us in exact proportion to the degree to which they can be used like all good tools: simply, directly and as extensions of us rather than the other way around.

The point of this book is to help you do just that.

Besides putting together a few home offices of my own, I've covered other peoples' home office projects as a magazine writer, and I've helped dozens of friends, acquaintances and colleagues who operate out of their houses. I've seen some awful workspaces—poorly planned or stupidly concerned with style over substance—and I've seen some great ones, which display a common, fundamental concern for efficiency, flexibility and utility. My real favorites add economy to that short list.

These are the elements this book concentrates on. It passes along hard-won, *practical* information and advice on everything from finding the proper space, through furnishing and equipping it, to tailoring it to your own needs and then dealing with the considerable stresses of functioning solo.

Now, although they have elements in common, good home offices don't all look alike. Most of us aren't able to carve out absolutely perfect spaces or to afford every electronic helpmate we could use. Virtually all of us operate within limits—financial, spatial or both. The book suggests compromises and alternatives—options I've seen or used that save space or money or time or aggravation. It doesn't attempt to give you an all-purpose blueprint, because we all operate in our own particular circumstances.

And that's the key point. Your home office is, after all, *yours*. This is a personal book about personal choices. Don't think of it as an arbiter or final authority, but as a friend whose brain you can pick for information and advice—some of it quirky but all of it real—that has worked elsewhere. Weigh what you read. Think about how it applies to your personal circumstances.

Then do what you want—it's *your* office.

2

Finding A Space

The first problem we all have to solve when we decide to establish a home office is where to put it. This can be a pretty tough question to answer, and it's one that is all too often answered wrong.

Because I got paid for years partly to travel all over the country looking at houses, I've had a chance to poke around dozens of home offices. Some of their locations were standard, some were brilliant, some were bizarre. A few were grotesque. All were food for thought. Before getting into particulars, though, there are a few generalities that I think are important to consider when you're trying to figure out where to put your home office.

YOU'RE IT

First, and most general, in a modern home office, with its computer and other electronic devices—you are executive, secretary, mailroom clerk, receptionist and custodian all rolled into one. You'll be using a whole range of tools to perform all kinds of jobs. Your home office itself is not, despite frequent repetitions of the phrase in national magazines, "a tool of the trade," any more than a stadium is a baseball bat. It's an *environment*—one that should help you use your tools conveniently to get all those jobs done smoothly. This fact leads naturally to the next basic point.

A ROOM (OR AT LEAST AN AREA) OF ONE'S OWN

Good work requires concentration, so to the extent that it's possible, your home office should provide privacy, both spatial and acoustic. In many homes, this privacy can only be symbolic, and often it has to be guarded by rules and clocks rather than walls or doors. Sometimes a simple rug on the floor can mark the limits of your office. Sometimes a plant or a low table can do the trick. Sometimes an arrangement of light can suggest a separate space. But try your hardest to find a location where you'll be able to establish some barrier, even if it's only implied or psychological, between you in your work space and others outside of it.

SPACE, AND MORE SPACE

Finally, you'll *always* need more room than you think, and you'll always fill up whatever space you've got. For almost four years after I started working at home full time, I operated out of an eight-by-twelve foot nook off our house's dining room. It held fourteen linear feet of cheap but carefully planned work surface, two file cabinets, a four-drawer telephone stand and yards of bookshelf. Not bad at all for a home office. And yet, I was quickly overrun.

My computer took up two feet of desk space. So did my printer. Eventually a photocopier expropriated almost three. Trays for active files sprouted on the desktop. Bulk cartons of stationery, manila envelopes, Federal Express mailers, copier cartridges, computer paper, and strapping tape piled up under the desk. Dead files and completed projects filled storage boxes piled up between an overflowing lateral file and a groaning bookcase. And this was with everything squared away and ship shape—the odd weekend afternoon, maybe, or right after we'd spent a week in the mountains and I hadn't had a chance to mess things up. Normally, notes, clippings, books, magazines and discarded drafts covered every surface in great, unstable heaps that occasionally cascaded gracefully to the floor to join the other mounds that I had carefully tossed there over my shoulder. I was inundated.

You're better organized and neater than I am (I say this with little fear of contradiction), but you too will find that your space is nibbled away by the very work you do there—not to mention the fax machine or the scanner or that wonderful new combination phone, answering machine and food processor. And remember that when you work at home, you have no central filing system, no corporate library, no supply closet down the hall, no mailroom in the basement, no maintenance staff. You handle it all. You store it all. Take it as an article of faith: in home offices, *Bigger Is Better*.

So. We're looking for a place where you can establish at least symbolic boundaries, where you can accumulate and efficiently use the necessary technology, where you can do all your work and where you might even feel comfortable about leaving it in progress. I've broken the possibilities down into a few types. There's obviously going to be some overlap in my classifications—a wall office could conceivably be a nook, a nook could be a conversion, a conversion could be a wall office and Bad Space can be found anywhere. Don't get hung up on my sub-headings. They're just a convenient form of organization. Now let's see what we can find.

UP AGAINST THE WALL

The most common arrangement is simply laying a workspace out along a wall, usually in the living room or bedroom. You've probably seen set-ups like this—maybe you even have one. The room retains its original function, but one edge is given over to the home office. This is an especially common solution in apartments, where there's simply no other room to squeeze out of the place. I had a living room wall office once, back in those simpler, pre-computer days. It was built around the classic door-across-two-file-cabinets desk. I loved it because I was just a few steps away from the couch and the easy chair in case I needed to do some serious, ah, contemplation. Of course, I was single then. There was no one else around to distract me or to be annoyed by my clutter—or my snores.

Living rooms

With a roommate or family around, you'll probably have to screen your living room wall office somehow. A simple dressing screen works, if you've got the space. Or you could buy or build work furniture that can close up to hide your equipment and files—a variation on the old roll-top desk.

In theory, if you're very neat with your papers and you're into the high-tech look, you can simply append your office and its electronic equipment to your entertainment center with its stereo and TV. I've seen this suggested, and even illustrated, in magazines, but it strikes me as fundamentally unreal—too many competing functions and too much pressure to be fastidious. Then again, I've met a lot of people who strike me as fundamentally unreal. As always, consider what will work for you.

Screening your office

Of course, if you don't live alone privacy will be a problem with this sort of office. You'll probably be able to suggest the limits of your work area, but you won't be able to build-in quiet, so you'll have to schedule it. Think carefully about how difficult the negotiations are likely to be before you go ahead. Then ponder how realistic you're being about limiting noise. With the best will in the world, family comings and goings disrupt concentration. If the living room wall looks like your best space, *and* you think you can grab enough time between interruptions there, you're in business. But if you feel that traffic flow will be too heavy, keep looking.

Bedrooms

The issues with bedroom wall-offices are similar, but not the same. Bedrooms, for example, are usually smaller than living rooms, so they generally offer less work space. On the other hand, you can usually count on a bit more quiet and solitude there during most of the day, and this can be a decisive advantage to setting up near the bed.

But let's be realistic. The biggest problem with working in the bedroom is that you'll tend to take over the whole space with your paraphernalia. If you share the room with someone, this makes trouble. To most people, the bedroom is a haven—a necessary retreat from the pressures, worries and general untidiness of the outside world. Your mate may have strong feelings about finding the bed lumpy with papers, the floor covered with boxes and the flat surfaces humming with electronics and littered with empty mugs and aging sandwiches. For some amazing people, this problem simply doesn't arise. I have a consultant friend whose office is in the bedroom he shares with his wife. He's set up his transportable computer where his bedside table would ordinarily be, and he has a printer, a phone and a writing surface nearby. Nothing is closed off, nothing is hidden. It's cheap, it's efficient, and it works because both he and his wife are incredibly, compulsively, neat. In my household, a bedroom office would lead to divorce, if not homicide. Know thyself. Know thy mate. This is touchy turf.

Dining rooms and other options

Walls in other rooms can be used as offices, too, of course. The dining room, if you've got one, is an option, but it's less often put to office use than you might think. Even though many families use their formal dining rooms only occasionally, the occasions tend to be special, so they often prefer to keep the rooms free of equipment and clutter. No keyboards under the Thanksgiving turkey, thank you. No printers nudging the birthday cake, if you please. It all depends on how badly you need the space and how ruthless you're willing to be.

Sometimes you can steal space along a hallway. I know of one Japanese-style, shoji-esque office along a hall that's bright and useful.

All too often though, dark and dingy hallways are converted into dark and dingy workspaces. If a hall is all you've got to work with, pay special attention to lighting (see chapter 9). Pay attention to the width of the hall, too, or you may create a tight channel that's uncomfortable for workers and passers-by alike. Recessed built-ins may be a partial solution to this problem, but they can get costly because they will almost certainly require structural modifications. (You can't just eliminate the studs behind the plaster or sheetrock; you've got to install a header to carry the load.)

One of the niftiest wall offices I've seen was laid out along one side of an apartment's foyer, which was perhaps twice as wide as a normal hallway. It was a little strange to be welcomed into someone's home through an office, but the space actually made a lot of sense. The occasional guest passes through, usually at a specific time, but people don't hang around in an entry hall. The family is likely to be at least a wall away even in the evening. And you might even have a door to close between foyer and living area.

Wall Office Advantages:
- You can usually find useful space along a wall somewhere in your home.
- Wall offices can be cheap—we're usually not talking structural renovation here.
- If you live alone or if others are out during the day, you can count on at least a few hours of privacy no matter where you set up, and you may be able to negotiate for more.
- In the bedroom, you can usually find a measure of privacy during the day even if others are at home.
- Oddball locations like a foyer or hallway can also provide relative peace and quiet.

Wall Office Disadvantages:
- Almost none if you live alone—it's your place; you make the rules.
- If you share your living space, you'll probably have to schedule your work-time around other people's timetables.
- You may not be able to leave work in progress without stowing your papers and diskettes.

- The usefulness of your wall office may depend on the consideration and understanding of others—uncertain attributes in many households.

NOOKS AND CRANNIES

I've already mentioned my small office off the dining room. It was the classic nook—a little space out of the main flow of traffic that had no particular competing use. There wasn't really much to think about. We knew as soon as we looked at the house that this would be my office. And if you've got a similar space, you don't need a book to advise you to use it.

Landings

But in some houses there are little corners of unused space here and there that you might not think of as potential offices. In big old houses—or apartments carved out of big old houses—stair landings often offer lots of space and get little traffic. At the top story especially, they often open out into dead-end hallways with plenty of space for furniture and equipment. When I was a little boy, my grandparents lived in an apartment on the top floor of a big old Victorian house. They had a landing just like this outside their door, which they used as storage space for seasonal clothes and my uncle's musical instruments. If an area like this is secure—behind a door to which you have the key—it can make a terrific home office for an apartment dweller, because it's usually outside your living space. You can work there without bothering anyone else in your household, and without being interrupted often yourself.

Under stairs

In a house grand enough to have big landings, you may also be able to find some useful space *under* the first-floor stairway. In many older houses, this area contains closet space or has been converted into a powder room containing a toilet, a sink and not much headroom. The slope of the stairs is a problem for any space you want to use under them, but many people have fitted small offices into this triangle of space. Much of the area too low for sitting and working can be used for storage. And, of course, you can only consider the space in the first place if there isn't a second set of stairs directly beneath the first.

Nook office under the stairs

Lofts

The sweetest and coziest sort of nook is the loft. Everybody seems to like the play-house feel of lofts, and they appear in lots of new houses and condominiums. They are, virtually by definition, up and away from the hustle and bustle of the rest of the living space, which is good. But lofts are open to household noises. This can be good or bad. It's fine if you want to be able to hear the baby cry, but not so hot if you're perched right over the TV.

Many folks who build small, efficient houses plan a loft as a home office right from the start, often with the idea that it can occasionally be used as a guest bedroom as well. And rehabbers often have the same idea in mind—I remember a beautiful new loft tucked under the cathedral ceiling in a remodeled one-room schoolhouse.

My biggest problem with lofts as offices is that access is all too often by ladder. Maybe I've just gotten old and fussy, but I simply don't enjoy climbing the rungs with a briefcase slung across my shoulder, a bag full of books in one hand and a box of printer ribbons in the other. Make two trips? You've got to be kidding!

Another disadvantage is that lofts are where all the heat collects. Without good ventilation, you can wind up 10 or 15 degrees hotter than on first floor level.

In some houses, lofts and stair landings have mated and spawned spaces that are nooks only in the sense that they are apart from the other living areas. Typically, these areas are high in the house—sometimes along an open hallway, sometimes as more confined spaces. The one I remember best was in the home of a builder who had his drafting board and office set up at the top of stairs that wound around a tower-like structure at the core of his house. The space worked just the way he'd designed it to. It was bright and cheerful because of the sunshine pouring through big windows up there. It was peaceful because he was well away from the rest of the house. And it let him remain connected to what was going on downstairs because he could peer down directly into much of the first floor. There were only two problems that I could see. First, the bright sunshine could create glare problems in computer screens unless it were carefully controlled. And second, wonderful, cozy spaces like this don't offer much chance of expansion.

Nook and Cranny Advantages:
- Nooks are cozy precisely because they are a bit apart from a house's living space.
- Setting up in a nook often means putting otherwise wasted space to work.
- If you're building or remodeling, planning a loft is usually cheaper than planning another room.

Nook and Cranny Disadvantages:
- Nooks often give you spatial isolation without offering peace and quiet.
- They are usually impossible to expand as your operations grow.
- Access to areas like lofts can sometimes be a little more difficult than you'd like.
- Especially in lofts, which attract warm air, ventilation may be inadequate.
- The less obvious a nook is, the harder it is to evaluate as possible office space. When you start getting creative (putting an

office under the stairs, for example), you have to get more careful, too.

CONVERSIONS

Extra space

The classic home-office conversion is the unused bedroom. I've taken over bedrooms three times for offices, and I wouldn't be surprised if you've done it once or twice, too. The advantages are considerable. The space is usually good-sized and reasonably attractive. It's separate from the rest of the house, but not so far away that you can't keep track of children or listen for guests. There's a door, so you can guarantee a reasonable amount of both spatial and acoustic privacy. And there's a closet or two to hold supplies and old files.

Drawbacks? Well, for some, the office has to go when the baby arrives. But who wouldn't be content with that deal? Actually, the biggest problem with bedrooms as offices is that they are *too* good. There's so much space that people don't bother to do much planning. Layouts are inefficient. Many of the converted bedroom offices I've seen have seemed, for want of a better word, flabby. Despite my advice that Bigger Is Better, space alone doesn't solve all problems. If you're lucky enough to have an unused bedroom to put to work, plan it just as carefully as you would a tiny nook.

Recycled space

Bedrooms aren't the only rooms that home-workers regularly convert. Closets, pantries, laundries and enclosed porches are all potential—if somewhat less desirable—targets. When you're thinking about converting one of these spaces into a home office, your first order of business is getting your priorities straight. Equipping an unused bedroom is one thing, but taking over the pantry in a household with an enthusiastic cook may be another. And you need to keep in mind that a space that works well for another purpose may need a little help if it's going to become a good office.

I have a friend who lived a few years ago in an apartment that had a very large closet. He was single, childless and didn't need forty-eight square feet to store his suit, his tie, his wetsuit and his twelve-string guitar. He did, however, need an office, so he did the natural thing. He installed bookshelves in the big closet, set up a desk, moved in some file cabinets and got to work—or tried to. But the room still felt like a closet. It was on an inside wall and had no windows and no ventilation. The original light was a single bulb with a pull chain. With some thought about lighting and maybe a fan, this little space would have made an adequate office. But my friend had simply added a couple of desk lamps. The office remained so dark and uninviting that he hated spending time there. So he didn't. His conversion was a failure.

I have another friend, a teacher, who had a much smaller closet—a standard bedroom clothes closet with double bifold doors. He installed bookshelves and a work surface, set up a small shelf for his monitor, built in a sliding keyboard tray, turned his computer on its

Successful closet conversion

side on the floor against the wall, added two desk lamps to the room light that already existed and the natural light of the two bedroom windows, and got to work. His space is much smaller, but it was much more carefully thought out. His conversion was a success.

Conversion Advantages:
- Converting a space from one use to another often requires very little work—move the old stuff out, move the new stuff in.
- Most conversions give you a space to yourself—sometimes, as with an unused bedroom, quite a bit of it.

Conversion Disadvantages:
- Taking over a space sometimes requires a contest of wills—does the cook get to keep the pantry, or does the office win out?
- Some seemingly likely candidates, like my friend's closet, simply don't lend themselves to office conversions.
- Other great spaces, like an unused bedroom, may have to be abandoned when a higher priority—like a new member of the family—comes along.
- Many people simply don't plan well when they have a big space to convert into an office, so they wind up creating a less efficient work environment for themselves than they would have if only a small space were available.

BAD SPACE

The rule of Bad Space is simple. Never establish your home office in a location—no matter how great it may be in other ways—that will often be uncomfortable. This sounds simple, but it's not. Because Bad Space is invariably tempting space. Like my friend's hole of a closet, it often beckons with a lot of square footage in a part of the house where no one will bother you. But Bad Space is also too cold, too hot, too damp, too bright or too dark. Usually it's a combination of several of these unattractive traits.

My Bad Space Hall of Shame, for example, includes all those damp, chilly basement offices where somebody is hunched over a battered metal desk in the cold glow of a fluorescent lamp ruining his back in the rattly embrace of a twenty-year-old surplus office chair. Uncomfortable. And depressing, which is even worse. I'd rather be working on the thirty-first floor of the Massive Urban Traffic Jam and Paper-Shuffle Building, wearing a tight collar, a three-piece suit and uncomfortable shoes.

Attic space can be just as bad. Unless it's well insulated, it will be freezing in the winter and boiling in the summer. Not so depressing as a Bad Space basement, maybe, but even more uncomfortable.

Okay, a lot of people have established perfectly good offices in basements, attics and other potentially disastrous parts of the house. But they were either fortunate in the design and construction they found, or painstaking in overcoming existing problems. Along with dozens of folks who have set up terrible offices in mouldy basements or freezing sun porches, for example, I know two people—one a consultant and the other a writer of educational software—who have set up offices in strange little garrets up tight winding stairs in their nineteenth-century houses. Both were fortunate. They both had sufficient light, and special temperature problems never developed.

The key, really, is making sure that your potential office space would make reasonably comfortable living space. After all, you're going to want to spend a lot of time there. Think especially about temperature, drafts, humidity, lighting. If you find that none of these is a problem, your potentially Bad Space is, in fact, good. Good.

There's one more kind of Bad Space—the kind that looks good in every other way, but just doesn't suit your style or work habits. For example, I've got an outbuilding in my back yard. It's big and bright, a framed garden house with six double-hung windows. It's already wired for electricity, and it could be insulated and sheetrocked in just a couple of days. For years, I thought it would make a great office. I'd have lots of room, lots of light and lots of privacy. Then I thought more about the way I work. I often go back to the computer after supper or late at night. I realized that the thought of getting bundled and traipsing 150 feet through the cold dark drifts of a New England winter wouldn't be conducive to evening work. An unattached office might be great for people who work regular hours or live in a gentler climate, but it's not for me. In my circumstances, the outbuilding is Bad Space.

Bad Space Advantages:
- If it's truly Bad Space, there are no advantages at all. Don't be tempted by mere square footage in the face of inevitable future discomfort.

Bad Space Disadvantages:
- If your office is not comfortable—or if it's a real trial to get to—you will not use it as often as you want to, as you need to or as you should.
- In Bad Space, your work won't get done—or if you're really dedicated, it just won't get done as well as it could be.

BIG MOVES

After I finally came to my senses and rejected our outbuilding as potential office space, we had only one option left if I wanted to move my office out of the increasingly cramped little nook off the dining room. We'd either have to remodel a chunk of the house or add on to it. Actually what we wound up doing was a combination of both: we took over the garage.

If you're ready for such a big jump, garages often make good offices. They are often attached to the house, and when they're not, they're usually close by. (Ours, for example, was separated by several feet, which we enclosed and made into a mudroom.) They usually have a concrete slab floor. They are usually wired for electricity. And they're pretty good-sized.

Unfortunately, our garage was a sad old one-car affair. I couldn't just spiff it up a bit and move in my computer. We extended it a few feet, poured a new slab, re-framed almost everything, insulated with both fiberglass batts and foam board, re-wired for both electricity and telephone, and installed a new heating system. Technically, I guess, this was a remodel. In effect, though, it was an addition.

It cost an arm and a leg.

It was worth it.

I sit here now working in a space that I designed to suit my needs and habits. Everything has its place. I'm comfortable, productive and slightly smug even as I sit here cranking away to pay off the loan.

A variation on this theme is another garage-grab I've seen. The garage itself was turned into a small baby-sitter's apartment, but it was also popped *up*, and the second floor became the Macintosh-equipped wife's bright, spacious home office. Once again, it was partly remodel, partly addition.

This sort of thing isn't limited to garages, of course. One of the biggest and nicest home offices I've ever seen belongs to an editor friend of mine who added a partial second floor to his *house* to handle his full time home work.

With remodels and additions, your biggest limitations are financial, although other factors come into play, too. You may have to get zoning approval. You will need a building permit if you're playing by the rules (I do, many don't). And unless you're doing the construction work yourself, you'll also have to work with builders and, maybe, an architect or designer.

This sort of major project is not for everyone. I work at home all day every day. Most people with home offices don't. As a homeowner, I can tear things apart and put them together to the extent my pocketbook, line of credit and banker allow. Apartment-dwellers can't. Even if you're in a position to add on or undertake a major remodeling job, it may not be the best way for you to go. With so much money at stake, I don't need to warn you to think hard and plan carefully before proceeding with a Big Move.

Big Move Advantages:
- You are creating your space, so you can get pretty nearly what you want.

Big Move Disadvantages:
- Cost—not just for construction, but for heating and maintaining a new space.
- Hassle—this sort of project puts you in the realm of local building officials, builders and architects. Things could go fine, or you could find yourself in a running battle over regulations or money or the fine points of your design.
- You may face the loss of another function (like car-parking, for example) in a remodel.

DON'T SETTLE

Now that I've laid out these several approaches to finding space for your home office, there are a few more general suggestions you should keep in mind.

- *Be creative.* Easier said than done, I know. But use your imagination. Don't settle automatically for what exists—or seems to exist—in your home. Work hard to figure out what can be done. Think not just about spaces, but about how those spaces could be made to work for you.
- *Get help if you need it.* If you have several options, or seem to have none, consider calling in a designer or an architect, and use their creativity.
- *Be realistic.* This may seem to be the opposite of being creative, but it isn't. There are limits to all plans and desires. Finances come into play here, but you don't need me to tell you that you can't do something you can't pay for. Other issues are just as important, though. Can you really expect the living room to be quiet every evening? Is that attic room *really* going to be cool enough during the summer? Be realistic about your arrangements with others in your household, too. Will psychological or symbolic privacy work for you? Can your mate live with an office in the bedroom?
- *Get your priorities straight.* Perfection is rare, compromises inevitable. As with virtually everything else in life, you'll probably have to make some important basic choices when you set up a home office. If you make the right ones, you're in business. If you make the wrong ones, you've got problems—and so has everybody who lives with you. Because of my new office, for example, we no longer have a place to put a car. To us, that's no big deal. To you, or to someone in your family, it might be.

I'll be talking in a lot more detail about equipping and planning your home office through the rest of this book. The right place for your home office is the place that works best—not just for your work, but for your family's operation, too.

3

Furniture

All of us need the same basic things from our home office furniture. We need something to sit on, we need a surface for our keyboard, we need a space where we can spread out papers and write by hand, and we need somewhere to file our work material and store our junk. Some of us have special needs, like a drawing board or room for an oversized computer monitor or a fax machine or a small copier. And all of us have personal habits to keep in mind and space limitations to work around.

The buzzword in office furniture these days is *ergonomics*. Like a lot of other good ideas, it's been watered down by overuse, but it basically means achieving the most comfortable relationship possible between people and the tools they use. The idea is that if you're comfortable, you'll also be safe, healthy and efficient.

Anybody who's ever worked outside the home knows that the ergonomic urge is not universal. Many employers are simply not going to shell out just to make their employees comfortable. Others do their best but make mistakes, like supplying a too-small typewriter return for a computer-user's desk. In home offices, we can suit ourselves—a pretty good, down-and-dirty definition of personal ergonomics—but we have to think carefully if we're going to get it right.

THE IMPORTANCE OF A GOOD CHAIR

The first place ergonomics shows up in an office is in the platform you sit on. Even before I left my salaried job as a magazine editor, my first purchase for my new, full time home office was a chair. I saw an ad for a cut-rate "Scandinavian" number, modeled on the famous Balans chair. You've seen these—they're the funny looking chairs without backs that look as if they might be part of a Nautilus exercise-and-torture installation. I have a friend who calls them "kneeling stools." You sit lightly on a seat that is canted forward, then you balance and take much of your weight on your knees, which you place on padded "kneelers" attached to the chair's frame. Balans chairs were designed by doctors and physical therapists to balance your weight between seat and knees, and they're supposed to eliminate bad posture and keep you pain-free and comfortable. But true Balans chairs can be pretty expensive—$250 and up. Hence, my imitation version.

It didn't work out.

My back was fine, but my knees ached when I stood up, and they positively shrieked when I went out to run. Even when I added padding to the kneelers, my poor lower joints continued to complain. Scratch one cheap pseudo-Nordic seat. The lesson is obvious. If you're

Balans chair

interested in a Balans chair, get a Balans chair. The trademarked style is manufactured by Hag, Ryba and Westnofa. Each company makes several versions. Some have curved frames that let you rock a little to keep the joints loose. Some come with casters. All are well-made, properly angled and nicely padded, although long-legged people I've talked to claim they're forced to cramp up too much for comfort. If I'd replaced my fake with the real Scandinavian thing, I might have been perfectly satisfied.

But at the time, I still didn't think I could afford a real Balans chair. Besides, I'm a confirmed sloucher, and I like to put my feet up on my desk. With even a phony Balans chair, both those activities are impossible—preventing such unhealthy maneuvers is one of the purposes of the design. So I decided to buy a standard office model. I went off to the local used-furniture store and plunked down $70 for a well-preserved red job with arms and casters. It did what I wanted my chair to do: it rocked, it spun, it scooted across the floor. I assumed it would be fine.

It was a disaster.

My knee pains became backaches and I had to stop running altogether because of an interesting little flash that extended from just above my waist down into my (increasingly large) rump. I finally acknowledged that maybe I was being penny wise and pound foolish. My next move should have been my first: some serious research on what made for good office chairs. I went out and sat in as many examples of the genre as I could find. Here are a few basics that I came up with.

Legs

Excluding the Balans-type or other specialized designs, good office chairs have a base with five legs, not three or four. The result is stability—especially important if, like me, you tend to lean back and contort a lot. Many have what are called "dual casters," which look a lot like miniature versions of dual rear wheels on trucks. Some even have brakes, which come into play when you stand up and remove your weight from the chair.

Adjustability and lumbar supports

Good chairs let you adjust the height of the seat. This can come in handy if you're not sitting at a work surface that was custom-designed for you. With an adjustable-height seat, you can even raise yourself high enough to type comfortably at a dining room or kitchen table, although you may then need to rest your feet on a Webster's Unabridged. On more expensive chairs, the adjustment is handled pneumatically when you pull a lever. On others, it's a matter of turning a crank.

If you're going to be spending several hours a day in it, your chair should also have an adjustable backrest with a lumbar rest—a built-in version of the cushion you might be tucking behind your back when you drive long distances. The idea is to support your lower back where your spine curves away from the seat back. Lumbar supports are the most obvious hallmarks of ergonomically designed chairs. (Not surprisingly, phony lumbar supports have come to grace phony ergonomic chairs. Keep your eyes peeled for other legitimizing attributes and evidences of high quality.)

Along with the lumbar support, the chair's back should be adjustable vertically. This is just common sense—it lets you put the lumbar support where your lumbar region is.

The backrest on many good chairs doesn't just adjust up and down, it also tilts forward with you when you lean toward your desk or keyboard. This keeps it in contact with your back, where it can continue to provide support. And chairs with tilting backrests often have tilting seats, as well. When you lean forward, this tilt lets your behind angle forward, too, so you don't have to bend your spine.

Arms

For me, at least, a good chair includes arms. This isn't a universal belief. I have former colleagues who claim that arms on office chairs somehow "get in the way." I've never been able to see how they could interfere with anything but falling out of the seat sideways, and this would have been a great safety feature for more than one of the journalists I've known. Many good chair designs are offered with and without. Unless you're firmly in the Venus de Milo camp, get the arms—you can always take them off with a few twists of an Allen wrench.

Quality concerns

Avoid at all costs those rattly, old-fashioned versions of the so-called "secretarial" or "steno" or "clerical" chairs which not only don't have arms but which are dangerously unstable and don't have much of a backrest either. These pieces of junk are an insult to secretaries, stenographers and clerks.

In your search, be on the lookout for cheap construction. You'll find plenty of it, because there are plenty of people like me who can't believe (at first, anyway) they have to pay a couple of hundred dollars for a mere seat. An inexpensive, adjustable, adult chair that I bought for my daughter is reasonably good in other respects, but its backrest is insufficiently-padded plywood. Perfectly okay for a young child who spends only a few hours a week (if that) at her desk, but painfully inadequate for an adult planning on getting some serious work done.

Test drive

Partly as a result of my experiences I'd recommend never buying a chair that you don't have a chance to work in for a few days, if not a couple of weeks. This might be tough to manage on most mail-order deals, but you should be able to arrange some sort of trial period with a local office furniture store. You wouldn't buy a car without driving it, would you? Well, if you intend to work regularly at home, you'll be spending a lot more time in your chair than in your car. Giving it a test drive is just common sense.

The chair I finally wound up with is, unfortunately, called "The Incredible Sitting Machine," by its distributor,

"The Incredible Sitting Machine"

the mail-order office furniture house Frank Eastern Co., of New York City. It cost what to me at the time was a staggering $350 or so (the price is now a hundred dollars higher), and it was worth every penny. I actually ordered it because it not only conformed to the attributes of a good chair that I had been collecting, but it was offered on a two-week trial with a money-back guarantee. I got it, I worked in it, I kept it.Once you've tried out a few chairs and carefully chosen one, it's time to consider

THE DREADED CHAIR MAT.

Most people hate these foggy vinyl things that sit on top of the carpet. I think they remind a lot of us of plastic covers on living room furniture. Unfortunately, they're sometimes necessary. My carpet installer told me in no uncertain terms that I had to get one if I didn't want the carpet in my new office to pull, pill and generally look ratty fast. Even so, I resisted until I found that my chair's casters wouldn't move smoothly over the carpet, even though it has no pile to speak of.

Chair mats come in different sizes, from about three feet by four feet to about five feet by six feet, with and without lips that can fit into a desk's footspace. I got a big rectangular model, because when I'm not lolling about with my feet up, my technique requires a lot of sliding up and down my main work surface. As obnoxious as the mat is, it would be even more hateful if I kept rolling off one end or the other. So it is as long as the major part of my work surface, and it's wide enough to let me scoot around and use the returns on both ends.

Mats come in different thicknesses, too, and they have stickum or grippers on their down sides to keep them from sliding over different thicknesses of pile—in theory, anyway. Mine still slides, and I find it very annoying indeed to have to reposition the thing every morning. I haven't yet solved this problem, but I think I probably should have opted for a model with the longer grippers supposedly meant for high pile carpets.

If you do buy a chair mat, you'll probably wind up paying more than you expect. I've seen prices from under $20 for a small, thin mat up to close to $300 for a large, thick one. Mine cost a discounted $60, and I still think that's a lot for a big flat sheet of plastic. Finally, watch out when you open the box. Mats normally come rolled up and tight-ly strapped. Heed the instructions that you be careful when you cut the strapping. When the bond is cut, the mat will spring open with great force and a *whap* that sounds like a giant saw blade being bent and quickly released. Be especially careful to keep pets and children clear.

COMPUTER FURNITURE

Now that you're comfortably seated, it's time to decide on work surfaces. The idea is to achieve an economical but well-outfitted office with as much adjustability, flexibility and versatility as you can manage. I think adjustable furniture is great for a home office because personal setups change so often. You may move, or buy new equipment that you have to accommodate, or you expand into a different part of the house. It's also important because your best typing height may not be the industry-standard 26-1/2 inches, or because you may require a monitor set somewhat higher or lower than the usual five or so inches above desk height.

Commercial office furniture is often not suitable for a home office installation: it's simply too big and blocky. You can often find units that offer a similar amount of working area—or, better yet, similar functionality with less area—with furniture designed specifically for home use. On the other hand, a lot of "home office" furniture (by no means all) is a bit, well, chintzy. Shop carefully.

To decide on what you need, there are a few questions you have to answer.

- How big a space have you got?
- What kind of space is it—a room, a corner, a wall?
- What equipment will you be using? (Assume at least a computer, a keyboard, a monitor, a printer, a phone.)
- Do you have any special needs, like a drawing board or space for an oversized monitor?
- How much room do you need for spreading printouts or piling research materials?
- How much work will you be doing by hand—jotting down notes or using a calculator, maybe?
- How soon do you expect to need more equipment, more storage, more workspace?

For the modern home office, with its computer and other electronic equipment, work furniture can be broken arbitrarily into several types: the computer rack, the open cart, the computer cabinet; the desk, (which may accommodate a good bit more than a computer) and the table, which is so simple and versatile. There are all sorts of overlaps, of course (when does a rack get so fancy that it becomes a cart?), but it's helpful to think of distinct solutions to the problems of furnishing your home office—even though some of the best solutions are combinations or permutations of several of these. I'll be using one or two models as examples of each category throughout this chapter, but many companies make versions of each type. Use the addresses in the Appendix to order catalogues, and take a look for yourself. The manufacturers can supply lists of their distributors in your area. Then go out and scout around at office supply houses, furniture outlets and stores like Sears and JC Penney. Even upscale chains like Workbench are beginning to make a really big play for the home office market, with specialized furniture and literature.

The computer rack

These are the most skeletal of all computer-holders, although they are usually modular systems and are therefore flexible and expandable to some limited extent. The most basic type is typified by the PC Caddy, offered by the Omnium Corporation. For about $300, you get a simple, rolling metal stand with surfaces for a computer monitor and keyboard above a rack that holds the computer itself on its edge. Neat, clean and limited. It would work well if your main workspace was your kitchen or dining room table. Spread your papers out there, pull your Caddy over for computer work, plug in an extension cord for power, and go to it—but remember you'll need to make space somewhere else for your printer.

A bit slicker is something called Computree, by Frontline. The company claims this steel and plastic rack was "designed to minimize horizontal space limitations and maximize vertical space availability." It consists of a "trunk" onto which "branches" carrying small tables or work surfaces can be hung. The branches can be pivoted in to stack one over the other for storage, and the whole tree can be rolled around on a base with casters. The basic model (three branches) does about what the PC Caddy does, and costs about the same. The fanciest model (five branches) includes a roll-out printer stand and goes for around $500. Casters are optional.

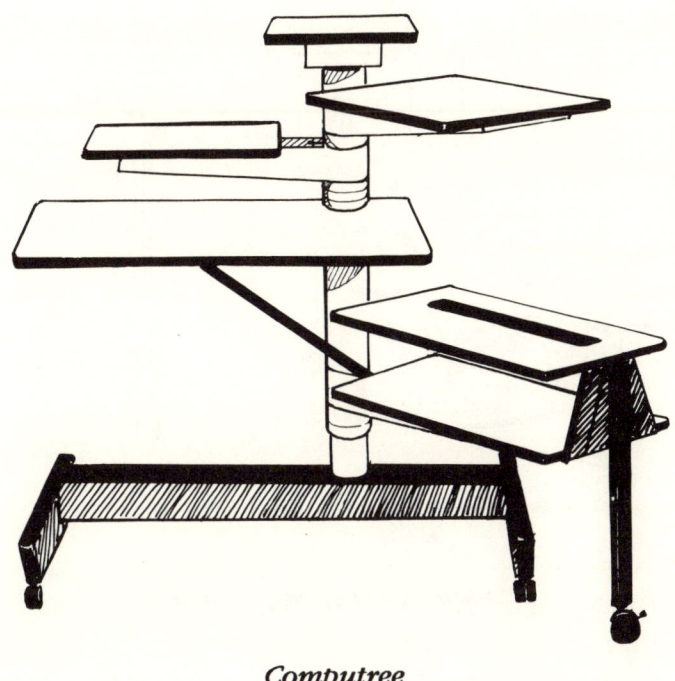

Computree

Another class of rack is represented by the Endura workstations from Luxor. These wheeled units look like a combination of your old metal typing stand from college and the audio-visual cart you may have pushed through the halls in junior high. They'll never win a design award, but they're functional in their various configurations, they offer a few modular add-ons—and they are inexpensive, starting at a little over $100 and running up to just over $250. Enduras even include a power cord and built-in outlets.

Another interesting variation is represented by Bretford's "Walltrak Shelving Systems." These are pretty much what they sound like: hanging wall systems that look like extremely sturdy bookshelves and that incorporate most of the traits of standing racks. The company offers a unit specifically targeted at computer equipment, but you can buy uprights ($35 to $43) and shelves ($80 to $123, including brackets) to customize your own arrangement. Wall systems can't be

Walltrak Shelving System

wheeled into the closet, but they might look better than a rolling rack in the living room or bedroom.

I like racks in general for their straightforward approach to holding equipment, and I appreciate most the systems that are modular, adjustable and expandable. Keep a couple of things in mind, though. First, even expanded racks don't offer you much space for anything but computer equipment. You'll need other space on which to spread out your papers and rest your phone. Second, the pictures of these things never show you the cables. In use, you'll have at least one power cable coming to your system, and you'll have connecting cables between your CPU and your monitor and keyboard and printer. Drooping, exposed cables can make a pretty picture ugly in a hurry. If you're thinking about an open rack system, ask in advance about where the cables go. (Luxor's Endura workstations, for example, include a "Cable-Track" cord management system. Other companies offer various solutions. Check them carefully. Make sure the number of cable clips is sufficient, that holes are drilled in roughly the right places, and that they are finished off properly, with no rough edges.)

Finally, open rack systems are just that—open racks. If you're not planning to wheel your unit off into a closet, remember that the equipment will be sitting there, staring you in the face, even when you're not using it. Think carefully about whether you—and others in your house—can live with all this raw electronics.

The open cart

You may get the most for your money with this class of computer furniture. The units, with elements of rack, cabinet and desk, generally offer a fair amount of space and comfort for computer work. Their biggest drawback is that they are seldom very attractive.

Many companies make open computer carts, but a good example of the type is "The Winner," by Hubbard, which costs less than $400

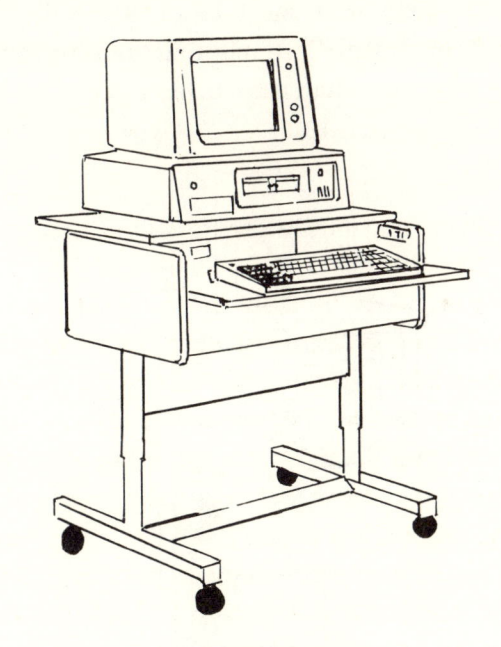

"The Winner"

and was recommended by computer columnist Jerry Pournelle as being a fine, simple workstation for the price. That it is. It's top surface, which carries your CPU and monitor slides back and forth so you can position it where you want it. The keyboard shelf beneath also runs on sliders. The whole thing sits on adjustable-height legs (that always rings the bell for me), and you can order "The Winner" with casters. There's no printer space, and no room for papers (although Hubbard, like most companies, offers a number of larger units). "The Winner" isn't pretty, but it has the utilitarian appeal of an old-time school desk—the kind that was bolted to the floor.

With its sliding work surfaces, this unit offers a little more flexibility than most similar work stations, but many of its competitors, like Royal's Model 5900, have adjustable legs, and most are available with casters. What they all have in common is a multi-level design, and a purely practical approach to supporting computer equipment. You can't pack them away in a closet like some of the racks, but you can park them in limited space, you can roll them into a corner when necessary, and you can fine tune them to suit your body size so that you can use them in comfort. They won't accommodate your printer, though, and they usually offer little or no modular expandability.

An exception is the AnthroCart, manufactured by the Anthro Corporation. It's more expensive than most other open carts, but it is high-

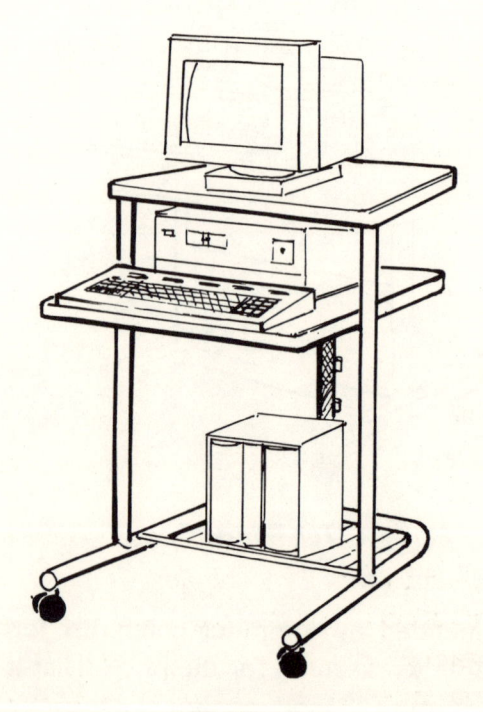

AnthroCart

ly expandable. For about $500, you get a metal rolling cart with two work surfaces whose heights you can adjust. This basic configuration will accept a standard IBM-style computer system—CPU, monitor and keyboard. No big deal in itself. But the company offers a number of options that turns the cart into a small, workable home office system. You can get lower shelves for storage, swing-out printer shelves, an upper extension shelf for more equipment, an attached six-outlet surge protector, along with various wire baskets and other gizmos. The company also makes larger and differently-configured AnthroCarts. It's a well thought-out system with a lot of flexibility, and while its basic components cost more than those of most other open carts, it's definitely worth a look.

The computer cabinet

I could just as easily have called these cabinets closed carts. They do more or less what carts do—hold your CPU, your keyboard, your monitor and maybe your printer—but they do it with more reserve. They look more like "furniture" than metal or plastic racks do, and they close up to screen at least most of your equipment from the rest of the room. I've discovered that if you go looking for a "computer desk" it's this sort of cabinet that you'll most likely be shown.

There are many variations on the cabinet theme, and units are made by dozens of companies. Many are painfully ugly, largely because they are often built of cheap materials and then stained heavily to hide imperfections and blemishes. I also find that many computer cabinets are just too cramped for comfort. Things are usually bearably tight above the waist, with sufficient space—just—for CPU, monitor and keyboard. But legroom is frequently a problem. Manufacturers, not wanting to waste space, build in shelves for a printer and, sometimes, paper or manuals. Bending under your keyboard to operate a printer at shin level is a great recipe for an aching back and a battered head. And keeping your knees comfortably clear of the shelves as you type is difficult at best.

But by no means all computer cabinets are ugly, cramped or inefficient. Some manufacturers have thought things over and come up with interesting solutions. One example is the Compucart built by the Versa Tec Corporation. It offers a "side printer pullout" for an extra $100 on most models (which run from $600 to $1,800, depending on style and material). This makes access to the printer much easier, but things are still a bit tighter than I like for the knees.

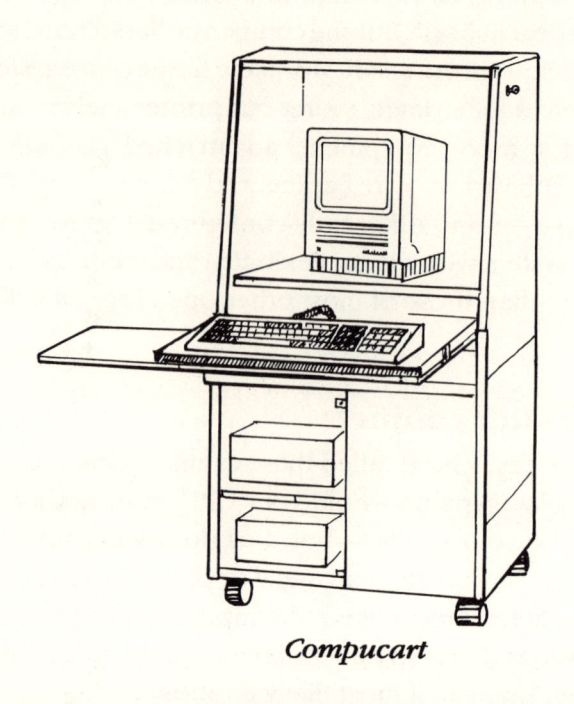

Compucart

The Tiffany Stand and Furniture Company had solved this problem with its unfortunately discontinued "Management Station One," which included a printer and paper compartment that swung out on hinges for use (a sort of closed version of the Computree). This arrangement not only put the printer in a more convenient location, but it opened up the area under the keyboard and CPU for your knees and legs. I haven't, frankly, spotted a similar unit offered by another company, but it's worth keeping your eyes peeled—this is a good design. One drawback: such systems tuck your printer, your CPU and your keyboard away, but your monitor remains perched on top. If this is a problem for you, look elsewhere.

One option might be Bretford's EC20 Microcomputer Security Center ($520). As its name implies, the concern here is protection, not beauty. This is basically a steel cart on wheels with a closable box superstructure. It will hold your CPU, your monitor, your keyboard and your printer (if it's not too big). It will lock them all up. It will give you plenty of legroom. And it will look institutional doing it.

Computer cabinets give the impression of doing it all. But of course, they don't. Like racks and open carts, they handle your basic electronic gear only. You'll still need a surface for papers, phone, Rolodex™ and the like. And that brings us to

Desks.

A lot of us have trucked big, serious "office" desks home at one time or another. When I was twelve or so my father borrowed a pickup truck one Saturday to salvage a beautiful old oak desk that was being disposed of by the company he worked for. It took up half my bedroom, but it was great—big enough to land a plane on, with file drawers and plenty of room for paper and pens and other supplies. I remember figuring out my high school batting average at that desk (and being despondent at the result), as well as puzzling there over calculus and chemistry.

I've used the desk since, too. Long before the advent of personal computers, it was the centerpiece of one of those back bedroom offices I mentioned in the previous chapter. And it's still in the family. My wife uses it these days, mainly as a big flat surface to pile papers on, in her study.

Desks like this are fine if you have the space for them and if you do most of your work by hand. And they're fine if you use them in combination with other units built with an eye towards electronic equipment. But even the ones fitted with those pop-up typing stands or built-in typing pads don't normally function well with a computer. A PC system, with its CPU, monitor and keyboard and cables, is bigger and much more unwieldy than the largest Selectric, and it's difficult to arrange the pieces conveniently, even if the desk incorporates a typing return. The biggest problem with these classic office desks, though, is that they are simply too big for most home offices.

Desks that do work well at home with computers and the related electronic equipment come in many forms from many manufacturers, but the most interesting units (surprise!) are the ones that start simple and offer modular expansion. This really makes sense. These pieces generally look pretty decent, they aren't terribly expensive, and you can add elements as you need to. Not desks so much as desk *systems*.

A good example is the Foremost Computer Desk, Model 4530, manufactured by the Sauder Woodworking Co. This is another unit that Jerry Pournelle has recommended, and he seems to know a good thing when he sees it. The 4530 is the simplest sort of desk—solid sides instead of individual legs, the obligatory modesty panel, and a top about four feet long by about two feet deep. No storage drawers. No book shelves. In many ways, no competition for my old oak.

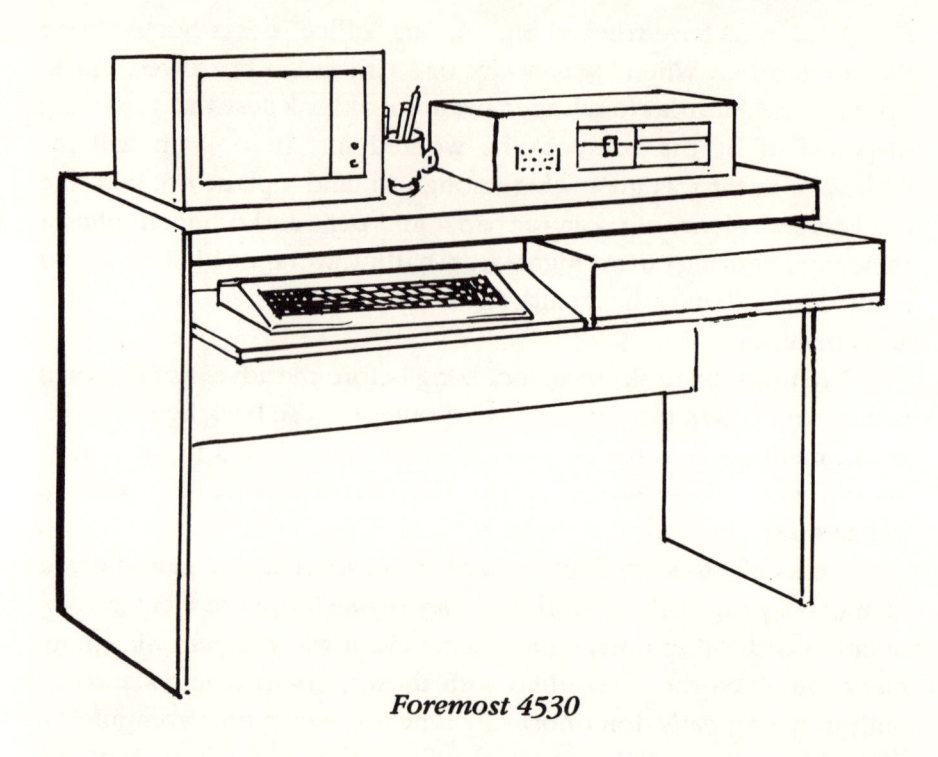

Foremost 4530

But the 4530 *does* have a slide-out keyboard pad that pulls forward next to a slightly raised flat surface on which you can spread out papers or set up a copy holder. With your CPU and monitor stacked on the main work surface, you still have room for a phone, a Rolodex™ and a few file folders. The 4530 doesn't hold a printer, but Foremost offers a separate, matching printer stand, along with a corner unit and a hutch that sets up on the back of the desk itself ($200-$300 for the whole shebang).

For very different-looking approaches to the same basic idea, take a look at Atlantic's "System Four" (about $800 for a desk with an adjustable keyboard pad, an overshelf unit and a rolling printer stand), and Tiffany's "Do-All Series", with its seemingly limitless options on desk size, keyboard pad location and add-ons (desks from $330 to $540, modules extra).

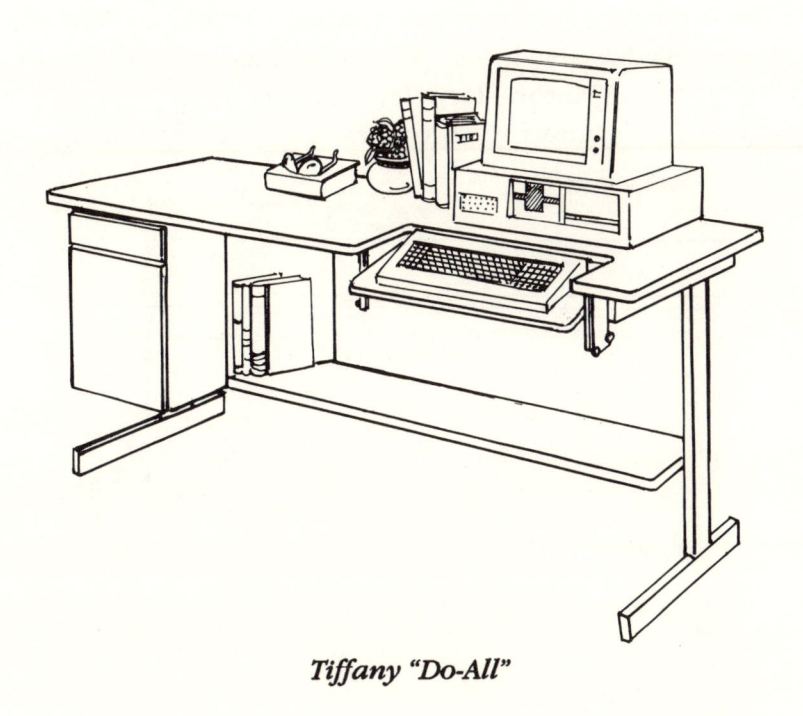

Tiffany "Do-All"

Take a good look at a few of these systems. By and large, they're better-looking than racks, open carts or cabinets, although they can grow to take up a good bit more space.

Tables

Tables aren't much different from the basic desks offered by systems manufacturers. But they're usually bigger and they're often adjustable. That's why I like them so much.

I'm not talking here about the perfectly reasonable idea of integrating your kitchen or dining room table into your office as supplementary space in conjunction with a rack, open cart or computer cabinet. I'm talking about tables as primary space: tables that either come at the right height to use for typing, or—much better—that can be raised or lowered to whatever height you please. Many such units can also be added to with modular extras like overshelves, drawer pedestals and the like. See? Just like desk systems, but bigger—and more adjustable.

My favorite example of this sort of thing is Krueger's Databoard system. Its centerpiece is a unit called, simply, a "Primary Work Surface." This is an adjustable-height table measuring either 52-1/2 or 62-1/4 inches wide by 33 inches deep (from $620 to $850, depending on size and finish). It's attractive, incorporates good cable-management

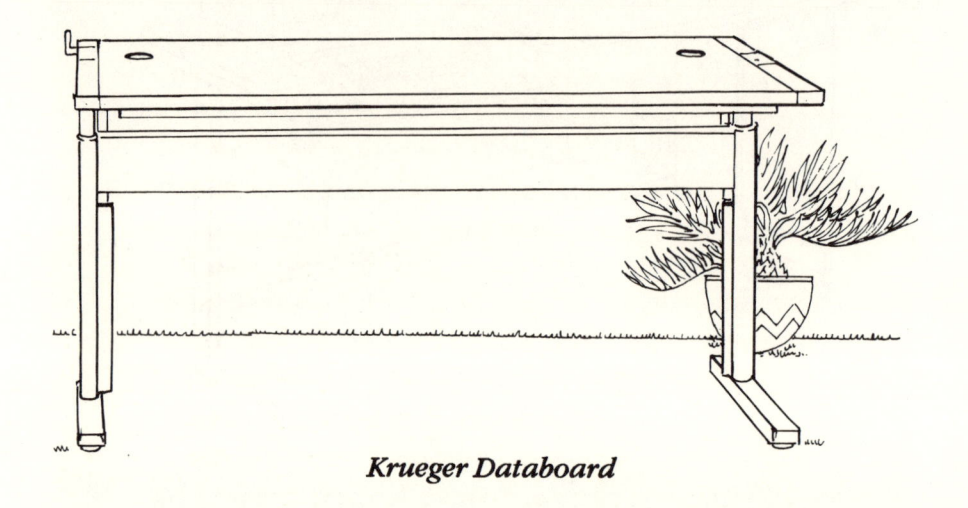

Krueger Databoard

features and works with a coordinated line of extensions, pedestal storage units, racks and specialized surfaces. Expensive but terrific. I've got an empty space in my new office that I'm saving up to fill with a Databoard table.

The Databoard is an especially elegant and versatile version of the table breed, but many other companies offer adjustable tables. They often come without add-on options and with utilitarian names like "work station" or "machine stand," and they're seldom featured either in catalogues or in showrooms. I think manufacturers may eventually join Krueger in promoting such flexible units, but for now you may have to work to search them out.

I've found that for my style of work a big flat surface set at keyboard height does the trick. It holds computer equipment, a printer, a phone, a lamp or two and a few file trays—with room left over for clipboards, loose files and my inevitable toss of papers. I work mainly on the keyboard, and I've found that when I need to take notes

Tilt!

Most computer set-ups waste precious desk space. Those of us who aren't using a dedicated computer rack, cart or cabinet usually plop our computers down in the middle of our work surface. If we're using an IBM clone or a Mac II, our monitor goes on top of our CPU, with the keyboard out in front. This works all right for computing, but it hogs working room that most of us could put to much better use.

There's no reason in the world why your CPU has to sit on top of your desk, nor is there any law that says you can't stand it on edge. I've got mine tucked out of the way under my work surface—on the far side of a support, so I can't inadvertently kick it. How about the monitor? Well, mine sits on an articulating arm that is bolted to the desk. The result is a vast increase in usable space where my CPU-monitor stack used to lurk. The monitor arm has a little rack that you can pull out and store your keyboard on, but I never use it—I simply push the keyboard to one side, and the desk in front of me opens up all the way to the wall. I have room to spread out papers, to open two or three reference books at a time, or to stand on when I need to reach the bookshelves high overhead. The amount of found elbowroom is astonishing, and the sense of smug accomplishment I feel for

to page 39

by hand (during phone calls, for example) or when I just need to break a momentary writer's block by pushing a pen for a change, scribbling on a lower than normal surface is no big problem. And with an adjustable unit, I could always raise the table up if I knew I'd be working largely by hand for a longer period.

I've been surprised to find that a lot of folks I've talked to consider this approach radical, if not idiotic. Salespeople often seem incredulous when I mention it, and most office workers and manufacturers clearly assume that the basic height of a work center should be "desk" height—that is, the 29-1/2 inches that is considered normal for handwriting chores.

But think about things for a minute. Most home office types these days simply don't *do* much sustained hand work. Like me, you probably spend most of your time hacking away at the keyboard, maybe talking on the phone, and generally doing no more with a pen or pencil than jotting notes or doing simple addition. Now, it's no harder to grab a handset on a 26-1/2-inch high surface than it is on a desktop set a few inches higher. And it's no big deal to scratch away in a notebook or on a document laying at keyboard height, either. But it is *very* nice to have a single, large space to spread things out on, rather than a surface broken up by level changes meant to accommodate several tasks. My idea may not be standard, but it's neither radical nor idiotic. It's just common sense. The whole point is that it's *my* idea. It suits *me*. The nice thing about an adjustable table (or an adjustable anything) is that you can fiddle with the basic unit until it fits *you* and *your* style.

BUILT-INS

The most obvious way to suit yourself is to build your own work surfaces or to have them built to your specifications. Actually, I don't think it's usually a great idea to build in too much of your first home office. As you work at home for a while, you'll gradually learn things about the way you go about tasks when you're unsupported by secretaries and some of the other structures of "big" office life. If you've built everything in, it's hard to make adjustments.

Your first home office will almost inevitably be something of a laboratory. It's a good idea to stay flexible. Use the most versatile, adjustable, non-built-in furniture you can find and afford. And keep track

having puzzled out this simple (and not uncommon) solution out is quite satisfying.

There are other ways to achieve more or less the same result. You can pop your CPU onto a shelf above or below your working surface, and you can do the same with your monitor.

In some circumstances, your desk may be the only place you've got for the CPU. Okay, but maybe you can tip it on edge and push it way over to the side of the surface.

Many companies make racks and stands to hold your CPU on edge, and just as many seem to offer pedestals and arms for your monitor. If you decide to tip your CPU onto its side, a stand is a good idea. If the chassis somehow thumped back to the floor, it would wreak havoc with your delicate, fast-spinning hard drive. You'd be lucky not to lose some data, and you might well lose the drive as well. For the same reason, don't

to page 41

of every drawback, every inconvenience, every niggling pain in the neck. Your time will come, and when you *do* build in, you'll not only get what you want, you'll get precious little that you *don't*. And you'll probably want to keep—or at least duplicate—a good part of the flexible system you've evolved.

Having said that, I've got to tell you that I built in most of the elements of my first full time home office, (or rather some very good friends built things in for me). But I'd been working at home part time for years, and I had my act more or less together. More important, though, building in my work surfaces let me use my quirky, limited space most efficiently. I couldn't put everything exactly where I wanted it, but I was able to make the best of an eccentric space.

One more important point. Because of the help of my friends, I was able to build in my work surfaces at a reasonable cost—much cheaper than all but the least expensive units I've mentioned here. If you are handy, or if you have skilled friends who are also extraordinarily generous, you can probably build cheaper than you can buy.

This isn't a do-it-yourself manual, and I'm not going to get deeply into construction techniques. But building a simple work surface is a fairly straightforward task. In most cases you can use wall cleats to support horizontal stringers, which in turn carry the surface itself. You can get a lumberyard to make you up a simple plastic laminate countertop that you can scribe and set in place. If you take this route you'll probably want to order a slightly textured, solid colored laminate to avoid glare.

We took another approach in my nook office. We simply laid down a plywood base over the stringers and covered it with a sheet of 1/4-inch tempered Masonite™.

I can hear you now. "Masonite? Yech!" Well, I happen to love the stuff for work surfaces. It's cheap (which was a vital consideration at the time), it's hard (have you ever tried to write with a sharp pencil on a soft pine desk?) and it's easy to work with. With a few coats of varnish, it's even nice looking, especially if you edge it with strips of some nice wood—we used cherry.

That's all I'm going to say about building work surfaces. It's not much, I agree, but if you need a book to tell you how to do the job, you really shouldn't be doing it—you'd probably save time and money buying inexpensive commercial units. If you insist, consult one of the put the computer in a spot where it can be kicked, bumped or jiggled by you or a passerby, and don't put it where it can't adequately exhaust the heat its power supply produces.

There's one other space-saving or space-creating technique you should know about. A sliding keyboard tray can make computing possible on a table or desk that simply isn't big enough for CPU, monitor and keyboard. Typically, the CPU and monitor are stacked in the standard way, and the tray is attached to slide out from beneath the table. But there's no reason not to reclaim the table top from computer equipment with an edge stand and a monitor arm *and* use a sliding tray. Note, though, that some of these trays only work properly when attached under a desk or table that is *writing* height. If your work surface is already down at typing height, be sure to buy a tray that scissors up to desk height. I happen to hate sliding keyboard trays—probably a legacy of too much work on a rattly, off-level early version. Many friends—in professions from writing to real estate to accounting—use them, though, and they have nothing but good to say about the whole, space-saving idea.

A couple of general warnings. First, if you move your CPU off your desk, you will probably need extensions for your monitor, keyboard and printer cables. This is no big deal technically, but

to page 42

> make sure you're sitting down when you check the prices of computer cabling of any kind. Extensions can easily run over $30 each.
>
> Second, if you don't have a hard drive, moving the CPU chassis off the desk has its drawbacks. It's a lot less convenient to swap disks in and out of a computer set on its side under your table than it is to manipulate drive doors set right in front of you. This is another situation in which you should consider standing your computer on its edge way off to one side of your desk or tucking it above your table on a shelf.
>
> However you do it, though, grab that space!
>
> •

many do-it-yourself books out there. *Sunset's* "Home Offices and Workspaces" includes a bunch of plans for the self-built home office.

FILES AND PAPER HANDLERS
File cabinets

Fancy interior designers often poo-poo the standard file cabinet for home office use. It's too big and too commercial-looking and too ugly, they say. But then they go on to suggest that you use an antique Transylvanian linguine press to store your papers.

Sure.

Besides, I *like* commercial file cabinets. They do very well exactly what I want them to do: hold my current but not especially active files in a secure and organized way so I can find them when I need them. My favorites are lateral files, which accommodate the legal-sized folders I like to use. I don't work on legal documents, but I stuff my overwhelmingly 8-1/2- by 11-inch papers in oversized folders so edges and ends don't usually stick out of even thick files. Lateral files—the kind with the drawers that pull out sideways—are simply easier to find room for up against walls, beneath windows or under counters. A quality, two-drawer lateral file will run you from $300 to $350 or so if you buy it new, but there are used office equipment stores in most cities where you should be able to find the same thing for under $200.

I'd recommend steering clear of the cheapest file cabinets you can find. Typically, their drawers don't have decent suspension systems, nor do they have the interlock that keeps you from pulling too many drawers out at once and overbalancing the unit.

You don't have to share my particular prejudices about size and orientation to understand the appeal of real file cabinets to people who have real files to keep track of. You don't even have to share my tolerance of ugly metal furniture. You can save money by going for cabinets that hold "letter-sized" folders. If you prefer, you can choose the old straight file rather than a sidewinder. And you can buy file cabinets that are wood, wood veneer or covered in plastic laminate.

More important to many people setting up home offices, you can get all sorts of sliding and rolling file bins, baskets, and cabinets. Rubbermaid, for example, makes a simple rolling file bin that glides right under a standard-height desk. Tiffany, Sauder and many other manufacturers offer various versions of file cabinets on casters or wheels. If your space is limited, you can roll these units into a closet

Rolling files

or out onto a porch or just into the corner to get them out of the way. And no wires to worry about!

Yes, it's possible to use a grocery cart. Or a laundry basket. Or a plain old cardboard box. You could probably use your child's little red wagon if you wanted to. But the humble file cabinet—in any one of its many forms—does the job better. Most of the time.

File trays

Actually, lots of my files aren't in my file cabinets. They're on top of my desk in stacking plastic file trays—legal sized, of course. (Rubbermaid, about $3, from Quill) This is where I keep my "active" files. For example, there's at least one tray (two or three in most cases) full of material for each chapter of this book. There's a tray or two for each of three magazine articles I'm supposed to be working on. There are three trays leaking outlines, queries and sample chapters of another book I'm trying to interest publishers in. And I must admit that there are also a few trays holding older files that I should move down into a file cabinet. Maybe tomorrow.

But most of this stuff I need to get my hands on, if not daily, then frequently and quickly. I also like being able to see these files. I enjoy being able to gauge how much work I've done and how much I have to go by looking at the full and empty trays. And I'm a lot more likely, slob that I am, to toss a folder into its tray every night than I am to tuck it away in a cabinet if I know I just have to dig in and haul it out again in the morning.

There are other paper holders out there, including some very slick little "paper management accessories" available from Tiffany and others as part of their modular desk systems. They're generally more expensive than stacked trays, but they allow even quicker retrieval when the phone rings and you need the right contract.

I also have dead files around, and you certainly will, too—stuff like details on business transactions that have been completed, or information on old clients, or ancient newspaper clippings about you, your service or business. I could toss a lot of my dead material and never miss it, but some it's safer to keep. Unless you've got a lot of excess space in your file drawers, you'll probably want to store old stuff away separately. I've bought a bunch of heavy cardboard boxes bought for the purpose from BrownCor (sales price here and elsewhere usually around $2.00 each), which have the advantage of being the same size and shape. You can just as well use any sort of recycled boxes, although you'll probably want to make sure they have tops to keep out dust, ice cream drips and such.

NEW OR USED?

In almost any even marginally urban area, there's an active market in used office furniture. You should always check this market out when the time comes to outfit your workspace at home. Used office furniture stores or warehouses are a terrific source for things like file cabinets, industrial-strength waste-baskets, bulletin boards, steel shelving and folding work tables. They're also full of basic, corporate desks and chairs. Some of these may suit you, most will not.

When you visit these places, bring a measuring tape and a notebook along. Sketch units that catch your eye, then jot down their dimensions. Go home and play around with the possibilities. There's no rule that says you have to use a piece of furniture for its precise corporate purpose. Maybe you'll come up with a nifty rolling widget that was built to carry electrical parts, which you can use as a portable file holder. Used furniture can definitely meet some of your most basic needs, but if you use you imagination, you can sometimes come up with great solutions to more particular problems, too.

Chances are, you won't be able to (or even want to) outfit your whole office with used furniture. Your chair, especially, should probably be new. And lots of decent carts, cabinets and work surfaces are reasonably priced in mass-market outlets. A step or two up the scale are furniture chains like Workbench, which are beginning to catch on that the home office market is a big one. Units on this level tend to be well-designed and well-built, without being out of sight financially. You start running into really high price tags when you start looking at furniture designed with the corporate market in mind. New corporate office units that are neat and flexible enough to be used at home, tend to be pretty expensive. If you've got the money, though pieces like the Krueger Databoard are definitely worth it.

PRIORITIES

Many new home office workers can't get everything they need all at one time. You might have to ease gradually into collecting the furniture you need for a complete and efficient work space. If this is your situation, where should you start? Well, when you begin hiking a lot or skiing even a little, you quickly learn that the most important item of equipment is your boots. They are your foundation, and without comfort and function there, the best pack or pair of skis in the world isn't worth a nickel. When you set up your home office, think of your chair the same way. You'll probably be welded to it for at least a few hours each day, and if it's not well-designed and comfortable, you're in trouble—and your work will suffer. If you can only afford one new item, let it be a good adjustable chair. Try to negotiate a trial period of at least a few days so you can make sure your choice really suits you. With a good, versatile chair, you can improvise for a while to meet your other needs.

After the chair comes your primary work station. This could be a rack, an open or closed cart, a desk system or a table. Generally speaking, you should go for the biggest, most adjustable and expandable unit that you can afford and that will fit into your available room. Keep cable management in mind, and keep an accurate list in your head of the equipment and work requirements that you have to accommodate. Be wary of dark stain, which all too often obscures bad workmanship, and favor modular systems over individual units.

Storage comes third, but it's not unimportant. Being able to put files away neatly and safely can mean the difference between success and failure in a home office—especially if you share your home with others. Take a look at real file cabinets instead of trying to make do forever with leftover wine cartons. Explore the used market, but also be aware that many modular desk and table systems include rolling file cabinets that scoot under or fit nicely next to the basic work station.

To keep things simple, just remember three words:
Adjustable.
Versatile.
Modular.
Ponder them in the context of one short, imperative sentence:
Suit yourself.
You won't go far wrong.

4

Computer Hardware

A computer isn't magic. It won't turn lousy work into a contract-winning presentation any more than GM's huge budgets and swollen bureaucracy guaranteed that it could turn out cars to compete with the Japanese. But if there is no magic, there is still a certain enchantment about the personal computer. It's the enchantment of *power*—not power over others, but the precious capacity to control more of our own lives. Owning a personal computer is possessing at least the possibility of greater personal independence.

Personal computers inspire dreams. With a PC, the full time consultants or entrepreneurs among us can compete with a whole company—and retain the advantages of creativity and flexibility. If we work in a corporate office, we can seamlessly extend our workday at home—after a precious hour or two with the family—rather than slogging on into the night in some empty high-rise. If we moonlight, we can slickly assemble and massage the data necessary to begin to put together a small business—without tipping off potential clients or customers that our work is being done in a former closet or the guest bedroom.

A few years back, a "home computer" was a small, relatively inexpensive machine that was often bought, played with, and then—like most toys—tucked away and forgotten. These old home computers amused, but they really didn't do jobs that people needed done. Today, though, true business machines, with their enormous power and potential, are within the reach of millions. It's turned out, as Apple CEO John Sculley and others have noted, that the true home computer is the home *office* computer.

THE CHOICES

What makes a PC a "business" PC? In a way, I guess, any computer used for a business function qualifies. But the real answer is probably this: *software*. A computer whose potential and capabilities entice developers to write lots of standard business applications programs—word processing, data base, spreadsheet and so on—becomes a business computer.

The king of the hill, running thousands of such programs on millions of machines, is the IBM-PC family and its clones. These machines are sometimes called "DOS" machines, after the operating system (DOS stands for "Disk Operating System") that runs them. Developed by the Microsoft Corporation, PC-DOS (developed specifically for IBM) and MS-DOS (sold or licensed generally) are essentially the same.

The Avis to IBM's Hertz is Apple's Macintosh, specifically the Mac Plus, the Mac SE models and the Mac II in one or another of its configurations. For a long time after the Mac first appeared in its original slow and underpowered incarnation, most serious computer users considered it a toy. If it ever really was, the Mac is a toy no longer. Driven first by the boom in "Desktop Publishing," for which it is admirably suited, and then by the introduction of the more potent SE and the whiz-bang Mac II, the Macintosh has begun to make real inroads among heavy computer users, taking over about ten percent of the business market.

That's it. These are the only two types of PCs that are widely used by American business, and the only two with great numbers of business software packages that are considered standards by users. This isn't to say that your old Apple II or Commodore 64 is worthless. If you're happy with what you've got, by all means stick with it. But if you're buying a new computer for serious work at home—one that will give you access to standard business programs and the ability to exchange data easily with other business users—head for either the IBM-compatible world or the Mac universe.

Software first

How do you choose between the two? There is one absolutely fundamental point to remember when you're shopping for a computer: *Your software determines your hardware*. For example, well over ninety percent of my work at the keyboard is with the word-processing program *XyWrite*. I'm used to it, I've customized it to suit my working style, and—perhaps most important—it's the standard for many of the magazines and publishing houses I deal with. In other words, I'm not about to shift to *Tolstoy* 2.5 or *Hackwriter* V. This being the case, my basic hardware choice has already been made. *XyWrite* only runs on IBMs and compatible machines. No Mac for me. If, on the other hand, I were interested in, say, *HyperCard* applications, I'd have to have a Mac, because that's where this kind of action is.

Cost

But maybe you have no hard and fast software requirements. You want to do word processing, perhaps, but you don't really care what program you use as long as it does what you need. If this is you, there are four important points to ponder. First, IBM compatibles are much cheaper than Macs. For example, at the moment, Whole Earth Electronics in Berkeley, California, a company with a good reputation for quality and service, is selling an IBM-AT clone, to which you could add a good monitor, a full memory board and a hard drive (I'll deal with this jargon presently—hang on) for a total of about $1,200 for the complete system. A competitive, roughly equivalent mail-order Mac SE runs between $2,500 and $3,000.

The major reason for this price differential is that IBM created its PC with an "open architecture." Very few of the components in the IBM-PC belonged to IBM. Other folks eventually got hold of basically the same parts, put together their own IBM-style PCs, entered the marketplace and drove the price down. The plummeting price of DOS machines was one of the most evident successes of the free enterprise system during the 80s. Back in 1983, you would have paid over $3,000 for an IBM personal computer. Today, you pay a third of that for a faster machine with much more memory and quicker, vastly more convenient data storage capability in the form of a hard disk.

Apple, on the other hand, has kept the architecture of the Mac closed. There are no clones, so there is no direct competition in the marketplace. This keeps profits high for Apple and prices high for you.

Most of us setting up home offices go looking for an "entry level" computer—one that does the job we want it to do at the lowest possible cost. For the purposes of a majority of people, that's a DOS machine. In fact, you could argue that the $1,000 IBM-style machine *created* the home office market. That doesn't, of course, mean you have to buy this kind of computer. Cost may well be less important to you than other concerns.

Installed base

The second consideration is that IBM-type machines are ubiquitous—more than 20 million of them have been sold since 1981. Macs are by no means rare, but you can't count on nearly as many businesses owning one. If you already know that your customers, clients or colleagues use Macs, the IBM dominance doesn't matter. Otherwise, it's something to think about.

Ease of use

Moving to the other side of the ledger, the third point is that Mac software has what's called a "consistent user interface." What that means is that all programs that run on the Mac are controlled in a similar manner. If you're familiar with a Macintosh word processing program, for example, you'll probably be able to navigate, in at least a rudimentary manner, a Macintosh database program (although Mac owners are beginning to complain that too many new software packages seem to be leaving this friendly attribute behind—"interface incompatibility" is the dreaded term they're muttering).

In the IBM-compatible world, where each program is a law unto itself, interface incompatibility has always been the name of the game (although there are "integrated packages" that put together several types of programs with more or less the same feel).

Partly as a result, Macs are less threatening to technophobes, most of whom feel more comfortable pointing at the little symbolic pictures (called "icons") on the Mac screen than they do typing in commands on the more "computerly" IBM-compatibles. Especially if you don't have an experienced computer-user to help you get started, the Mac's superior ease of use may be worth its higher price to you.

Words or pictures?

Fourth and finally, while IBM compatibles are "character based" and therefore great with words and numbers, the Mac is "graphics based" and is supreme with pictures. If you are a writer or a number-cruncher, you might lean toward the IBM world (not because the Mac can't handle words or numbers, but because Macs, except for the expensive Mac II, come with what we might charitably call a rather small screen). But if you are a graphic designer, say, or a newsletter publisher who uses lots of diagrams and drawings, the Mac is probably the tool for you. The Mac library is full of graphics programs. And this comes close to closing the circle and returning us to the first law of computer-choosing, which is worth chanting softly again: *Your software determines your hardware.*

Forget the Holy Grail

One more word of advice: watch out for true believers. In talking to co-workers, friends and suppliers before you make your choice, you'll discover that fanaticism and prejudice are alive and well in the personal computer world. There are grizzled DOS users who wouldn't give a Mac space in a trash compactor. "Too cute," they growl. "Typical California feel-good nonsense. Let's just get down to work."

On the other hand, there are Mac zealots to whom IBM is a four-letter word. "The Mac is a people's machine," they chant. "It's easy to use and it's non-threatening. More personal, less corporate."

Forget all this nonsense, and discount the advice of people whose eyes mist over or whose ears steam when they get onto the topic. Both DOS machines and Macs make fine home office computers. One path may suit you better than the other, but be sure to make your decision based on your real needs, not some techno-ideologue's propaganda.

LEARNING THE LINGO: BASIC STUFF

I'm not a computer expert, and I don't intend to go into deep technical detail about these wonderful machines. But there are a few things you need to know—if only to talk intelligently to a salesperson. Keep in mind, though, that things change so fast in the computer industry that this month's hot tip can be next month's stupid idea. It's not at all a bad idea to stand back and let the tidal wave of technological advances race right by. Then you can paddle along after it in the calm and comfortable sea of the tried and true.

DOS choices

In the IBM-compatible world, there are basically three kinds of computers: those based on Intel's 8088 chip (and the similar 8088-2, 8086 and NEC V-20), those based on the 80286 chip and those based on the 80386 chip. The 8088 machines are the basic PCs and XTs—the technology of the early 80's. (XT was IBM's designation for what was basically a PC with a larger power supply, more slots and a hard disk. (XT: *Extra Technology*.) These are so-called "8-bit" machines, because they move data eight electronic bits at a time. The 286 computers are the 16-bit AT-class machines that came into prominence in the mid 80's (IBM again: AT stands for *Advanced Technology*). And the 32-bit 386 machines became the state of the art in the late 80's. (But the beat goes on. Computers based on the 80486 chip have arrived—and the 80586 is already on the horizon.)

Although things are immensely more complicated than this, for most users the biggest difference among computers built around the three different chips is pure speed. In the future, though, the fact that 386 (and subsequent) machines can run a number of different programs at the same time may become important to some of us. (If you do most of your work with spreadsheets, for example, you'll be able to switch over to your word processor to write and print out a letter without terminating your session. And you'll be able to easily juggle all sorts of data into a single document. This is called "multi-tasking." Pretty neat.)

Virtually all current 8088-style machines offer a "turbo" mode that runs them much faster than the early PCs and XTs. You'll often hear these computers described as "XT clones," and for several years, this was where most of the action was among the compatible builders. Prices were driven down ruthlessly, and today you'll see stripped-down versions advertised—often as the "Turbo" something or other—for under $1,000. That price point has made the XT-style machine the basic home office computer—the machine that made office-power affordable to hundreds of thousands of us who work where we live—or want to.

Luckily for us, the same sort of competition has sent the cost of 286 "AT clones" plummeting downward as well. As I write, basic models cost less than $1,500, and you can get one fully configured for around $2,000. At the moment, 386 computers run about $1,000 more, but the price is dropping there, too. In fact, machines based on the cheaper 386SX chip have really come on like gangbusters, selling for little more than 286 cost.

XT clones

If you're on a tight budget, the old, unexciting 8088 XT clone will still serve you well. Properly configured with enough memory and mass storage (don't worry—information on this kind of stuff is coming up), it will handle word processing chores superbly. It will work fine for many spreadsheet and simple data base applications, too.

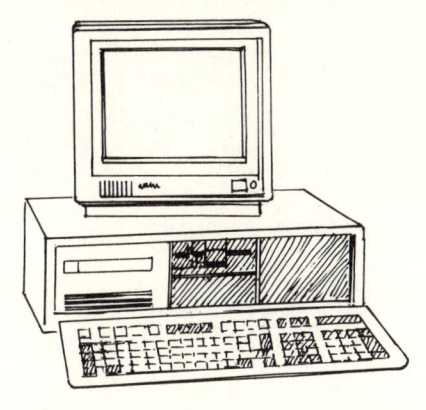

XT clone

XT clones are inexpensive and proven. They're still being bought by the tens of thousands. But by computer standards, the 8088 is old technology—obsolescent if not obsolete. It's not sexy. As a result, it's been common to read something like this in computer magazines: "The competition between AT clone-makers has driven the price of 286 machines down to within $400 or $500 of XT-type computers. For that kind of money, it's silly for any buyer not to go for the faster and more powerful machine."

In Computers, Speed Doesn't Kill, It Just Makes You Crazy.

Computers do things in a hurry. Even the slowest old 4.77 MHz clunkers are quick by human standards. If you've never used a computer before, you'll be thrilled with the way spreadsheet calculations ripple across your screen, or with your ability to effect nearly instantaneous block moves in a document that you're working on.

But as the Olympics show us every four years, there is fast and there is *fast*. XT-type computers are merely fast on their basic setting. In turbo mode, they are *fa*st. With a hard disk, they become, maybe, *fa*st. They are certainly quick enough in their handling of basic spreadsheet, database and word processing tasks to satisfy any sane person—*until the moment that that person uses a faster computer.*

Because, as many of us know to our sorrow, using a *fast* (or even a merely *fa*st) computer inevitably induces an insidious—and permanent—form of insanity. To those without the strength to resist peeking, a vision of *fast* transmogrifies mere fast into slow. Crawling. Tortoise-like. Snailistic. *Slow*. An XT user who's spent illicit hours with a 286 or an even racier 386 machine will never be happy with what's at home again. Lust for speed becomes all-consum-

to page 55

ing. Previously happy relationships between human and machine inevitably crumble under the strain. Bank accounts suffer horribly.

The way to avoid this horror is simple: never use a computer—at least for a familiar task with familiar software—that's faster than your own. If you do, you will become insane and there will be no helping you.

Take it from one who knows.

•

This may indeed be good advice if you're not penny-pinching, but before you follow it, keep three things in mind. First, people who write for computer magazines are exposed every day, as part of their jobs, to the cutting edge of technology. They're spoiled and fussy. Second, they are often writing to the big-business market, not to you and me setting up our small offices at home. And third, they don't have to pay for the computers they test.

Consider. If you save that $400 or $500 on your computer, you'll have it to spend on a small photocopier, or a pretty good printer, or a two-line phone and an answering machine with enough left over for a really good desk chair. Or, if you prefer, you could look at that money as paying for your hard disk. If you have no special processing needs—giant data bases, huge spreadsheets, serious graphics manipulation—don't feel the least bit embarrassed or wrong-headed about shopping for an XT clone if the cost of an AT-style machine is just too big a stretch.

XT clone Advantages:
- These are the least expensive business computers available. They are, in fact, the machines that started the home office boom by offering industrial-strength computing at the magic $1,000 price point.

- They have been around for a long time (by computer standards). The technology is proven.
- Especially if you intend to do mainly word processing, where there are no recalculations or sorts to wait for, an XT clone's lack of speed isn't a serious problem.
- Most programs written for IBM-style computers run on XT clones. Some are too sluggish, and a few of the most recent were written for OS/2 (see page 63) rather than DOS.

XT clone Disadvantages
- These computers are dead ends as far as new OS/2 programs are concerned. This is no problem now, but may become a drawback over the next few years.
- Compared to 286 or 386 machines, these computers *are* slow. This could be a problem if you plan to be manipulating big spreadsheets or databases.

AT clones

The main advantage that these 286 machines have over 8088-based computers is that they are faster. The AT clone is still the standard in business, even though the 386 is beginning to make serious

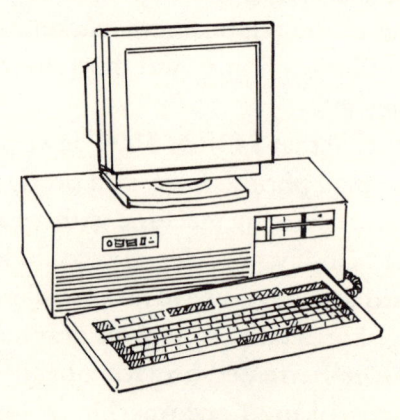

AT clone

inroads in the corporate world and the cost-competitive 386SX looks poised to knock the AT clone off its perch.

Until the emergence of the 386SX, 286 machines probably offered the most bang for the buck in home offices, too. Their quicker proces-

Why Buy A Clone?

Many new computer buyers who want to enter the world of DOS wonder why they shouldn't just buy an IBM. Those three little initials have an enviable ability to soothe anxiety and quiet skepticism.

The answer is that those three little initials are expensive.

Goodness knows there's nothing wrong with IBM machines. My first computer was an early IBM-PC. I bought it before there were many reliable clones out there, and long before the big price drops of recent years. It served me well. I upgraded it in various ways over the next few years before moving on to the more powerful machine I needed for certain specific tasks. My daughter has the IBM in her room now and it's still going strong.

But today, there are a number of reliable companies selling DOS computers that are the functional equivalents of IBMs—and that cost hundreds of dollars less. There are also, unfortunately, some less ethical companies selling boxes that are carelessly slapped together and that use inferior components.

How do you distinguish between the pearls and the pig swill? Just as you do when you shop for any expensive item. Make believe you're looking for a new car. Check the ads in your local

to page 58

paper. Talk to everybody you know who has ever used a PC. Quiz salespeople about service, guarantees and warranties. Most important, I think, find a library that subscribes to *PC Magazine*. Go through back issues. Check out the reviews of various machines. Read the ads and new product announcements. Before you know it, you'll have developed a feel for the market, for the companies in it and for the quality of their products. (Remember, we're talking about DOS machines here. There are no pseudo Macs at the moment.)

My current computer is a Northgate 286 machine—an AT clone with a huge chassis (bad) and a responsive keyboard (good). Although it's worked fine for me, I'd be just as happy tapping away on an IBM. But I'd also be a thousand dollars poorer.

•

sors can be a great boon when it comes to recalculating gigantic spreadsheets, sorting through massive data bases or working on big desktop publishing projects. And these AT clones *will* be able to run OS/2.

AT clone Advantages
- First and foremost, speed.
- A fine cost-performance ratio.
- The ability to run OS/2 as programs written for this new operating system become more widely available. (Frankly, I don't think this is that big a selling point—DOS is still very much alive.)

AT clone Disadvantages
- Although they give you a lot of performance for your dollar, they *are* more expensive than XT-style computers.
- Just as 286 machines superseded 8088s, 386 computers have come along to surpass 286s. The AT clone is no more at the cutting edge than is the XT clone. (Of course, that's only a disadvantage if you're the sort of person who has to be on the cutting edge.)
- Most tellingly, the more capable 386SX machine now on the market cost very little more than AT clones.

386 and 386SX Machines

Predictably, some of those same magazine writers are recommending that we skip the "dead end" 286s, and head right for the top shelf and the 386. At roughly triple the cost of an XT clone, this is questionable advice for the home office, unless you have very special needs indeed. To most of us at home, a full-bore 386 machine simply isn't worth the money

But—and this is a very important but—now that the 386SX has dropped down so close to 286 prices, these writers are correct. The SX shares many of the traits of the more powerful 386, including its multi-tasking capabilities. If your choice comes down to similarly-priced 286 and 386SX computers offering similar performance, the SX is definitely the way to go.

386 and 386SX Machine Advantages
- Speed.
- Multi-tasking capabilities.
- Cost. The 386SX, with many of the full 386's capabilities, nearly matches 286 prices. 386SX machines offer an excellent cost-performance ratio.

386 and 386SX Machine Disadvantages
- Cost—a legitimate 386 (not an SX) at the moment runs a cool $1,000 or more over the price of a good AT clone.

CONFIGURING YOUR MS-DOS COMPUTER

Whichever chip you choose to power your system, you still have to consider the way in which your computer is set up—its configuration.

First, be aware that some of the prices you'll see advertised are misleading. They often don't include a monitor, for example, or sufficient storage in the form of disk drives or a hard drive. Be sure to add the extra cost of these devices when necessary, so that you're comparing apples to apples (oh, dear) when you shop. Here's a list of things to look for.

Speed

This is usually expressed in Megahertz (MHz). The original IBM-PC operated at 4.77 MHz. A modern XT clone's "turbo" mode should run at something in the range of 8 to 10 MHz. 286 machines are typically flying along at 10 or 12 or 16 or even 20 MHz. There's some overlap with 386 computers, which run at 16, 20 or 25 MHz, and by the time you read this some will be revved up to 33 MHz. Speed isn't terrifically important if you do mostly word processing, but it is helpful unto necessary if you work with large spreadsheets or big, complex relational databases.

Memory

This is expressed as RAM, which stands for "random access memory." This so called "volatile memory" is where the characters you type onto your screen exist until you save them to a diskette or to your hard drive. It's also where at least part of the program you're working with—a word processing program, for example—resides once you've told it to get to work. So the larger the program is, the more memory it requires.

DOS can work directly with up to 640 kilobytes—"640K"—of random access memory. ("Kilo" stands for 1,000, and a byte roughly corresponds to a single character, so 640 kilobytes is—roughly—640,000 characters.) The original IBM-PCs came through with just 64K. When I bought my first computer in 1984, I thought 256K would be plenty. But software packages are getting bigger and bigger, and there are more and more small and helpful programs that you might want to keep in memory as you work, so you'll want at least 512K of RAM, and preferably the full 640K.

Actually, you'll often see 286 machines advertised as having a full megabyte (a million bytes, or 1,000K) of memory. The extra 360K is

PS/2, OS/2, MCA, EISA......SOS!

This whole abbreviated area is a confusing mess. Salespeople and magazines tend to toss these initials around, so you should know what they mean—and what they portend.

PS/2 stands for *Personal System Two*, the second generation of IBM personal computers that begins with the little, limited Model 25, and tops out—at the moment—with the 386-based Model 80.

MCA stands for *Micro Channel Architecture*, IBM's proprietary arrangement for moving electronic instructions around inside the computer—to and from the microprocessor chip, the memory chips, any enhancement boards you might add, and so on. A particular system for doing this is called a *bus*. MCA succeeds the older AT bus, is meant to handle the extra tasks that 386 computers can perform and is used in most (not all) PS/2 computers.

EISA stands for *Extended Industry Standard Architecture*, a competing bus established by nine personal computer manufacturers who decided they didn't want to pay IBM a lot of money to license MCA. Unlike MCA, EISA would accommodate cards sized for the AT bus, as well as allowing the use of future cards that would take advantage of the 386 machines' ability to move data in 32-bit streams. This "backward

to page 63

what's called "extended memory." The 286 chip was designed to be able to address up to 16 MB of memory. Unfortunately, DOS won't allow applications to use more than 640K. For my money, extended memory isn't really good for much—the only exception, for DOS 3.0 and higher, is VDISK, a so-called "RAMdisk" program that lets you use extended memory as if it were a storage device (a disk or hard disk) as long as the computer is powered up.

If you really need more than 640K of memory, though, you can get it by adding an "expanded memory" board to your computer. (A *board*, or *card*, is an electronic component that is slid into a *slot* [a fancy plug] under the computer's hood.) Expanded memory uses some technological prestidigitation to offer a potential 8 MB of *useful* memory to XT and AT machines. These boards conform to the expanded memory specification ("EMS") developed by industry giants Lotus, Intel and Microsoft. The add-ins are often called "LIM" boards in honor of the three companies who developed the standards. They can cost anywhere from several hundred to several thousand dollars, depending on manufacturer and the amount of memory you buy. The main drawback of LIM boards is that expanded memory can only be used by software specifically written to work with the EMS specifications. Some popular DOS programs work with expanded memory. Most don't.

Storage

Once you've created a file of data, you'll want to save it somewhere. You store it to either a floppy disk or a hard disk. The old standard on IBM-style machines was a 5-1/4-in. floppy that held 360K of data. Then a similarly-sized disk was developed that can hold 1.2MB of data. Within the last few years, the 3-1/2-in. disk, holding either 720K or 1.44MB of data, has been coming on strong. The current standard for the Mac is a 3-1/2-in. disk with a capacity of 800K. ("MB" stands for Megabytes, or a million bytes. Instead of MB, you sometimes see "Meg.") The smaller disks are easier to cart around, for one thing, and are better protected against damage.

(Note: Zenith has just introduced a laptop machine that uses 2-in. disks. It's too early to know if this new size will become popular.)

Consider sticking to the most basic technology. More people out there have disk drives that can read and write to 5-1/4-in., 360K disks compatibility" has been a big selling point for EISA backers.

OS/2 stands for *Operating System Two*. Like PC-DOS, which it is meant eventually to replace, it was developed by Microsoft for IBM. It will run only on 286 and 386 computers. It can run most DOS programs, but doesn't do so any better than DOS, even though it lists at a hefty $325. OS/2 does offer potential benefits, though. Eventually, when applications are written to take advantage of its power, it will let IBM-style computers run a number of programs at the same time, and it will also, using something called *Presentation Manager* ("*PM*"), give the IBM environment a graphic look and feel similar to the Mac environment.

Even the pundits, of whom I am most emphatically not one, are confused about all this stuff—not about the abbreviations or about the software coding or electronics, but about what will actually happen in the marketplace.

IBM established the PS/2 line and its MCA in an attempt to gain back the business it had been losing to cloners of the open-architecture XTs and ATs. MCA especially, was developed as a way for IBM to regain control over the PC market by supplanting an open architecture with one that could only be licensed—at great cost—from IBM.

It doesn't seem to be working. Consumers are well aware of how well the open architecture

to page 65

than anything else. If you'll be exchanging disks with others, that's important. And in a home office, floppy disk capacity isn't likely to be critical, especially if you have a hard disk. Keep in mind, though, that 3-1/2-in disks are coming on strong. If you can't afford to add a small drive when you buy, you may want to make one an early add-on.

Hard disks just sit there and store vast quantities of data. There's no floppy disk to press in or pop out. Also known as hard drives, fixed drives or Winchester drives, hard disks were exotic beasts in the early 80's, but they've become standard equipment on PCs today. This is largely due to the astonishing drop in price they've experienced. Today, you can get a 40MB hard drive for less than $400, and that's a great deal compared to the old days.

Most hard disks simply slide into one of the spaces that would otherwise be occupied by a floppy drive. But there are so-called *hard disk cards*, too. These are hard disks attached to cards that fit into slots under your computer's hood. They are generally somewhat more expensive than the standard variety, but if your machine is short on floppy drive bays but has a few extra slots, hard drive cards can be the best way to go.

There are also *removable* hard disks, which are made to be popped out of their bays and carted to another, similarly equipped machine. A pretty good way to move vast quantities of data under certain circumstances. Both Tandon and Plus Development make good removable hard disk systems.

Data gets to and from a hard disk much faster than it does to floppies, so installing one really speeds up the computer's internal operation. And because its capacity is so large (20 *million* bytes in a 20 MB hard drive as opposed to 360 *thousand* bytes on the standard floppy), a single hard disk can hold all your programs and data. You don't have to keep swapping disks in and out as you move from application to application or task to task, so it speeds up your own act, as well. Many new software programs assume that they will be used with hard drives, and they act like real clunkers if you don't supply the goods. Buy one with your computer if you can possibly afford it. If not, get a second floppy drive (maybe a 3-1/2-in. number) and make a hard disk your first add-on. (Hard drives are rated for their *access times*—how long it takes them to find a random byte of data. As a rule of thumb, hard drives used in AT-class machines should be rated at 40 milliseconds or less, of the first generation of PCs has served the user, and there's a great reluctance to support a system that will guarantee higher prices and less competition. As a result, EISA is getting a lot of support in its battle with MCA.

The PS/2 line alone certainly isn't recapturing market share for IBM, because most individual consumers still don't see good reasons to pay the IBM premium, and they feel comfortable with the types of machines they've been using. Actually, during 1988, IBM's share of the PC market plummeted from about 40 percent to around 26 percent. In an attempt to recoup some of those lost sales, IBM has brought back the AT bus in its Model 30 286. The message? The PS/2 line has a long way to go before it dominates the personal computer market. Don't worry about it.

Finally, few users are yet convinced that they'll need OS/2 anytime soon. It's clear that it will be a very long time before OS/2 displaces DOS as the IBM world's primary operating system, and it will be a much, much longer time before DOS—with thousands of powerful applications programs written for it—disappears as a useful operating system.

For now, don't worry about the alphabet soup. For most home office users, it spells very little that's important.

●

while fixed disks in XTs should have access times rated somewhere between 40 and 80 milliseconds.)

To make your storage media—whether floppy drives or hard—talk to the computer, you have to have a controller card plugged into the guts of your machine. Make sure one is included in the price quoted, and make sure that it has the capacity to handle at least two floppy drives and a hard disk.

Connections

You will want to attach your computer to a printer, and you also may want to hook it up to your telephone by way of a modem. To do either of these things, you will need *ports*, which are basically special plugs in the back of the computer. Make sure your new machine includes at least one *parallel* port and at least one *serial* or *RS-232* port. These are often part of a special board that's slid into one of your computer's expansion slots. The board often includes a clock, also. You do want a clock, not to tell time by but to automatically note date and hour that a certain file was last worked on. Some programs can also grab the date from the internal clock and drop it—on command—into any document you want.

While you're at it, check to see how many of the computer's slots will be free after the disk controller and the parallel and serial ports are installed. You may later want to install other boards—an internal modem, for example—and you want to make sure you'll have room. Three free slots is probably enough. Five would be better.

Monitors

If it's not bundled in, you should be able to get a good monochrome monitor for less than $150. A standard for years has been the Amdek 310 series. Monochrome monitors generally show green, amber or white characters on a black background. I've used all three, and all three are fine. As with your disk drives, you need a card—this time called a "video card" or "video board" to connect the monitor to the computer's innards. With an inexpensive monochrome monitor, be sure the card you get is "Hercules compatible." This will give you high-resolution letters and numbers, and also the ability to display certain graphics.

If you want a color monitor, be careful. The least expensive and still the most common color monitor runs on a card called a Color/Graphics Adaptor (CGA). New users are sometimes seduced by a color screen, but CGA resolution is simply not acceptable for regular work with words and numbers. The characters are fuzzy, in contrast to the crisp look of those generated by a Hercules-compatible card on a (much less expensive) monochrome monitor. Do your eyes a favor and resist the CGA temptation.

Color aficionados will be quick to point out that there are color monitors and cards that yield higher resolution than CGA. Something called EGA (Enhanced Graphics Adapter) has been pretty well supplanted by something called VGA (Video Graphics Array). Although most people think of VGA as a color system, there are also VGA monochrome monitors and cards, which are descending in price toward Hercules levels. Keep your eyes on them, especially if you expect to be doing much graphics work. VGA offers fine resolution for letters and numbers, along with a true gray scale.

So-called "multi-scan" monitors can handle both EGA and VGA input and more. But we're talking monitor-video card combinations that can push $1,000 here. Color can be a great help in keeping spreadsheets clear and easy to use. It can also differentiate items nicely in database applications. For word processing, its benefits are dubious. If you want color and you can afford a *good* color system, by all means go for it. If you want color and you can't afford a decent system, consider going with an inexpensive monochrome setup until you save up enough for a color card and monitor combination that won't do more for your optometrist than for you.

Power

Original IBM-PC's had tiny 65-watt power supplies. Most turbo systems today come with a 135- or 150-watt supply. AT-type machines and 386s often have 200-watt power.

Convenience

Most DOS computers have their power switches on the right rear. This is okay, but it means a blind reach every time you turn the unit on or off. Favor machines with power switches sensibly located on the front panel.

Likewise, give points to a computer with a *reset switch*. Every once in a while computers get "locked up"—the cursor won't move and you can't get anything to work. Even the old "control-alt-delete" combination won't register. A reset switch lets you restart things without turning the power on and off. You shouldn't get locked up very often, so this isn't a really big deal, but it's the kind of virtually cost-free convenience feature that indicates intelligent thought behind the computer's design. Similarly, especially if you keep your CPU in the traditional position under your monitor, favor computers whose keyboard cable plugs into the front of the unit, not the back (and good luck in finding one).

Keyboard

Some clones come with good keyboards. Some come with the mushiest pieces of junk imaginable. If you find you can't stand the one you get, replacements are available for around $100. The best known are from Key Tronic, DataDesk and Northgate. Most of the people I know consider the Key Tronics *blah*. The DataDesks seem to have a soft but solid feel, and the Northgates come closest to duplicating the crisp clickiness of the excellent IBM keyboards.

DOS

Your new computer needs a copy of its operating system to run. At the moment, the latest version of DOS is 4.0, but it is considered expensive and full of bugs. For now, the best advise is probably to stick with the previous version, 3.3.

Many computer deals include a current version of MS-DOS (which comes on a floppy disk with a manual) as part of the purchase price. Some vendors try to get you to pay $70 to $100 for it. If this happens to you, bargain—just as you might for floor mats or rust treatment in a new car. Few dealers will let the price of DOS break the sale.

BASIC CLONES

Most IBM-style clones look something like the original: a box containing the guts, a separate keyboard attached by a coiled cable and a monitor, also linked by cable, usually sitting atop the box.

The trend lately has been toward smaller boxes to contain the computer's innards. This is a fine idea, especially for home offices. Just be sure that the smaller container still has room for enough empty slots to cover any future upgrading you may have in mind.

Companies like Epson have long been offering reasonably priced units through retail computer stores. Other respected names to look for include AST, Compaq, Everex, Tandon, Tandy (Radio Shack) and Zenith, although some of these companies don't compete strongly on price. Dell (formerly PCs Limited) sells highly-thought-of DOS machines by mail order. So do CompuAdd, PC Designs and Northgate, among others. Many computer stores and mail-order companies offer "house brand" computers. These can be great deals, but don't leap unless you've heard a ton of good reports about the model you're considering. Low price is nice, but piece of mind is more important than squeezing the last possible dime out of your computer's cost.

Whichever brand catches your eye, make sure you understand what's being offered for the price. Remember that many retailers offer what seem to be phenomenal deals—until you notice the fine print that reads "monitor not included." These guys know that most of their customers are probably after a machine configured pretty much as I've just laid it out—full memory board, ports, floppy drive, hard disk and monitor included. In answer to a straight question, they should have the price of that useful machine at the tips of their tongues. If they don't, they don't know their business, so take a walk.

PACKAGE DEALS

Several manufacturers of DOS machines have begun to realize that there is a market among students and folks working at home for basic, modestly-sized XT-type computers that can be bought, brought home, plugged in and used without much fuss. IBM's small Model 25 fills the bill, although it is—typically—quite a bit more expensive than the competition. Companies like Zenith, with its eaZy pc, have spotted this niche, too. So have Britain's Amstrad and Texas's Tandy.

One of the best known packages has been offered by HeadStart. Their very basic XT-clone Explorer lists for about $600 without a monitor or hard disk, or about $1,400 with a 40 MB had drive and a CGA monitor (although there's no reason you couldn't buy a simple monochrome model from a third party). The machine also comes "bundled" with some basic software programs and a graphical interface that's meant to ease the way of new users and timid computer-phobes. Looking to its laurels, HeadStart has now begun offering computers (list $2,000 for the XT-clone, $3,000 for the 286, without monitor) that include compact disk (CD) hardware, along with a solid bundle of CD software that includes everything from a Grolier encyclopedia through the *Chicago Manual of Style* to the wonderful *Hot Line* telephone utility (see page 116) and a good bit more.

These packaged systems make sense. They are small, reasonably-priced and they've been designed to be simple for beginners to set up and use. There are a few things to watch out for, though.

- First, keep in mind that almost everyone who frequently uses a computer wants to upgrade in some way at some point. Be sure you have at least one free slot to do so. I'd feel a lot better with three.
- Second, lean toward systems that will accept standard-sized expansion boards, which are invariably cheaper than proprietary cards. The fine Tandy units, for example, have long required more expensive Tandy cards.
- Third, be careful if the system ties you to special equipment. Amstrad, for example, has its power supply strangely tucked into its monitor. This means that the motor is far away from the electronic components and needs no cooling fans, and so makes for a very quiet-running PC. But it also means that you have to use an Amstrad monitor.
- Fourth, think carefully about the benefits of whatever bundled software you're offered. Some companies offer you useful stuff, while others seem to toss in whatever obsolete or mediocre packages they've been able to cut a good deal for. Then, of course, you may already know what software you'll be using.

LAPTOPS AND PORTABLE COMPUTERS

These are really two different breeds of cat. Laptops are (or should be) small enough to cart around in briefcases. Some are actually small and light enough to use comfortably on your lap. Most run on batteries as well as AC current. Portables, sometimes called "transportables" or "luggables," can be carried conveniently, but not without some effort. Because they are larger and heavier than laptops, they often offer greater power and speed, as well as more readable screens. They usually require AC current.

Over the last couple of years, true laptop DOS machines have real-

Laptop

ly come into their own. Toshiba and Zenith lead the pack, but laptops are offered by companies like IBM, Epson, NEC, Data General, Datavue, Sharp, Kaypro, Hewlett-Packard, and Grid (now owned by Tandy-Radio Shack). They have several advantages for home-office workers.

First, their size means that you can use them on your old typewriter stand or the laundry work counter.

Second, because virtually all of them run on batteries, you don't have to run extension cords halfway across the room to use them. This can be a real convenience if you want to set up every evening on the kitchen table or the back porch.

Third, although some of them are quite a load, you can carry these computers with you when you travel or when you visit clients. The Toshiba T1000 at about seven pounds, has recently been displaced as the lightweight champ by the disk-less NEC UltraLite at about four and a half, with other models ranging up to an arm-stretching 15 pounds and beyond.

But laptop computers have their drawbacks, too. In the first place, stuffing all that technology into a small package isn't cheap. Even the stripped-down, least expensive models rival standard XT-type desktop machines in price. To get anything like the speed and capacity you'd want in your only computer, you'll pay $800 to $1,000 more than you would for a desk model.

And the screens on many laptops, while adequate for a few hours' work here and there, aren't easy enough to read for full-time labor. Many of them, like the Toshiba T1000, use *super-twist LCD* technology, which means adjustable gray-black characters on a light gray background. Good, but definitely not great. An increasing number of laptops are offered with much more readable *backlit* super-twist LCD screens. Zenith is famous for its laptops' eye-popping backlit screens, though most other manufacturers now market computers that display similarly sparkling characters. The price you pay for such clarity is not just money, but battery life as well.

In my experience, laptops make terrific second computers, but unless your "home office" is actually your briefcase or you have insurmountable space problems where you live, they're not quite ready to take over as your main machine. I use my Toshiba T1000 when I travel on business or around the house if I feel like working away from my desk. It also gets a regular workout as a backup device for certain files on my main computer's hard disk. I use a cable and a special software program called *LapLink* (see p. 120) to copy data onto the Toshiba's 720K disks. Having up-to-date copies means I can take the portable off somewhere and continue work on my current project, and it also means I can replace vital files if they somehow get trashed on my main machine's hard drive.

Then again, maybe your main machine doesn't live where you do. An editor friend of mine bought a Zenith 181 laptop as his only computer shortly after that model, with its wonderfully readable screen, came out. It was a good choice for him because, although he was doing a lot of work at home and on the road, he still spent most of his time in front of an IBM-PC in the office of the magazine he edited. The laptop gave him the flexibility—there's that word again—he needed.

Portables are a different kettle of fish. Many of them, like the classic Compaq Portable, were shaped like portable sewing machines (and weigh about as much). Some, like the newest (and very pricey) Compaq Portable 386 and the Sharp PC-7221, are smaller and lighter,

Portable

shaped more like a big lunch box. Still others, like the costly high-end Toshiba 3000 and 5000 machines, are "clamshell" designs. They look like big laptops. All of them require AC power. Like laptops, portables are generally a good bit more expensive than standard XT clones, although mail-order prices on the remaining basic XT-type models are often under $2,000.

A portable can be a fine home office machine. Most have keyboards and screens good enough to support full-time labor. Most are configured with the ports and components you need (the exception may be a hard disk, which you can add yourself). They're self-contained and easy to move around, so they're easy to set up and put away. You can, with relative ease, cart them to and from another office. They offer a home-office worker a lot of—here we go again—flexibility.

(Late note: There is now a Mac portable. Expensive—over $6,000, list—and heavy—more than 16 pounds—but otherwise terrific.)

MACS

If you decide to go the Mac route, you have several choices: the Mac Plus, the Mac SE and the Mac II (and its various upgrades). The Plus and the SE both look like classic Macs—that little upright box with its small screen. The Mac II looks more like an IBM-AT—a CPU box with a separate monitor usually sitting on top.

The Mac II is a very powerful and versatile computer, roughly equivalent to an IBM-style 386 machine, but with the Macintosh's consistent interface and ease of use. Many people think that it's pointing the way for all of personal computing. But the Mac II is also very expensive—at $5,000 or more, much more expensive than most 386 machines—and unless you are planning to use big, specialized programs, you just don't need it.

Down at the other end of the Mac spectrum is the Mac Plus. Apple marketers have talked about a $1,000 Plus as necessary for their "push into home offices," so they understand the problem. Right now, though, the street price of the very basic Mac Plus is still up around $1,400. The Plus comes with a single internal 800K, 3-1/2-in. floppy drive and 1 MB of memory. It has no slots, so it's tough to expand—additional memory is no big problem (except for its cost)—but the only way to add other enhancements is by way of the ports on the back of the machine.

My Mac friends tell me that a hard drive is at least as desirable on a Macintosh as it is on an IBM clone. You can add one to a Mac Plus by way of its Small Computer System Interface (SCSI—pronounced "scuzzy") Port, but that, unfortunately, would run the cost of the machine up to about $2,000.

The graphical nature of Mac software gobbles up memory, and depending on your applications, the 1 MB in the Plus may not be adequate. At the moment, memory ain't cheap—$300 per MB is a pretty good price.

The Mac SE is becoming the Mac of choice for many buyers. It's faster than the Plus and has an expansion slot. Unfortunately, it carries the traditional high Apple price tag. The current street price for SE with a 20 MB hard drive and 1 MB of memory is about $2,600. Strangely, the keyboard is often not included. This is because Apple is offering either a standard keyboard (for about $100) an extended, IBM-style keyboard that includes function keys and a separate numeric keypad (for about $170). Just as with IBM clones, replacement keyboards are available—DataDesks are the best known—for less.

Mac SE

I like Macs. I like the fact that (except for the Mac II) they're small and can fit easily onto cramped working surfaces, and I've never really minded their small nine-inch screens. I also like the ease with which they handle certain tasks. In many ways, they are terrific home office machines. But there are two major drawbacks. First, they're expensive—a reasonably set up Plus, for example, could easily cost you twice what a solid XT clone would go for. And second, they are not easily ex-

Mac IIcx

panded. If you don't think you'll need more than a hard disk and some more memory, then you should be all right on this score. But if you want to move on to accelerator cards and large-screen monitors, you may be in for some tricky figuring.

All the same, anybody setting up a home office these days should look at a Mac if software or other considerations don't put you irrevocably in the MS-DOS camp. The Mac was originally promoted as "an advanced productivity tool for knowledge workers." It delivered. Macs *are* more friendly than IBM-style machines. They *are* easier to use. Especially if you're scared to death of computers but know you have to enter the electronic age, the Mac may well be the way to go.

BUYING YOUR COMPUTER

There are basically two ways to buy a new computer. You can go to your local retail computer store or you can opt for mail order—usually at a significant discount and sometimes with superior service as well.

Computer stores

Theoretically, a newcomer to computers should buy from a nearby store. The idea is that you pay a bit extra, but that you can lean on the knowledge of the computer experts on the store's staff while you're making your purchase, and you can rely on nearby help if you need service after the sale. Peace of mind.

The theory holds up if the computer store is a good one. Unfortunately, I've found that the level of expertise, service and professionalism at most of these places is a joke. I'm not alone. Almost everyone I know has been infuriated by the same syndrome, and you can read occasional angry tirades on the subject in the pages of many computer magazines.

I've talked to salespeople who didn't know that a Plus was a Macintosh. I've had salespeople urge me to "move up" from my word processor, which happens to be particularly suited to my work, to *DisplayWrite 4*, an IBM program that was designed for secretarial use. I've shared the common, almost typical, experience of waiting with money in my pocket while a "sales representative" ignored me in favor of hunching over a keyboard to blast bogies in *F-15 Strike Eagle*.

On Buying Computer Hardware

1. Choose your software first, and buy hardware to handle it.
2. When you have no special software in mind, choose it (and thus your hardware) based on what the people you'll be working with—or want to be working with—use.
3. Never buy a product—computer, software or peripheral—until it has entered the mainstream and established a solid track record. Stay away from the cutting edge if you don't want to be the one who gets sliced.
4. Don't expect accurate information or helpful service from retail computer stores. A moderately well-informed consumer knows more than a clear majority of computer salespeople. Do your own homework. Make your own decisions.
5. If you do find a retail computer store that provides good service and helpful advice, give it your business and mention it to friends. These rare places need encouragement.
6. If you're cautious, buying computer equipment by mail can be the best way to go. There are a few mail order companies that are as famous for service and good business practices in this field as L.L. Bean and Lands' End are in theirs. And they generally offer highly competitive prices.

to page 78

> **7.** Find a guru or join a users group. No matter what kind of system you buy or how comfortable you are with the technology, you will need help. Many problems, especially standard beginners' mistakes, can be solved quickly with a short friendly phone call to an amenable, experienced acquaintance
>
> **8.** Once you've got your feet on the ground, be sure to return the favor by helping other beginners freely.
>
> •

Part of the problem is poor training. That can account for ignorance and even sloth. But how about the rotten advice? This is often the result of "spiffs"—incentives paid to salespeople by manufacturers and software companies. This "push money"—not the buyer's needs—often dictates the products that salespeople recommend. This despicable practice preys on customer ignorance, so it harms precisely those of us who wander into retail stores looking for help. Knowledgeable users don't get hurt, because they simply ask for the product they want. The moral? Do your homework. Check the computer magazines. Talk to friends and acquaintances. Don't rely on the vendor for advice. If you must ask for help and you have the moxie for it, ask about spiffs, too.

Truly good computer stores *do* exist, although they are the exception rather than the rule. One way to find one is to contact a computer users group in your area (you can often get a line on user's groups through local colleges or even high schools). People who have been using computers for a while will inevitably have formed opinions about nearby retail outlets. If there is a consensus that one or more of them is a good place to shop, go ahead.

If you buy locally, you'll almost certainly pay more. Again, do your homework, let the salesperson know that you're aware of the "street price" of the merchandise you're interested in (the more-or-less standard discount price available from mail-order firms). Ask him or her to match it. Local stores can almost never compete with discounters, but they will often drop their price at least a bit, while stressing the benefits of having service nearby. At a good store, this benefit is real.

Mail-order

Personally, I'm a confirmed mail-order man. (This is an obsolete term, actually. Like most other people following the same route, I order by phone. And my purchase is usually handed to me, not by Don or Helen at the post office, but by Mitch or Dean the UPS guys. In the vast majority of cases, there's no mail involved in mail-order shopping. But then there's not much foot in football, either.) I've bought computers, peripherals and software this way, and while not everything has gone as smooth as silk, my problems have been endurable, the prices have been right—and I've consistently gotten more accurate information and better advice over the phone than I have in retail shops.

Actually, my first experience with mail order wasn't a good one. Back in late 1984, I needed a dot-matrix printer that had a letter-quality print mode and that would accept extra-wide paper. I did some research and settled on the now long-discontinued Toshiba 1351. Then I checked the ads in the computer press. The best price I could find was from a place called the PC Network in Chicago, so I unlimbered my credit card and made a call. The printer wasn't in stock, but I was assured that it would be arriving in a week and would be sent out to me immediately. I now know that they might as well have told me that my check was in the mail. A month later, the printer had still not arrived. I made call after call to Chicago, and was frustrated almost every time in my attempt to get through to anyone at PC Network who could help me. The printer was finally delivered on the day I was planning to cancel my order. By mail.

The printer was fine, the price was good, and nobody actually tried to swindle me, but the transaction was a hassle. I never dealt with PC Network again (the company eventually slid into Chapter 11), and this unpleasant experience taught me to value convenience and credibility over rock-bottom pricing.

Since learning this lesson, I've had no more problems with the companies I've dealt with, but I have had two minor problems with equipment. The first was with a monitor I ordered from PC Connection of Marlowe, New Hampshire. When I uncrated the thing, plugged it in and started working on it, I realized that I was writing down hill. The manufacturer had somehow installed the tube slightly askew. I called New Hampshire, explained the trouble, was issued a return authorization number, and had a replacement monitor two days later.

My second problem was with the hard drive in a computer that I'd ordered from Northgate, a mail-order clone manufacturer in Plymouth, Minnesota, which also makes those excellent replacement keyboards. When bad sectors on the hard disk began to multiply like a rabbit colony run amok, I made a phone call to Minnesota and an express service delivered a new hard disk to my door the following day.

While they both offered highly competitive prices, I'd chosen to do business with both of these companies largely because of their reputations and policies. PC Connection is the L.L. Bean of the computer world. People on the phone from Marlowe are invariably well-trained, knowledgeable and polite, and the company is famous for its good service, excellent customer support and trustworthy business practices. Northgate is nowhere near as smooth, but in researching my computer purchase, I found that the people I talked to up there were equally polite and knowledgeable. And you can bet I was well aware of the next-day replacement guarantee that I eventually needed to take advantage of.

Many other mail order firms are reputable, helpful and pleasant to do business with. But you still have to be careful. An infamous scam in California took hundreds of gullible bargain-hunters for a ride by advertising ridiculously low prices and demanding payment up front (no credit cards). The criminals involved never contemplated a legitimate business. They simply skipped with the proceeds. You can avoid this sort of outright fraud pretty easily. Be skeptical of prices that are too good to be true, and never deal with an outfit that demands payment up front.

But most mail order problems are the result of cash flow troubles, not fraud. You want to be doing business with an economically sound company, not one that's going to declare bankruptcy after taking your money but before supplying your merchandise. Unfortunately, there's no way to be sure of a firm's bottom line. Your best bet is to check back issues of computer magazines to see if the company has been in business for a significant length of time. You can also ask other users for their recommendations. Neither of these approaches is foolproof, though. Protect yourself by using a credit card for all of your mail order purchases. Then if there's a problem and you don't receive your merchandise, the issuing bank will usually reverse any charge that may have appeared on your account.

FTC rules require that when you place an order through the mail or over the phone, it must be shipped within thirty days. (Actually, 30 days is ridiculous. If the company can't ship your order immediately, you should try another company.) If the company finds that it will be more than thirty days, it has to notify you and give you a chance to cancel your order. If you cancel, the company has to refund your payment if you've made one. It can't force you to accept a store credit or an exchange instead of a refund.

These government regulations cover the basic rules of the mail-order game. But you should be operating with a set of rules of your own:

1. Don't send cash. Don't send a check, either. Phone the 800 number and use your credit card. Ask if the company runs your card immediately, or only after your order is shipped. Try to do business only with companies that expect payment *after* they've supplied your needs, not before.

2. Confirm the price and the specific merchandise you're interested in. Get the brand names of components (such as hard disks or monitors) if none were mentioned in the ad. Make sure that the offer includes everything you want, and that you won't have to pay extra for standard items like cables.

3. Check availability. If what you want isn't in stock, you might want to try elsewhere for quicker delivery. The best of the mail order companies can almost always get your merchandise out the day after you place your order—you can even get next-day delivery from some of them.

4. Ask about warranties. Some companies sell so-called "gray market" equipment on which manufacturers don't honor warranties.

5. Be certain that you can return something if it turns out not to be what you wanted. Ask about the company's refund policy.

6. Note your order number. Ask the salesperson for it if he or she doesn't offer to read it to you. Keep a record of your order, the price, the date and time, and the name of the salesperson.

What you're looking for when you buy your computer—and your other equipment, too—is a solid, competitive price, few hassles and as little anxiety as possible. The price is usually pretty easy to pin down—even if it takes microscopic reading of an advertisement or careful quizzing of a salesperson. The hassle and anxiety factors—which can be even more important than cost to a computer novice—can be tougher to sniff out. Just be sure to keep your nose in the air and your wits about you.

GURUS AND USERS GROUPS

Choosing a system, buying it, setting it up, and getting yourself working productively on it—this whole process is full of stress. The pressure can be radically reduced if you can get a little help from your friends. When I set up my first electronic home workspace, I relied heavily on a friend who was the "computer guy" at the publishing house where I worked at the time. He helped me choose my basic hardware, and later my memory and hard disk upgrades. Watching him work on the company's computers demystified the technology and gave me the confidence to handle simple tasks under the hood of my new machine. He also knew my word processing package from top to bottom, and he always seemed to have the answer that saved my bacon when the program confounded me—which it often did in the early days. He acted as my counselor, my consultant and my troubleshooter. He was my computer guru.

If you've got access to a guru of your own, you're in clover. Wine him and dine him. Wash her car every Saturday. Offer to handle the shopping, the child care and the mortgage payments. It will all be worthwhile.

But gurus don't grow on trees. You may not know anyone with computer expertise. Or you may not like the ones you know. Your best bet then is a users group. These organizations sometimes form around a specific computer type or software package. Especially in large cities or college towns, there's a good chance that you'll be able to find a group dedicated to IBM-style machines or Macs. Finding users groups can sometimes take some detective work. If your city has a regional computer magazine (*Computer Currents*, for example) it might run a listing of area groups. If you can't find a published directory, check bulletin boards at college computer labs. Ask at computer stores.

Once you find a group, attend a few meetings. I must admit that I have found some UG meetings a bit off-putting. Membership can sometimes be a bit inbred, and the very expertise of some members can be frightening. Hang in there at least long enough to sense whether you'll be able to get some helpful advice either from individuals or from the group as a whole. It has lately become common for some members to charge for helping novices through their early trials. This isn't especially friendly, and its a far cry from the way early UG's operated, but it's by no means criminal for someone to ask compensation for services rendered. If you like the person, you think he knows his stuff, and the price seems reasonable, consider cutting a deal.

5

Computer Software

What software you acquire depends not just on what you want to do and how you want to do it, but also on what any colleagues or customers may be using and whether you've already gotten used to a specific program on another job.

If you know you'll be exchanging data, for example, with clients who use Lotus *1-2-3* (Lotus Development Corp.), it makes sense to buy *Lotus* for yourself. If in your corporate job you've gotten used to storing and retrieving data using *dBase IV* (Ashton-Tate), it's silly not to stick with the package you know if you think you'll be doing similar work at home.

A lot of people setting up home offices fall into one or the other of these categories. Their software choices—at least for their primary purposes—are cut and dried, and if you're one of them, you can skip a big chunk of this chapter.

But a lot of us start without a clue. We have neither previous experience nor colleagues nor clients to help us make our choices. And we've often got a few special problems of our own to overcome:

- We're worried about money. This home office stuff can run into big bucks, and these three and four hundred dollar price tags give us the willies.

- We're nervous about computers. We know we need one, and we know they can do wonderful things, but we also know they are mysterious, truculent and vindictive.
- We're concerned that we're too ignorant to make smart choices. We don't even know about many general software applications, let alone what to look for in particular packages.

One solution for those of us weighed down by one or more of these concerns is to go out and spend $90 to $150 on something like *PFS:First Choice* (Software Publishing Corp.) or Microsoft *Works* (Microsoft Corp.) which are both available in either DOS or Mac versions. These programs are known as

INTEGRATED PACKAGES.

The reason is simple: they include modules for word processing (with spelling checkers and thesauri), spreadsheet work, simple database management, communications and graphics—the so-called "big five" applications. That's the first big benefit: they do it all.

Second, these packages are inexpensive. While big time, big buck integrated packages like *Symphony* (Lotus) and *Framework* (Ashton-Tate) exist, they haven't caught the imaginations of users the way *First Choice* and *Works* have. With these more modest programs, you spend between a third and half as much for all five capabilities as you would normally pay for a heavy-duty single-purpose word processing, spreadsheet or database program.

Third, you save the time and emotional energy that you'd otherwise spend looking for the "perfect" program. This is no small benefit: I've seen people tie themselves into paralyzed knots of tension at the thought that they might make The Wrong Choice.

Fourth, while each function is simpler and less powerful than the big guns in each field, they still offer virtually everything 90 percent of home office workers will need.

Fifth—and maybe most important to a vast number of nervous computer beginners—these packages are designed to be quick to learn and easy to use. Keys have similar functions in each application. Text, data, numbers and pictures can be swapped among the modules. Everything fits together neatly and simply. I have one friend who's been using *PFS:First Choice* cheerfully for over two years and has yet to crack the manual.

Another nice thing about these inexpensive integrated packages is that you can use them to gain computer experience and confidence. Then, if you find it necessary, you can move to something more powerful for your primary job—word processing, say, or data base management—while retaining the four other capabilities at what remains a bargain price. In the process, you will have become comfortable using a computer, and you will have given yourself a chance to refine your ideas about exactly what you may require in that more powerful program. Based on my experience with new users, though, the chances are that one of these packages will be all the software a novice user will need for a long time to come.

CHOOSING INDIVIDUAL SOFTWARE PROGRAMS
First, relax

Okay, for your own good reasons you don't want to take the easy way out with an inexpensive integrated package. Or you're ready to go for that heavyweight program in your primary application. But you still have no special insight, and no particular reason to buy any given package (no colleagues to swap disks with, no happy past experience). How do you decide which one of these Big Busters will be best for you?

Well, start by giving yourself a break and dropping the idea of "best." Or at least be certain that you are not defining "best" as "perfect." I can't tell you the angst I've seen produced by Type A novices (*not* novice Type A's) giving their ulcers a workout while frantically researching to find their ideal software package. While there may be a program that is better than all others for your purposes, there are certainly several others that are almost as good. The difference just isn't worth worrying yourself into a tizzy over.

Here are a few things you should be checking out. Calmly.

Who uses what?

First, is there a standard in your line of work? In my line, for example, the standard word processing package is *XyWrite* (XyQuest) It's used by lots of newspapers, magazines and publishing houses, and they like to get copy on disks that they can just pop into their drives and get to work on. In fact, the contract of the book I wrote before this one included language requiring me to submit my manuscript either in *XyWrite* or in a format directly readable by *XyWrite*. Clearly, using this program is a good idea for a writer.

But, you know, if I used *WordPerfect* (WordPerfect Corp.) or *Word* (Microsoft) or *WordStar* (WordStar International)—as hundreds of writers do—and I liked it and worked smoothly in it, I'd be okay. These are all fine, well-known programs (now that *WordStar* has shaped itself up), and despite my last contract, most magazines and publishing houses can handle them with no trouble at all. They can handle lots of others, too. I lucked into *XyWrite* by working for a while on a magazine that used it. But if I'd trodden a different path and come up with *Final Word* or *Volkswriter Deluxe*, there'd be no big problem. Facility with a program is more important than some subjective concept of perfect suitability.

Second, is there an overwhelming market leader? In the IBM world, Lotus *1-2-3* in spreadsheets and *dBase IV* among databases both leap to mind. Neither one of these packages is any longer the technological leader in its field. But incarnations of each were early market leaders and they've been upgraded sufficiently to remain the targets everybody else shoots at. If you're a novice, it's not a bad idea to plant yourself squarely in the mainstream. There will be lots of people out there speaking your language and more books, articles, courses and add-ons available when you're ready for them. And while a market leader may not be the slickest package out there, you can be sure it's not a dog. It's a safe choice.

SOS

Third, and related to the first two, is there one program you'll be able to get especially good help with? One important fact of life for most home office workers is that, just as we do without secretaries and mailrooms, we also struggle along without corporate training sessions or computer centers. But maybe your spouse or best friend uses *Rbase* (Microrim) all day every day instead of *dBase*. That alone might determine your choice of a database program. Although a *PC Magazine* survey shows that most people learn how to use new software either by

Viruses

What a scare! These awful programs—"Trojan Horses," "Worms," or, more commonly these days, "Viruses" are getting into people's computer systems and mangling precious data.

These insidious bits of computer code gain entrance, then often simply go to sleep until awakened on a certain date or by a specific sequence of events. Then they go to work. Sometimes they just leave harmless messages and then go away. Sometimes they play little jokes, bringing up an irrelevant screen or a funny picture. But sometimes they maliciously destroy vital sectors on your hard disk and leave you with a disaster on your hands.

The good news for home office workers is that it's very unlikely any of us who are not linked up to a computer network will be bothered by viruses.

The term virus is helpful, because it makes you think in terms of infection. Your system won't catch a virus unless it has contact with an infected piece of software. Most infections are carried over networks. You should watch out about downloading shareware programs from bulletin boards. I've been told that the system operators (sysops) of the bigger boards and the major online systems check new shareware programs to be sure they aren't infected, but

to page 89

that the sysops of little boards often don't have the time. I'm not so sure about that. Some little boards have wonderfully dedicated sysops and great reputations. Nonetheless, these days I get most of my shareware directly from the author, not by downloading files or from someone handing out disks at a users' group meeting.

Many companies are now offering what they call "Vaccines" to recognize and alert you to any programming code that looks like a virus. *Mace Gold* contains a vaccine that, I confess, I don't use.

You don't need to be paranoid about viruses. They are nowhere near as prevalent as media hype would have you believe. But they do exist, and it only takes one to wipe you out. So use common sense.

•

reading the manual or simply by experimenting on screen, don't fail to consider the value of a little help from your friends.

A little over a year ago a friend of mine bought an IBM-XT. She wanted a full-featured word processor to help her handle some very sophisticated volunteer responsibilities. Three or four packages would have done the job, including the one I use, but I didn't recommend *XyWrite* because it's tough to learn (or it was—it now comes with an optional menuing system that removes much of the sting) and it isn't widely used outside the publishing industry. Following consideration two, above, I recommended *WordPerfect* because it's the most popular of the major word processing packages, and I thought it likely that my friend would be exchanging information on disk with other WP users.

This turned out to be a mistake. *WordPerfect* has all the capabilities my friend needed, a fine tutorial in its manual and a terrific technical support arrangement, but it's still no easier to learn than *XyWrite*. My friend, who is neither a dummy nor a timid soul, got confused and frustrated. And I couldn't help her much since I don't know more than the most basic *WordPerfect* functions, either. Her computer now sits in a corner, barely used.

In retrospect, it's obvious that my friend would have been much better off if I'd recommended *XyWrite* — relative obscurity, steep learning curve and all—because I could have walked her through every step, answered all her questions, made sure she began to get work out soon, and generally kept her angst to a minimum. She'd be using that computer today, instead of walking past it and feeling silly. When you're looking for software, the availability of a potential private tutor may be the most important consideration of all.

Easy to use or easy to learn?

This talk about getting help with a program opens up a real can of worms. What you really want is a program that you can not only learn to use in a flash, but one that will do everything you might conceivably need done in a particular area and one that will be smooth and easy to use when you're up and running with it. Forget it. These three things don't go together.

Here's an example. Frightened by my friend's disaster, you choose a package that is easy to learn. It has a very fine menu system, which lets you make a series of choices to get the program to do what you want. No problem. But a year later, you're thoroughly familiar with the software and with the tasks you need to accomplish with it. You're sick of paging through menus to accomplish every little thing. You want a quicker, more direct way to tell the program what to do. One solution is the option of turning off the menu system and using direct commands. Some programs offer this option. Most do not.

In the best of all possible worlds, all software would be both easy to learn and easy to use. Unfortunately, precious few programs combine both traits. So there are usually choices to make.

If you're going to be using the program a lot—a few hours every day or two, say—its power and its eventual ease of use are probably more important than its initial ease of learning—as long as you either have help to call on or understand from the outset that figuring things out may be a long and difficult process.

On the other hand, if you're new to computers, don't have a friend who can help much—and especially if you're feeling a little threatened by the whole electronic smorgasbord—then ease of learning should be close to the top of your list. You want something that will get you over the hump quickly, and you should be willing to trade off a few fancy features and supreme slickness somewhere down the road.

This is why I think inexpensive integrated packages are such a good idea. You can get up and running, gain confidence, and *then* switch—if you really need to—to a powerful, free-standing program that might be tough to master. You won't have wasted any money, because the other applications in your integrated package remain useful, and you'll have a simple program to fall back on—if you need to—until you master Big Buster.

In any event, whether it's hard, easy, integrated or free-standing, don't try to learn a software package in its entirety all at once. I'm always surprised at the number of people who get worked up over footnotes or list sorting when they don't yet know how to format, save and print out a letter. You'll inevitably feel overwhelmed at times, but you'll avoid a lot of frustration if you thoroughly master what you need to do basic tasks, then gradually pick up more sophisticated techniques as you come to need them.

It's so hard to find good help these days.

Before you make a final choice, find out all you can about a package's manual—what in computerland is usually called its documentation, as if it were a resident alien. Although some companies issue manuals that are models of organization and straight talk, the mass of software documentation is notorious for its turgid worthlessness. If you're able to check manuals yourself, fine, but the best way to get the word on a package's documentation is by reading the software reviews in magazines like *PC Magazine*, *PC World*, *PC Week*, *Mac World*, *MacUser*, *MacWeek* and *Info World*.

A manual isn't the only tool a software house should provide to help you out. Sometimes you get stuck and the book doesn't seem to cover the situation. This is when you turn to the phone and what's called "technical support." *WordPerfect* has the best technical support in the industry—a toll-free number and unlimited free help for all registered users. This is very popular, and has probably sold thousands of copies of the program to cautious customers, but because it's expensive, other software companies seem reluctant to follow suit. Many answer questions for free, but make you pay for the call. Some have 800 numbers but make you pay by the minute once you're connected. Some make you pay all the way. Some offer support for only sixty or ninety days. Some don't offer any formal help at all. Some offer it but don't install enough phone lines, so you never reach anything but a busy signal. Some are known for putting you on hold seemingly forever. As with documentation, I think the best place to get information on the merits of the technical support offered by a range of companies is in the reviews run by the computer press, although you should be able to get basic answers either from a software retailer or by contacting the companies directly.

One last point. It's usually wise to stay away from release 1.0 of anything. The first version of virtually all software programs is full of bugs and other minor problems, most of which will be fixed pretty quickly for release 1.1 or 1.2. Be just as careful of major upgrades (the jump, say, from 1.3 to 2.0). These tend to contain little unpleasant surprises, too. If you're jogging happily along using *UltraCalc 4.4*, and the UltraCorp offers you an upgrade to *UltraCalc Plus 5.0* for a mere $50, take it, but beware. And call or write for what should be a free version 5.1 to be sent to you as soon as the biggest bugs get fixed.

SOFTWARE TOUR: If it's Tuesday, this must be *The Norton Utilities*.

Like most home office workers, I don't have a personal "big five." I have, basically, a big *one* and a number of littles. My big one, naturally, is a word processing program. For my friend the financial planner, it's a spreadsheet. For a sales rep, it's likely to be a database program. Of course, that doesn't mean we don't use and need other software. I may spend ninety percent of my time at the keyboard writing, but I often use communications software to send my copy to one editor or another. The financial planner and the sales rep both write letters, reports and memos to their clients, customers and contacts. And we all probably use one or two smaller programs to help with specific chores every day.

But we all have different styles and needs. I'm not covering the waterfront here—just offering a brisk, non-technical tour of some standard applications, along with a few of my favorites programs and types of programs. My purpose isn't to delve deep or to recommend specific programs, but to give you a sense of what's available, what it's good for and what choices you might have to make.

In fact, one of the great pleasures of computerdom is successfully matching your needs and style with the appropriate software. Don't just hang by your fingernails, using—as so tentative users do—the easiest bare minimum of your primary application. Jump in. Test, push, question, experiment, kibbitz. *Learn.* You'll make some mistakes, spend some money and ultimately—if you stick with it—control a system, based on your own experience and a few particular software packages, that fits you like a glove.

WORD PROCESSING

This is the most common use for computers in modern home offices, and even antiquated or crippled word processing systems look like magic to someone who's used to typing or writing longhand. Even moderately competent packages can handle an amazing range of tasks. You can move chunks of text quickly and painlessly. You can reformat documents without retyping them. You can dump whole pages of boilerplate into letters or briefs or reports at the touch of a few keys. These days, most programs offer built-in spelling checkers. Many give you a thesaurus, too. And some can do more. Automatic footnoting. The generating of tables of contents and indices. Automatic page numbering with running headers and footers. The insertion of lists of names and addresses into vast numbers of letters or documents. And on. And on. And on.

The big two in this area are *WordPerfect* and Microsoft *Word*, which each have large chunks of both the DOS and the Mac markets. They are both "full-function" programs that do everything but correct your penmanship. On IBM-type machines, *WordStar* and *XyWrite* compete in the same market, *WordStar* as the former leader trying to win back defectors and *XyWrite* as a sort of cult favorite.

A number of the DOS packages got their start as imitators of dedicated word processing systems. *MultiMate* (Ashton-Tate) and *Office Writer* (Office Solutions, Inc.) were developed to feel like the Wang system, while IBM's *DisplayWrite* mimics—what else?—Big Blue's *Display Writer* system. These programs have always struck me as being really clunky—layers of menus and a "page orientation" that makes you flip from "page" to "page" instead of scrolling smoothly through the whole document. But if you've been trained on a dedicated Wang or IBM system, you'll feel at home pretty quickly with them.

A few other DOS programs are famous mainly for being easy to use. *PFS:Professional Write*, which is essentially the same as the word processing module of *PFS:First Choice* has been the best known of these packages for years. But the big noise these days is *Q&A Write* (Symantec), which combines simplicity and power to an unprecedented degree.

PC-Write (Quicksoft), while offering both great speed and a constantly growing range of features, is best known for being a terrific deal (see the box on the facing page).

Sprint (Borland) has recently checked in as a chameleon. You can set it up to use the command keystrokes of any one of several popular word processing programs.

And there are special-purpose word processors for DOS computers, too. *Nota Bene* (Dragonfly Software) is based on the *XyWrite* engine, but has added an integrated text database (sometimes called a "textbase"), specialized "style sheets" that conform to academic standards, and amazing foreign alphabet capabilities to become the program for scholars.

Lotus *Manuscript* was developed specifically to handle long, scientific and technical documents, which must often be accompanied by detailed graphs, charts and diagrams.

MacWrite (Claris) used to be the best known "easy" word processor on the Mac, but in its new form as *MacWrite II* it's become more powerful—and more complicated. *WriteNow* (T/Maker) is the easy-to-use word processing program of choice for the Mac these days. Microsoft *Word* is far and away the most popular word processing program for the Mac. It's awfully powerful, but many users consider it a bit clunky. *Word*'s strongest competition in the DOS world, *WordPerfect*, hasn't really made a big mark among Mac users. Ashton-Tate's

Shareware

Back in the early days of the IBM-PC, a man named Andrew Fluegelman wrote a wonderful communications program to allow people with computers and modems to communicate electronically over the phone lines. But instead of starting up a company and marketing *PC-Talk* through retail channels, Fluegelman, in the best hacker's tradition, put his program in the public domain. Users plucked it, free, from online services, computer bulletin boards and user-group distribution disks. Some users even changed *PC-Talk*, improved it, and added their names to its credit list.

Over the next few years, true public domain software transmogrified into the catchier-sounding and more businesslike shareware. Like public domain software, shareware steers clear of normal distribution channels. But it's copyrighted and isn't generally open to modification. Its authors intend to make some money on it, but have chosen for reasons either philosophical or financial to focus their "marketing" on word of mouth and easy digital distribution.

Although new computer users might find that some shareware companies offer limited support, limited documentation and limited concern for the uninitiated, there is, in fact, an awful lot of very good shareware out there. *PC-Talk*

to page 97

FullWrite Professional is a popular, powerful Mac word processor, although it requires an awful lot of memory to work at its best. *MindWrite* (Delta Point) is a writer's word processor—it includes a terrific outliner, and it can handle files created in a whole host of other programs. Despite gripes about "interface incompatibility", it's fair to say that even comprehensive Mac programs are easier to use than their DOS counterparts.

The fact is that most users never need more than fifty percent of what their word processing programs give them. On the other hand, it's not always easy to gauge what capabilities you'll use, especially if you're not familiar with the species as a whole. Here are a few questions to ask, based on my experience and that of a number of friends.

- *Does the program let you create macros?* These let you store a whole series of actions under a single key. Anybody who writes very much will wind up doing certain things over and over. Macros makes doing them quicker and less tedious. I use macros, for example, to open and close my letters and to pull the address off the page and print it on an envelope.

- *Does it let you delete or move words, lines, sentences, paragraphs and specified blocks of text?* Even some terrific programs aren't so hot here, limiting your options to words and blocks. That's a pain.

- *Does the program offer mailmerge?* This is the ability to merge a list of names and addresses (or anything else, for that matter) into a form letter or similar document. Lets you write to the entire House of Representatives in a flash. Or create your own junk mail. I especially enjoy using this feature, because it makes me feel as if I'm getting back at the cretins who send huge, funny-looking envelopes, imploring "MR. MARK, you *must* return the enclosed coded disk, slipping it carefully into the tiny cellophane packet after first rubbing off the coating to display the *unique* code number that has been issued *only* to the MARK family. You are *already* the *winner*, MR. MARK, of a ONE MILLION DOLLAR MANSION, an INCREDIBLE FERRARI SPORTSCAR, a SIXTEEN CARAT DIAMOND RING or a free subscription to next year's fantastic contest brochure."

- *Does the program include a spelling-checker? A thesaurus?* After scoffing at both these features in the past, I now consider has been overtaken by programs like *Q-Modem*, *ProComm*, *Boyan* and, for the Mac, *White Knight*—all shareware, and all at the top of most lists of fine communications programs. *PC-Write* has long been considered among the swiftest and most powerful word processors. *PC-File* is nearly a standard among simple flat-file database programs. And there are hundreds of other useful shareware programs available on bulletin boards or through users groups. The biggest obstacle many of them face is that they are so cheap that potential customers wrongly assume they can't be much good.

Ah, yes, price. Although you can obtain shareware programs at no cost, you're expected to pay a small fee to the author if you like them well enough to use them regularly. (I've seen everything from $5 to $75 or so—most seem to cluster around the $35 to $45 mark.) When you pay this registration fee, you usually receive a printed instruction booklet to supplement the documentation that came on the disk. You also generally qualify for limited technical support, and you'll receive notice of modifications, upgrades and new products.

Needless to say, a lot of people use these programs without paying the fee. This is theft. Some of us are thieves on purpose, while some of us are thieves by oversight. Sometimes it's hard to judge whether a certain program has

to page 99

a spelling checker a necessity and a thesaurus highly desirable. Both are available as stand-alone packages if the word processor of your dreams has everything but. There are grammar-checkers too, but I'm resisting on the ground that I don't want to know how bad my seventh grade teacher would think my writing is.

- *Does the program include an outliner?* These can be pretty amazing, helping you organize levels of thought and relating them to each other. As befits my undisciplined brain, my outlines tend to be simple lines of freeform text, which I shuffle around and play with until they become fullblown paragraphs of drivel. I wouldn't know what to do with a formal outlining system. But many people claim they simply couldn't function without them.

- *What does the screen look like?* All things being equal, uncluttered screen displays are best because they are the least distracting to someone trying to create reasonably intelligent prose (or poetry, for that matter). *WordPerfect* is probably the champ here. It offers you an almost perfectly blank screen to write on—no ever-present menu bar or distracting lines of information. In *XyWrite*, I can modify the screen display to be cleaner or to contain more information as I please. In some other programs, menu lines or lists of functions can be toggled on and off.

- *Does the program offer on-line help?* This is a sort of manual on disk, which you call up when you're stuck. I never use it (maybe because early versions of my word processing program offered a worthless example of the breed), but many folks seem to rely upon it.

- *Does the program automatically save your document to disk periodically?* This can save you considerable anguish in case of a power failure or a (virtually inevitable) careless move on your part. My word processing program doesn't offer this feature, apparently because its designers consider it a sissyish safeguard that slows things down intolerably (there is a momentary electronic gulp as the system swallows your data). But as one who has more than once unaccountably activated the "abort" sequence and fired hours of work out into the been incorporated into your quiver or not. For example, I registered my copy of *PC-File* right away, because I was using it regularly right away. But it was over a year before I registered *XWord*, a program that converts documents written by one word processor into the format of another. Because I use *XWord* only occasionally, and for a moment or two at a time, I simply didn't stop to realize the degree to which I relied on it, and that I really should pay the fee.

Here's the way I now judge whether to pay the shareware registration fee or not. If I'd be just as glad to erase the disk and use it for something else, I don't pay (and I *do* go ahead and erase the disk). Otherwise, I send in the money. You should, too. Somebody worked hard to produce these programs, and if you use them—or even simply rely on their being there—the least you can do is express your appreciation—at bargain rates.

Besides users groups, electronic bulletin boards and online services, there are a few other places to get shareware. The best known is probably PC-SIG (PC Software Interest Group), which will send you a directory for $12.95 from which you can order programs for a few dollars each (you still have to pay registration fees). Before you get started collecting shareware, though, get a look at a book entitled *How to Get Free Software*, by Alfred Glosbrenner (St. Martin's). It's the authority on this topic, and it's available in many libraries.

●

ether unsaved, all I can say is I sure wish it did. Boy, do I wish it did.
- *Does it offer automatic page numbering?* You'll appreciate this if you write anything longer than one-page memos or letters. It's exactly the kind of thing computers should handle for us.
- *Does the program support most currently popular printers?* This shouldn't be a problem, but check. And if you already have a printer, or if you know what printer you are going to buy, check for sure.
- *Can you bypass the menus when you become familiar with the program?* Awright!
- *Does it handle footnotes, headers, footers, indices and tables of contents?* If you are a grad student or a lawyer or a consultant or something, this stuff comes in handy. If you're a normal person, you'll never use most of it. Note: in some programs, automatic page numbering is a function of the header capability.
- *Will it output side-by-side columns? Snaking columns?* Snaking columns are the kind you find in magazines—the bottom of one column jumps to the top of the next. These capabilities might come in handy if you handle your organization's newsletter. I've used side-by-side columns writing industrial video scripts: words for the narrator in one column, suggestions for camera shots and angles at the appropriate spot in the other. (These suggestions are always ignored by the director and the camera operator, but they impress the guy who's paying you.)

Other people you talk to will no doubt mention other features you might want to consider. Keep in mind that while many programs don't offer all these possibilities, many offer all this and much more. Every year or so, *PC Magazine* runs comprehensive, comparative reviews of dozens of packages. It's worth digging out.

SPREADSHEETS

The first time I saw an electronic spreadsheet in action, I couldn't believe it. In the late 70s, I helped negotiate several teachers' contracts as a member of the local board of education. I well remember going laboriously through hypothetical pay schedules, working the math on a calculator for each step on each line. It took hours to figure totals on just a few possible proposals. A few years later I watched over a colleague's shoulder as he played with his department's budget in Lotus *1-2-3*. He'd enter new options, push a button, and watch as revised figures rippled across the screen. Magic!

Even the simplest spreadsheet programs can do much more sophisticated tricks than that, but most people gratefully use them for essentially the same purpose: the quick, convenient manipulation of data to answer twin sixty-four dollar questions, "Where are we?" and "What if?". You can use a spreadsheet to work up a budget or a financial proposal, track income, outgo and expenses, calculate your taxes and help dozens of other money tasks.

The first spreadsheet was the now-defunct *VisiCalc*, which was written to work on the Apple II, and was largely responsible for the success of that early machine. Lotus *1-2-3* was inspired by *VisiCalc*, but was from the beginning written to take advantage of the more powerful IBM-PC. It sold like hotcakes from the start, and still remains at the top of most software charts. *1-2-3* dominates the spreadsheet market in a way that no other program in other areas approaches. There have long been other great, full-featured spreadsheets—many people have considered *SuperCalc* (Computer Associates International Inc.), for example, to be superior to *1-2-3* in some areas—but they've had to settle for a small part of the market.

Because *1-2-3* is so dominant, hundreds of "templates" have been written for it. These are the numeric equivalent of form letters—you plug in the one that best handles the task you have in mind, maybe make a few small changes, and then get to work without having to "program" the things yourself. My favorite *1-2-3* templates convert the spreadsheet into a tax form and let you play with various alternatives as you try to figure out how to get a refund from the IRS while avoiding a long jail term.

1-2-3 lists for close to $500, and usually costs a little over $300. Not cheap. Several programs have tried to make headway by looking as much like Lotus *1-2-3* as possible, but charging much less. *VP-Planner* (Paperback Software) and *Quattro* (Borland) are the two best known. They both add a few extras of their own, but their main appeal

Pirating And Copy Protection

Pirating is stealing software, and almost everybody's done it at one time or another. It's very simple. You just copy a software package onto a new disk or set of disks and pass it on to a friend or co-worker. The result is two programs—or three or five or a dozen—for the price of one. There are times when that's pretty hard to resist.

But resist we should. Pirating isn't just the theft of a disk, it's the theft of somebody's work. As a writer, I'm especially sensitive to that. I want people to buy lots of copies of this book, not just buy one, make photocopies and pass them around. (I know, people are always passing books around. But only one person reads a book at a time. That's the difference between a legitimate loan and a theft of someone's work.)

One common justification for pirating is that a lot of software is overpriced—especially for an individual user, as opposed to a corporation which can often swing a great deal on pricing. This is true. A lot of software at least *seems* to be grotesquely overpriced. That's where the temptation comes in. But a lot of houses are overpriced. We don't steal them because it's not an easy thing to do.

Another rationalization is that nobody in his right mind wants to spend a few hundred

to page 103

dollars on a program until its clearly the *right* program. So give me a copy, old friend, and let me try it out as if it were shareware. I have a lot of sympathy with this point of view, as long as it's honestly stated. And I really don't see any harm in making a copy for this purpose. But if you find you don't like the program, you should reformat the disk. And if you find you do like it, you should buy your own copy. This is where the process often breaks down.

To combat piracy, many software manufacturers used to burden their programs with "copy protection"—a few lines of code that wouldn't allow the package to be copied more than the once or twice necessary to back it up and install it on your hard drive. Some also required an obnoxious so-called "key disk" be in the A: drive of your computer.

This was intolerably clumsy to many honest computer users (and simply intolerable to many dishonest ones), and manufacturers of programs that overcame protection found a brisk market. A short, sharp arms race seems to have led to the defeat of the defense. Copy protection is now rare on software other than games.

Piracy is wrong. Copy protection is ugly. "Testing" a package is hard to condemn. Play fair.

Besides, you need the manual.

•

is that they work with *1-2-3* files and look and feel like *1-2-3* while costing perhaps half as much at standard discounts.

Other programs have decided to stay simple to appeal to folks who need neither a lot of sophisticated capabilities nor the ability to generate a huge spreadsheet. The shareware program *PC-Calc* (Buttonware) is probably the best known of these.

Lately, some heavy hitters have attacked the *1-2-3* hegemony by offering, not just more power, but whole new capabilities. The leader of the new pack is *Excel* (Microsoft), which was first offered for the Mac, but is now available for the 286 and 386 IBM-type machines as well. It's got way too much power and sophistication for me—think of a Volkswagen driver dropped into an Indy car—but anybody expecting to be doing serious financial workups can't afford not to look at the *Excel* option.

If your work at home is going to entail the manipulation of a lot of financial data, you probably already know a lot more than I do about spreadsheets. If you're not sure whether you need a spreadsheet or not, you have several options. First, don't forget that *PFS:First Choice* and Microsoft *Works* include good spreadsheet modules. Second, you can check out shareware programs like *PC-Calc* at very little expense, and register only if you find that you have a need. Third, just wait. There's no rule that says you have to own a spreadsheet just because you're working on a computer at home. If your business is simple and straightforward, you can profitably rely on those old standbys, pencil, paper and calculator—just don't tempt yourself by watching an electronic spreadsheet in action.

DATABASES

The first database I ever used—or tried to use—was the original MS-DOS version of *dBase II*. I turned on the machine, called up the program, and was greeted with ... a dot. Nothing else. No instructions, no options, no real acknowledgement that the program was ready to go to work for me. That was my introduction to the infamous *dBase* "dot prompt." Needless to say, I didn't get much done that day. And when I asked for the program's manual, all I got was a horselaugh. Those were the good old days, when men were men and if you didn't already know how to use *dBase II*, there was seemingly no way for you to learn. Databases have come a long way since then. Many of them can actually be negotiated by mere mortals.

There are basically two kinds of database programs. "Flat file" programs or "file managers" are generally simpler and cheaper. They let you search for data in one file only—which for many people is quite enough. "Relational" programs or "database managers," on the other hand, are usually more complex and more expensive. They let you pull information out of several files, *relating* information in one to information in others.

For example, in my flat file database, I have a list of members of a local organization. I've got names, addresses, phone numbers, areas of interest, and the names of subcommittees these folks are willing to serve on. If I want to, I can pull out everyone who's ever told me they'd work on the newsletter or the entertainment committee. I could refine things further and ask for only those willing helpers who live on a certain street. And if I wanted to I could eliminate everyone named Smith. In short, I can set up almost any set of requirements I want to—as long as all the information to be culled exists in the single file where I keep the information.

But what if I was keeping lists for two organizations which for some reason or other wanted to merge? I might want to find out how many people already belonged to both. Well, I'd have to pull complete lists from each organization's file and compare them by hand—unless I was using a relational database. Then I could simply ask it to spit out the names that appeared in *both* files.

Of course, there are fancier uses for relational databases than comparing membership names. You plug into one of these systems when you order something out of a catalogue and the person on the other end of the phone asks for your name and zip code, then proceeds to read back your address, bank card number and life history. When that happens, you've just come into contact with a sophisticated relational database management system—one that, for all its power, you can essentially emulate at home if your work calls for it.

Big time relational database programs like *dBase IV*, *Rbase for DOS* and *Paradox* (Borland) can do amazing things, and they can be "programmed" to offer customized screens and operations. In fact, a whole class of dBase programmers and consultants is making a very good living doing just that for companies of all sizes. But because they incorporate good menu systems (which you can override as you become more expert), these big guns are all a lot easier for normal people to use than early packages used to be. If you think you'll need relational power, you'll probably be able to manage a relational program. *dBase* is still the standard, but there are dozens of competitors out there, including the two mentioned above. An especially interesting relational database is *FoxBase* (Fox Software), which speaks *dBase*'s language but is considered by many users to be a superior program at a lower price. *VP-Info* (Paperback Software), at a discounted $60 or so is a sort of low cost *dBase* clone, just as *VP-Planner* is an inexpensive *1-2-3* alternative. *PowerBase* (PowerBase Systems) is a powerful relational program that is known for exceptional ease of use.

My needs are such that a flat file program serves me fine. I use *PC-File* (Buttonware), a shareware package that I think cost me about $40 to register (it's about $70 now). *Professional File* (Software Publishing) has been the standard in this field for years, and it remains a simple, useful program. But at about $150 from mail order houses, I think it's just too expensive—especially when compared to *PFS:First Choice* and its database module. A popular option these days is *Q&A* (Symantec), which combines a file manager with a nifty word processing module that was upgraded a bit and turned into the stand-alone *Q&A Write*. The most spectacular thing about *Q&A*, though, is that it offers a so called "natural language interface." In other words, you can ask it to handle certain operations by typing a sentence in English, rather than by flipping through menus or by entering arcane commands. For occasional users especially, this capability is a terrific convenience—and it works.

COMMUNICATIONS

This is one of those areas where there's a considerable gap between theory and reality. In theory, you can plug a modem into your computer, hook into your phone line and then send and receive files digitally to and from similarly equipped systems anywhere in the world.

In practice, electronic communication is often frustrating, infuriating and costly—subject to glitches of every kind. Time after time, it's taken me hours, multiple phone calls and goodness knows how many dollars to send simple 3,000-word manuscripts over the phone. Sometimes the problem has been an error on my end, sometimes it's

On-line Services

One of the most seductive elements of computerdom is the idea that you, sitting comfortably at home, can push a few buttons on your keyboard and tap into all sorts of information, expertise and digitized wisdom.

Generic
When people talk about going on-line, they're usually talking about being connected to one of the general purpose services like *CompuServe*, *Delphi*, *GEnie* or, most recently, the much-ballyhooed *Prodigy*. Thousands of people are registered users of these electronic supermarkets, which give them a little of everything— you can play games on them, send messages to other members, check the current headlines or scores, converse on line, consult with experts in special interest groups, download interesting software, and buy all kinds of products.

You can usually access these services through a local number at little or no cost, but they're anything but free. Most of the general services charge a registration fee (often discounted) from about $20 to about $40. You pay little or nothing in the way of phone charges, because they all offer packet-switched local calls in most areas. But you do pay access charges that often vary according to day, time and the speed of

to page 109

been a goof on the other. And sometimes we just haven't been able to figure out *what* the trouble was.

As you can probably tell, I'm a little grouchy about communications software. Nonetheless, the idea of being able to move data instantly from computer to computer is irresistible. And it is possible to set up a system that works—newspapers regularly receive electronic copy from all over the place filed by reporters who are anything but digital wizards.

For me, without the aid of consultants and programmers, the key is a communications program that is easy to use, but that still offers at least a limited "script language"—a programming feature that lets you automate repetitive tasks much as do the macros in a good word processing package.

Complex, powerful programs like *Smartcom III* (Hayes Microcomputer Products), *Crosstalk Mk.4* (Microstuf), *Relay Gold* and *Relay Silver* (Relay Communications) offer advanced script languages and the ability to do fancy turns: things like communicating in the background while another application is working in the foreground, or managing a complex electronic bulletin board, or even sending and receiving data at the same time.

If you need something this sophisticated, by all means do your homework, check with your electronic correspondents and go for it.

Otherwise, I think the simpler the better. Solid programs like *Boyan* (Boyan), *ProComm* (Datastorm Technologies) and *Q-Modem* (The Forbin Project) are all available as shareware, they're all cheap ($35 to $50) and they're all fairly easy to operate. (*ProComm Plus*, at $75, offers a few more features than its older sibling and is offered through normal retail channels—it's been getting raves in the computer press.) Give a few of these programs a try. If one of them does what you want, send in your registration money and consider your search over.

For Mac users, *Red Ryder*—now called *White Knight* (FreeSoft)—is a near-standard. It's available either through retail channels or as shareware (around $80). *Microphone II* (Software Ventures) is a more powerful program with an elaborate script language, but it also has the reputation of being relatively easy to use ($295 list).

I don't have very complicated needs. I just want to get my copy where it needs to go in one, painless try. Most people working from a your modem—anything from $5 per hour up to $20 or so. Some charge monthly minimums, regardless of your use. The exception is *Prodigy*, which charges a flat $9.95 per month, regardless of on-line time.

Most of the on-line folks I know started by signing up with one of the general services— usually the one that gave them the best financial deal through free hours or promotional pricing. If you have a computer and a modem, you should probably at least try out one of these systems. They can be enjoyable and valuable in their own rights, and they each have a number of "gateways" to other, less general services. *CompuServe*, for example lets you send MCI Mail and gives you access to the *Dow Jones News/Retrieval Service*. And *Delphi* lets you open the door into *Dialog*, a huge collection of dozens of specialized databases.

I use both *CompuServe* and *GEnie*. Although I don't sign on very often, it's nice to know that I can when I want or need to. What keeps me from being a devoted user is the fact that, as a general rule, on-line services need to become easier to use if they're going to attract anything approaching universal appeal. Despite all sorts of manuals and sporadic practice, I find that it's not all that easy to navigate on-line. I always seem to be cycling through the same sets of menus, or jumping back to a level where I don't

to page 111

home office are probably in very much the same boat, and these programs will do the trick.

One more thing. If you're going to be communicating with the same person most of the time, it's a good idea for both of you to settle on the same program. I don't know how many times I've traced a problem to the fact that we had two inexpert users driving two programs that didn't use the same words for similar functions. And the fact that many communications software manuals are horrible—even by normal software standards—didn't help.

Remote computing

There is a special segment of the communications software market that is especially interesting to people who collaborate with colleagues who aren't nearby. Many of these programs were actually invented to let an expert at the home office help someone in the field when a computer problem arose. But they also let you and your collaborator see the same screens, and let you work on them together. Most also work well to help you actually use your computer at work *through* your computer at home. Lots of possibilities for the home worker here.

I've never used a remote computing program, but the best known is *Carbon Copy Plus* (Meridian Technology), which is bundled with some brands of modems. Others are *Co-Compute* (Harmony Technology Associates), *Co/Session*, (Triton Technologies), *In-Sync* (American Video Teleconferencing) and *PC-Anywhere* (Dynamic Microprocessor Associates), which also offers something called *PC-MacTerm* for situations when there's a Mac on one end of the line. To use them you need two copies—one running on each computer. And to use them effectively, you really need two phone lines—one to talk over and one over which to move data.

Electronic mail

This is digital communication with a twist. Instead of dialing another computer directly, you dial a "post office" and send data to your correspondent's "mail box." There are some real advantages to sending data this way. First, you can simultaneously send the same message to multiple mail boxes if you wish. And second, you can send and want to be. Actually, I'm fairly sure that if I made a really concerted effort, I could crack the code. But as a home office worker who pays his own bills—no corporation to pick up the tab here—I can't justify the expense of a concerted effort.

Communications

Electronic mail (or "E-Mail") services like MCI, Western Union's EasyLink, and AT&T Mail excel at getting information from here to there instantly. They're commonly used by business people rather than the sort of computer-users who make up such a large part of *CompuServe's* membership. I use MCI, coupled with Lotus *Express*, and find it a terrific combination for moving formatted digital documents of virtually any size. You can also send flashy MCI "letters" through the U.S. Mail, deliver hard copy the next day, and even transmit faxes through the system—to multiple correspondents.

E-Mail companies bill in various ways. Monthly or yearly charges for your "mailbox" are common—MCI gets $18 per year for its basic service. Some charge for use by the minute. Others, like MCI charge by the size of the document you're transmitting—45 cents for the first 500 characters, $1 for up to 7,500, and $1 for each additional 7,500. Special services cost extra. The main three E-Mail services are roughly competitive in price, and for an average sized document

to page 113

receive your mail at times that are convenient to you—not to the person or people on the other end.

There are lots of electronic "post offices" out there. You can send E-mail through *CompuServe* or other online services. Or you can use any of the specialized services like AT&T Mail, Western Union's Easy-Link or MCI Mail.

MCI is my favorite mainly because of a program that makes using it easy. Lotus *Express* was designed specifically to automate and facilitate your use of MCI Mail, and it does its job supremely well. At its simplest level, it will, on command, call the MCI access number in your area, log on to the system, check to see if there's any electronic mail for you, and download any it finds—all automatically. It will operate with similar ease if you have documents to send. It can be customized to look for mail from specific senders. And it will keep track of documents sent and received.

Although it gobbles up a lot of memory to do this, *Express* can be set to run in the background, automatically polling your mailbox periodically while you work in another application. *Express* retains the formatting commands in my *XyWrite* files, so that I can send and receive documents with proper margins, line-spacing, centering, headers and page breaks. It also handles complex *1-2-3* spreadsheets flawlessly. *Express* is a limited program—you shouldn't consider it as an all-purpose communications package—but if you expect to be sending a lot of electronic mail—and if your most frequent correspondents have MCI accounts—it's a smooth option.

DESKTOP PUBLISHING

This application is hot, and with good reason. These are page-layout programs that, at their best, allow an individual computer user to design and lay out an attractive book, magazine, brochure, newsletter or advertisement. No T-squares, no X-Acto™ knives, no wax machines and paste-up. Who wouldn't be fascinated?

The two best-known packages are *Ventura Publisher* (Xerox) the IBM champ, and *Pagemaker* (Aldus), the top Mac program (which also comes in an IBM version). They are both expensive, and while *Ventura* is the more complex, neither is exactly a snap to learn. But they're both are *much* cheaper than, say, Federal Express. A standard chapter that I transmit might cost $4 or so by MCI. Sending hard copy by FedEx would cost $14.

Databases

Dialog isn't the only encyclopedic database available on line. There are dozens, hundreds, perhaps thousands. Among the best-known are *BRS*, *NewsNet*, *Wilsonline*, *Infoline*, *Orbit*, *Vu/Text*, *Lexis* and *Nexis*. Most of these are expensive to join and expensive to use. (How does $75 an hour suit you?) They are also difficult to navigate—the province, for the most part, of practiced research librarians and other highly-trained professionals.

Both *Dialog* and *BRS* have made an effort to bring database access to the multitudes, with *Knowledge Index* and *BRS After Dark*, which operate in the off-peak hours after 6 PM and on weekends. These are both scaled-down, simplified versions of the two companies' real heavyweights, but they still offer a vast range of databases on dozens of topics, and they've both earned a strong following among writers, students and others who need to locate odd information—often at odd times.

It costs $35 to register with *Knowledge Index*, then $24 per hour on-line. You can also purchase copies of articles and documents you

to page 115

terrific and they've both been used by professional designers for several years now.

I've used *Ventura* in a rudimentary way for a couple of years, and I find that while it has power to spare for big jobs, it's a bit musclebound for smaller ones. I've also had the chance to play with *Pagemaker* on a Mac, and I really liked its more direct approach to smaller documents. There are dozens of other packages out there, mostly less expensive and less powerful. GEM *Desktop Publisher* (Digital Research) is a good example of a capable but not full-bore package. Simpler, less capable and cheaper are *PFS:First Publisher* (Software Publishing) and *Newsroom Pro* (Springboard Software). And an interesting thing is happening. As time goes on, full-function word processing programs are picking up more and more desktop publishing features, like column manipulation, the ability to integrate graphics into text files and very sophisticated printer control. For simple tasks like newsletters, I find myself using my word processor with a laser printer and special fonts rather than calling up *Ventura*. The newer versions of *WordPerfect* and *Word* offer even more possibilities.

One of the raps on desktop publishing is that it has given enthusiastic incompetents access to design power, resulting in ugly documents full of funny fonts. If you're an enthusiastic incompetent who aspires to better things, and a Mac user to boot, help is at hand. Broderbund is offering *DTP Adviser*, "stackware" written to work with Apple's *HyperCard* environment. It's a combined tutorial, project planner, glossary and database that helps you get your DTP chore done reasonably well and on time.

If you're intrigued by the possibilities of desktop publishing, check the iconoclastic *Personal Publishing* magazine for solid reviews and good information. *Publish!*, a more mainstream periodical offered by the publishers of *PC World* is glitzier and less gritty.

This is a woefully inadequate appreciation of desktop publishing. But DTP is a major application that has so many implications that I don't want to short any by mentioning only some. And if I tried to cover everything, I'd be writing a book. Read up on this one, and try to get good long looks at a variety of programs—either at retail stores, computer shows or the offices of friendly graphic designers. For many home office workers, desktop publishing can open whole new worlds of opportunity.

> locate for $7.95 plus the cost of the document or 25 cents a page for articles. You also get two free hours when you register so that you can learn the system without a lot of pressure. Registering with *BRS after Dark* costs $75, and you're committed to paying a $12 monthly minimum. Depending on the actual files you're looking at, on-line charges start at $6 and go up to as high as $48.
>
> •

TSRs

Remember when I said that Lotus *Express* could operate in the background while another application was on your screen? In that format, *Express* is being used as a TSR—a Terminate and Stay Resident program. These packages are designed to be loaded into your computer's memory, but to remain out of sight until you trigger them (or, in *Express*'s case, until they are triggered by your computer's clock). Hence, their other names—memory-resident or RAM-resident programs.

The best-known TSR is Borland's *Sidekick*, a so-called "desk accessory" that offers a notepad, a calculator, an appointment calendar, a phone dialer and a table that displays the 256-character extended ASCII character set on screen. (ASCII stands for American Standard Code for Information Interchange, and this feature is mostly for programmers). There are lots of other desk accessories on the market, all offering more or less the same sorts of features pioneered by *Sidekick*. I've tried *Sidekick*, but it always just seemed to get in the way. My word processing package offers nine widows, so I've never felt the need of a notepad, I can find and dial phone numbers either from inside my word processor or by using another program (below), I can access an ASCII symbols table more quickly from within my word processor than through another program, I need my appointment calendar open in front of me if I'm not going to miss meetings, and I'm content to use a separate, desktop calculator.

But many, many people rely heavily on *Sidekick* and *Sidekick*'s competitors. To someone using a spreadsheet, for example, the ability to pop up a notepad without storing the worksheet and suspending the whole session is attractive unto addictive.

Borland now offers *Sidekick Plus*, which includes an outliner, a simple file manager, a communications module and all sorts of new and wonderful attractions. I'm still not tempted, but it may be just the ticket for you.

Hot Line

I *do* use TSRs, though. One is an element of the *Mace Utilities* (below), which is only called upon after a disaster. But the other I use many times a day. At base, *Hot Line* (General Information) is a gigantic list of phone numbers and addresses (compiled in *dBase*, by the way). For about $50 (discounted), you get 10,000 entries, covering a broad range of businesses, organizations and government agencies. Want to know how to call the Boston Red Sox at Fenway Park? The number's here. The American Bookseller's Association? Yup. The Venezualan Embassy? Uh-huh. You can create a personal directory, too, of course, and you can also buy specialized directories for about a dozen fields, covering ad agencies, public relations firms, publishers, newspapers, and radio and TV stations. This is terrific, and it's saved me plenty in directory assistance charges. But what I like best about *Hot Line* is that it dials my phone for me and keeps a detailed list of every number I call and how long I spend on the line. This comes in awfully handy when I try to separate business and personal calls, and when I need to submit expense accounts. *Hot Line* is one of those programs (you'll find your own) that dovetails perfectly with the job I do and the way I do it.

There are other good dialer-directory-record keepers out there. Borland's new *Sidekick Plus* offers a phone module that is vastly more powerful than the simple dialer in the original *Sidekick*. For Mac users,

Focal Point (TENpoint0) and *QuickDex* (Casady and Greene Inc.) can help manage phone business.

There are hundreds of TSRs on the market, and a lot of them are enticing. But since they all want to reside in memory, you can load only a limited number of them. At one point, I habitually loaded *Gofer* (Microlytics), a TSR that will search through files to locate a word or phrase. But with a large word processing file open, I kept running out of memory. Now I use *Gofer* the way I use *Express*—as a stand-alone program that I run from outside my major application.

PIMs

A PIM is a Personal Information Manager. In a way these are the big brothers of desktop accessories like *Sidekick*. The idea is that you should be able not just to computerize names, addresses, phone numbers, appointments and notes on various topics, but to *link* them so that their relationships can be viewed from different perspectives. Most of these programs combine the attributes of outliners, file mangers and text databases. Some of the best known for the IBM world are *Grandview* (Symantec), *Info-XL* (Valor Software) and *Agenda* (Lotus). For the Mac, *Focal Point* and *Hyperworks Organizer* both take advantage of Apple's *HyperCard*. (See the box on the next page.)

I've got to tell you that although this market is supposed to be hot, I simply have no use for these things. They sound good at first, but all too often they make a complicated, high-tech operation out of something that could be handled better by a pencil and a pad of paper. Or maybe my needs just aren't complex enough to require this kind of help. Or maybe my brain is simply too muddled. Even if I thought PIMs were the greatest idea since flannel sheets, there's a major drawback I'd have to overcome: if you rely on a Personal Information Manager, you'd better have access to your computer at all times. This isn't too realistic for me.

Even if you agree with me about PIMs per se, there are other types of organizers that might be worth looking at. One of the best is *ACT!*, which was written for MS-DOS machines to help salespeople track clients. But *ACT!* (Conductor Software) is great for anyone who does a lot of phone work that requires follow up action—letters, updating a tickler, a later phone call at a specific time, maintaining a log. Chang

HyperCard

Everybody defines *HyperCard* as "an information environment." Big help. Maybe my local library is *HyperCard*.

Bill Atkinson, who invented it, calls *HyperCard* "a software erector set." That's a little more helpful, but I'm still stumped, aren't you?

Let's check this out.

HyperCard is for the Mac—it's included when you buy a new model.

HyperCard uses as its basic metaphor a stack of cards, each one holding information—either text, graphics or sound.

Therefore, *HyperCard* applications—programs written to run with *HyperCard*—are often called "stackware."

HyperCard links related information. This is based on the concept of *hypertext*, a totally free-form text database in which words, sentences and paragraphs can be found and linked according to the user's needs and interests.

HyperCard and applications based upon it are non-linear. The idea is that you can use "buttons" to jump from card to card, following related subjects or ideas. Supposedly, this closely duplicates the way people think.

HyperCard includes its own script language. You can write *HyperCard* stacks yourself,

to page 119

or you can modify and customize stacks written by others.

In *HyperCard* applications, you can enter your own information (text, graphic, sound), you can find specific information, or you can browse through related topics.

HyperCard seems to be having trouble breaking into the business market, because it's too freeform.

HyperCard has been a great hit in the home and hobby markets because it's "neat."

Good *HyperCard* applications seem to knock out everyone who sees them.

To really understand what *HyperCard* offers, you really have to use it for a while.

There are now *HyperCard*-like products for character-based DOS machines. *Hyperpad* (Brightbill-Roberts) is the best known.

•

Labs' *C.A.T.* (which stands for contacts, activities, time) does similar work on the Mac. Programs like this are often called "Activity Tracking Software," and as a group they make a lot of sense for many home workers. They help you organize your life without trying to take it over.

CONNECTIONS AND CONVERSIONS

Once you've committed to doing virtually all your work on a computer, you'll inevitably run into times when you have to move data to or from another machine, or convert files created by one program into files readable by another.

The simplest situation comes up after you buy that little laptop you've been lusting after. How do you get your most recent draft of a report into the little machine so that you can work on it in the hotel room tonight? Well, maybe you can simply copy the draft onto a disk and pop the disk into your portable. But the portable uses 3-1/2-inch disks and your desktop machine is probably configured only with 5-1/4-inchers. So much for that idea.

Enter programs like the *Brooklyn Bridge* (Fifth Generation) and *LapLink* (Traveling Software). Combined with something called a null-modem cable, these packages make it easy as pie to move files from one machine to another. If you move files frequently between or among DOS machines with different sized disks, a program like this is almost required.

A tougher nut to crack—and one you're less likely to run into—is converting a file created in one program into another program without losing its formatting. For example, for a time I was doing a lot of editing for a small sports magazine. Authors were good enough to supply their copy on disk, but they used a variety of word processing programs. Different programs use different hidden symbols to create new lines, paragraph breaks, margin controls and so forth, and if I simply called the raw files into *my* word processing program, I got plenty of text, no clear formatting and lots of garbage. The solution was to *convert* those *WordPerfect* or *WordStar* documents into *XyWrite*. My favorite conversion program, which seems to get better all the time, is *XWord* (Roland Gans Software), a shareware program that is quick and slick. Other programs are better known: *Word-for Word* (Mastersoft) and *Software Bridge* (System Compatibility) for example. They don't all convert the same sets of programs, so check to be sure that your most likely subjects and targets are included in the program's conversion capabilities.

I also use a program called *Media Master* (Intersecting Concepts) to convert files written on old, pre-MS-DOS, CP/M machines. As time goes on, I see fewer and fewer manuscripts created on Kaypro IIs, the Morrows, Northstars or Osbornes, but *Media Master* has saved me a lot of time and trouble over the years.

Finally, and more important all the time as Macintoshes make greater headway in business, is moving files between DOS machines and Macs. *MacLink Plus* (DataViz) is a program that combines the attributes of the straightforward transfer programs and the more complex conversion packages. With it I could, for example, translate a DOS-created *XyWrite* document into a properly formatted Microsoft *Word* file on the Mac. *LapLink Mac* (Traveling Software), on the other hand, moves files neatly, but doesn't convert. (This may not be a problem if you're using essentially the same packages on each machine—*Word* is a good example.) On the way: disk drives and controllers that let you go either way—Mac or PC. The newest models in the SE and Mac II lines already incorporate disk drives that can read data created in the IBM environment.

CONTEXT SWITCHING

One of the hot computing concepts these days is "multitasking". This means running more than one application at the same time—having both of them working simultaneously. For example, you could have your database program running a monster sort at the same time you were plugging new numbers into your spreadsheet.

This is the sort of thing that 386 machines and OS/2 software will make common—in maybe five years. For now, though, most of us would settle for a way to pop back and forth between that database program and our spreadsheet without closing one, going back to DOS and starting up the other. Not real multitasking, just quick, efficient switching from one program to another.

The best known context switching program is *Software Carousel* (SoftLogic Solutions). It lets you pop back and forth among up to a dozen programs by storing those you aren't using in whatever Random Access Memory your system has free, including either expanded RAM or that otherwise useless extended RAM. Another such program, although it takes an entirely different approach, is *Switch-It* (Black & White International), which was originally conceived as a tool for *dBase* power-users.

I finally understood the need for such switching programs when I found myself having to quit my word processor repeatedly to start and run my desktop publishing program, and vice-versa. Now I jockey back and forth at the touch of a button. Nifty.

DOS SHELLS

This is a category that you Mac users can just sneer at. A DOS shell is a program that lets you avoid the uncommunicative prompt of the IBM-type operating system. Macs, of course, have a friendly "shell" built in.

Instead of having to learn and then type specific—and often obscure—commands, DOS shells let you choose from menus of choices. DOS shells make a number of operations a bit slower for experienced users, but for many people, they take a lot of the fear out of computer use—surely a worthy accomplishment. The current king of the shells is *Norton Commander* (Peter Norton Computing), which seems to get good reviews even from grizzled DOS veterans—probably because it keeps the old DOS prompt on the screen at all times in case you get the urge to type something arcane. The only shell I've used much is *X-Tree* (Executive Systems), which makes some housekeeping chores simpler, but which I call on only occasionally.

UTILITIES

Strictly speaking, software utilities are programs that do a single, limited task. There are many of them. Some print addresses on envelopes. Some stop your cursor from blinking. Some rotate your spreadsheets ninety degrees so you can run them across multiple sheets of fan-fold paper.

But the word "utilities" is often taken to mean something much more specific among computer users: programs that either save you from disaster or try to protect you from it.

The grandfather of all utilities packages is *The Norton Utilities*, originally written by computer celebrity Peter Norton. Hundreds of thousands of computer users owe *NU* their piece of mind (if not their jobs) for its ability to find and restore files that have been mistakenly erased from disk. *The Norton Utilities* and its closest competitors, the *Mace Utilities* (Fifth Generation Softwaree) and *PC Tools* (Central Point Software), can do much more than that in their most recent, highly sophisticated versions—specifically, they can help you recover from an accidental, and formerly catastrophic, hard disk reformat. For the Mac, *Symantec Utilities* (Symantec) does much the same thing, along with the Mac version of *PC Tools*. And they all offer all sorts of helpful methods for sorting your files and packing them efficiently on your hard disk. I've used Norton gratefully over the years. (Gratefully hardly covers it. I once mysteriously trashed a long manuscript that I'd been working on in my spare time for several years—no copies, of course—and while the normal, fast, restore function couldn't help me, the program let me laboriously locate and stick chunks of the story back together again. *Norton* got every bit of it.) But, churl that I am, I'm a Mace man, myself. Paul Mace seems to approach disk operations from the point of view that something *will* eventually go horribly wrong, and I find that strangely comforting.

For example, an advanced version of the *Mace Utilities* called *Mace Gold* includes a TSR called POP, which takes a picture of everything in memory every few minutes. For me, it helps make up for the fact that my word processing program doesn't have an automatic save feature. If you lose power suddenly, or accidentally fail to save properly, POP can reconstruct the contents of your RAM. I set POP to click its pic every ten minutes (you can choose anything from a minute to an hour), and work with much greater peace of mind.

Whether you have a hard disk or not, you really should invest in *The Norton Utilities*, the *Mace Utilities*, *PC Tools* or the *Symantec Utilities*. Sooner or later, everyone will blow a file by mistake, and everyone should have the option of restoring it instead of leaping from the nearest high window.

Other, more recent, utilities attempt to head off hard disk problems by monitoring and correcting the disk itself. The best known are *Spinrite* (Gibson Research), *Disk Technician* (Prime Solutions) and Mace's *Htest-Hformat*. You're messing with things at a pretty basic level when you put these guys to work, and you may not feel comfortable doing that. On the other hand, I recently bought *Spinrite II*, and seeing it work has given me a lot more confidence that the data on my hard disk will remain secure. That's pretty important to a one-man show.

BACKUP

If you have a hard disk, virtually all your work is sitting digitally on a small plate revolving at great speed within incredibly small tolerances. The wonder isn't that things go wrong occasionally, but that they don't go wrong more often.

Here's what Paul Mace writes on the envelope containing his *Mace Gold* utility package:

"When you use your computer to store valuable work you relinquish amateur status. As a professional you should recognize that making regular (daily) backups is a prudent necessity. One day, without warning, you will lose some or all of your data, due to the inherent risks of digital computers.... You should be prepared to reconstruct any information for which you do not have current duplicate copies."

Daily backups may put a strain on most people's self discipline, but even weekly backups can relieve anxiety—and save you at least some anguish when you "lose some or all of your data, due to the inherent risks of digital computers...."

There are a number of ways to back up hard drives for both Macs and IBM-style computers. The simplest and probably the best is to use a tape backup system based on the little DC2000 cartridge. I use an Archive tape drive. Other well-known names include Tallgrass, Mountain, Irwin and Jade. The great advantage to these things is that you tell them to run a backup and they do the job for you. My system backs up my current 20 MB or so of data in just about twenty minutes. The great disadvantage is that they cost a lot of money. I spent about $300 for my Archive drive and another $100 for a card called a "host adaptor" (you don't need one of these if you're running just one floppy disk instead of two). I also pay about $20 per tape cartridge.

Since tape systems cost so much, many home office workers turn to disk-based backup systems. These programs transfer your data onto normal floppy disks. The major drawback to this kind of system is that, while they strictly speaking work faster than tape systems, they aren't as convenient. You actually have to sit there inserting and removing disks as the program runs. You're liable to need upwards of twenty disks for each backup (which means at least forty dedicated to this purpose, because you should always have at least two sets of disks rotating). What all this means is that you're probably going to back up less often with a disk system than with a tape system.

The best known disk-based backup program is *Fastback* (Fifth Generation), but there are many worthy competitors in this market. Before I invested in my tape system, I bought a disk backup program called *Back-it* (Gazelle Systems), and found it most satisfactory. It saved

Backing Up and Storing Original Program Disks

When you buy a new software program, you should use the original disk or disks only once. Even if you have a hard disk, copy the original onto another diskette, then tuck it away in a safe place. This way, it serves as an ultimate backup in case of disaster. I keep all my originals at my parents' house two miles up the road. Some people go so far as to store especially important backups in their safety deposit boxes.

If you do have a hard drive, copy the program onto it from the diskette you copied from the original. Keep this disk at hand as a sort of proximate backup.

When I first started using a computer, I tended to scatter my disks—originals, backups and everything else—all over my desktop. I *still* toss them on the floor occasionally when I'm in full flight. This is really a lousy idea. Standard floppy diskettes are not especially robust. They can be affected by dust, magnetism (that little paper clip dispenser, for example), heat, and even the oil from your hands. I can also verify that they do not react well to being rolled over by your chair. I finally invested something like $8 in a diskette storage tray, and now I have four of them. Number one stays at my parents' to hold my originals, so that I can recover from a

to page 126

fire or burglary at my house. Number two sits on my desk and holds blank, formatted disks that are ready to use. Number three rests next to it, holding program backups. And number four sits just to the right of my monitor and holds the disks I'm likely to want to use regularly—mainly floppies that I'm backing up specific projects on.

Different companies call these disk holders by all sorts of different names, but they're all roughly alike—a tray to hold fifty or seventy-five diskettes, with a smoky transparent lid to protect them from dust and sunlight. Some have latches, some have locks, some have neither. You can also buy disk files that hold only ten floppies, and that are just the ticket if you have to carry diskettes with you on the road.

The newer, rigid, 3-1/2-inch diskettes are more robust than their larger cousins, but they're still best kept together in a tray or file. I only have a dozen or so of these smaller disks, and I store them all in two nylon "wallets" sold by Traveling Software.

•

me twice during hard disk problems, and—thank goodness—it restored everything flawlessly.

Of course, if you're working on a particular or particularly important project, daily or even hourly backups should be virtually automatic. When I'm working on a book, for example, I copy chapter drafts to (1) a 5-1/4 disk that stays in the disk holder near my computer, (2) another 5-1/4 disk that gets rotated every few days with another filed at my parents' house, and (3) a 3-1/2 disk that stays with my laptop computer. Before I bought my tape system, I also made a backup of my entire hard disk every Friday afternoon (well, almost), and exchanged the 25-30 disks with a similar package that lived in my father's clothes closet.

It's that "well, almost" that made me go to tape. Backing up onto disks is a hassle that I sometimes skipped. With the tape system I now have, I back up daily, letting the Archive software handle the whole thing during suppertime. And of course, that's the whole point. You can have the best backup system in the world, but if you don't use it, it does you no good. Listen to Paul Mace. Go pro.

WHERE TO BUY—AND WHETHER YOU SHOULD

With software as with hardware, I'm a fan of mail-order. Prices are lower than at most retail outlets and service isn't a significant issue. Your main concern is making sure you're getting the latest version. If you know specifically what you want, why not call for it?

On the other hand, if you're shopping for an application but you aren't sure about which particular program will suit you best, a good retail outlet is probably a better approach. Chains like the exemplary Egghead offer competitive prices, decent help, let you play with software, and let you return a package you don't like within a specific length of time. Retail outlets can also usually arrange training if you need it. At the retail level, I feel more comfortable dealing with a shop that specializes in software than with standard computer stores. But no matter where you buy, you should expect good service, competitive prices, knowledgeable salespeople and a chance to test the programs you're considering. If you don't think you're getting as much help or service as you want, use the phone.

A final reminder: I've written about a lot of neat stuff here, and there are hundreds, of other worthy programs and types of programs out there—some sound downright irresistible in reviews. But you don't actually *need* a lot of software to work efficiently. A utility package like Norton or Mace and a backup program, yes, but beyond that, consider sticking with the major applications you know you'll use from the start. Learn your primary program or programs thoroughly, get a solid fix on your own work habits and then maybe look around for packages that suit your specific personal needs.

I realized gradually, for example that a good phone dialer would really make my life easier, so with the help of a compu-wizard of a friend, I rigged one up from within my word processor. But with this system, I could only dial. Very convenient, but not much help at expense-report time. What I *really* wanted was a program that would keep track of who I called when and for how long. When *Hot Line* came along, offering all this plus huge directories of useful numbers, I grabbed it.

I've grabbed a few other programs, too, and most heavy computer users eventually wind up with a shelf full of software. But make your choices carefully and choose only programs you really need. Be skeptical of packages that will require you to change your style in some basic way. Habit is almost always stronger than the pull of a program's potential, and packages that work across the grain of your normal patterns inevitably wind up gathering dust on that shelf.

6

Computer Peripherals

For our purposes, let's define peripherals as elements relating to the computer system that enhance, expand or protect its operation. Not all peripherals exist on the periphery. Some are essential for almost everyone. Others are indispensable for certain kinds of work. The most common peripheral is virtually ubiquitous. Many people consider it part of the basic computer set-up.

THE PRINTER

This is the "output device" that makes a $2,000 personal computer system as useful as a $200 typewriter. I've known people who have bought computers without investing in a printer, but they all had one thing in common: they used their home offices at night or on weekends and had access to a printer at their day job. Even then, most of them eventually sank a few hundred dollars in an inexpensive Epson or Brother, or an Apple ImageWriter. For all the talk of computers foreshadowing a "paperless office," most of us still like to see our work in black and white. It's a commonplace among writers, students and executives alike that you get a whole different sense of your prose when you read it on paper rather than off the screen. Besides, whether you're checking a short story or a spreadsheet, manipulating actual pages lets you see more of your product at one time than a computer screen can. And, of course, if you're dealing directly with customers or clients, they'll almost always want your work on paper, not on disk.

There are several distinct types of printers. One has become the overwhelming choice of most home office workers, but when you start scoping out the possibilities, you'll run into several options and sub-options. Let's start with a formerly dominant technology that's no longer a good pick in most circumstances.

DAISYWHEEL PRINTERS

These are the old standards—the printers that are to the non-technical eye basically typewriters without the keyboard. They get their name from their flower-shaped printwheels of metal or plastic, the "petals" of which smack against a ribbon to transfer letters to the page.

Daisywheels were the choice of most offices for a long time, because they produced letters that looked "typewritten" rather than "computerized." Many of them—machines by companies like Qume and Diablo and NEC—were rock-solid workhorses. Tens of thousands of daisywheel printers are still churning out letters, memos, briefs and reports without complaint.

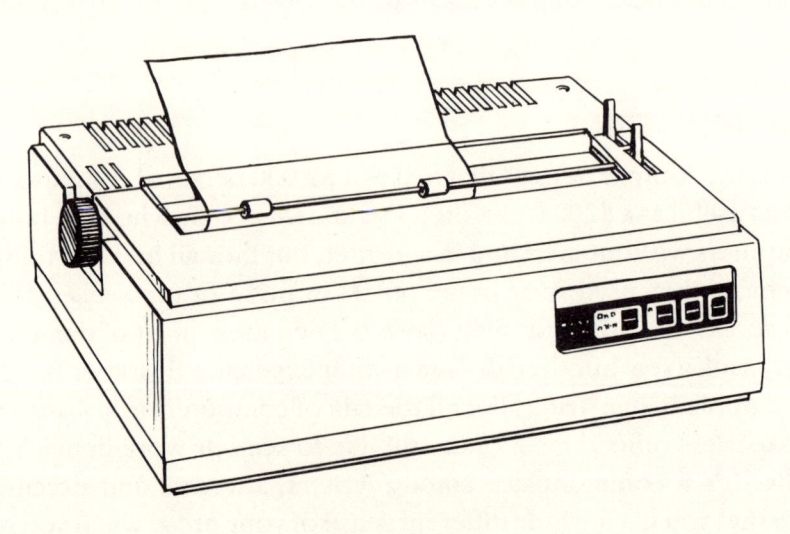

Daisywheel

But daisywheels aren't fast—many of them printed fewer than twenty characters per second (cps), and forty was considered very quick indeed. And they can't handle graphics. As speedier, more versatile dot matrix printers developed "near letter quality" ("NLQ") and then "letter quality" ("LQ") type, they began to steal the market away from their stodgy predecessors. A few manufacturers—Primages is a good example—have marketed fast daisywheels that can even handle limited graphics, but they cost an arm and a leg. For all intents and purposes, the daisywheel is dead as a general-purpose machine. You sometimes see models—usually *verrrrry slooow* ones—offered at temptingly low prices, but unless you have a very specific reason to prefer typewriter-style technology, you should resist. Most home office workers can get more of what they want for less money if they turn to

DOT MATRIX PRINTERS.

These are the machines that used to crank out only that ugly "computer" type—light, square, hard to read, and too obviously implying mass mailings or, at least, a lack of personal concern.

That has changed. Most models still spit out this sort of utilitarian print when they're set on "draft" mode and told to go fast (usually well over a hundred characters a minute—sometimes over two-hundred), but virtually all of them now offer handsomer NLQ or LQ type if you're willing to accept a slower speed—which is still usually equal to and often much faster than the daisywheel standard.

Like daisywheels, dot matrix machines are *impact* printers. They make letters appear on paper by punching their shape against a ribbon. But instead of a few dozen symbols on a printwheel, the single print head of a dot matrix printer houses a number of tiny pins—usually either nine or twenty four. These pins are electromagnetically fired against the ribbon in patterns to create the shapes of letters. You can see why early dot matrix printers created ugly type. Who wants to read a serious document in which the letters look like they've been dabbed on by Seurat? These days, though, you've got to peer through a magnifying glass or a loupe to make out the dots in letter-quality dot matrix output. Despite the carping of some ossified fusspots, LQ printers are entirely adequate for formal business documents.

My first experience with letter quality dot matrix printers was with an early Epson 1500LQ, back in 1984. It was still thought somewhat daring at the time to use a non-daisywheel for business correspondence, but the magazine I worked for made the move and never got one peep of negative feedback.

When I went out on my own the following year, I bought a Toshiba 1351, a letter-quality competitor of the Epson. I needed to be able to run drafts of articles very quickly, but also be able to send letters on my stationery that would stand up to the closest scrutiny of the pickiest correspondents—several of whom had the power of life or death over my plans and projects. The Toshiba ran drafts at 150 characters a second or so, and produced elegant letter-quality print at around sixty or seventy. It served me proud.

In 1985, the 1351 cost $1,800—and that was a *discounted* price. Today, I could get a machine I'd be happy with for over a thousand dollars less. Dot matrix printers are getting better—and cheaper—all the time. But there are different kinds of machines, and a number of considerations to keep in mind when you go shopping. One basic distinction in the dot matrix world revolves around the question

How many pins?

At the inexpensive end of the market—roughly under the $500 list price mark—print heads have nine pins. In this universe, you won't run across any true letter-quality type. Near-letter-quality is the name of the game, and there are some pretty terrific players. In the Mac world, things are very simple indeed. The standard here is the Apple ImageWriter II, available for around $500, although there are clones out there for as little as $250 or so. On the IBM side, the best-known line of inexpensive printers probably remains Epson's FX series, which has achieved workhorse status in homes, schools and offices all over the world. The basic FX isn't very exiting. It's just sturdy, reliable and, of course, Epson compatible. This last is important for printers of other makes, too, because in MS-DOS circles, Epson codes and sequences have become a standard that software writers conform to, so that what appears on your screen shows up properly on paper.

Epson markets an inexpensive LX line of machines, too, but the outstanding bargain among nine-pin printers over the last few years has been the Panasonic KX-P1091i, recently superseded by the KX-

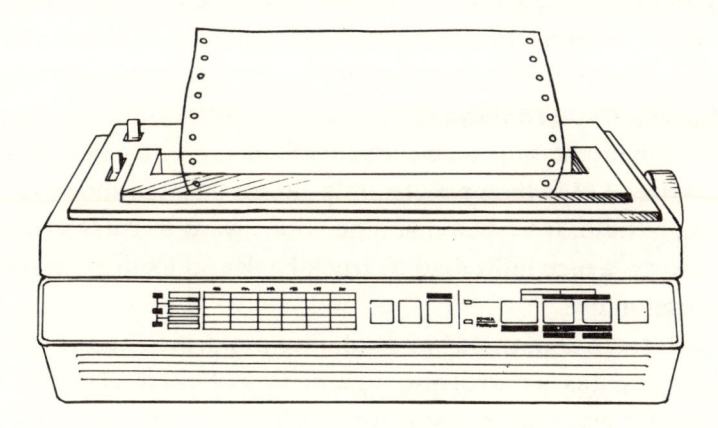

Dot matrix printer

P1191i. You can sometimes find this machine discounted to around $200, which makes it an absolute steal. It's Epson compatible, it includes a tractor-feed mechanism to handle standard edge-perforated fanfold paper, and it runs at about a hundred characters per second in draft mode and thirty or so in excellent near letter quality. This is a terrific home machine if you don't need truly high speed or absolutely knock-'em-dead print. By the time you read this, there may be a better printer out there for the price, but you won't go far wrong if you use the P1091i/P1191i as a bench mark when you go shopping for something in its price category.

Although I think some near-letter-quality type—like the Panasonic's—looks terrific, you may feel that some printers' versions aren't sharp enough for formal business documents. If you need impeccable print, you'll need to turn to a twenty-four pin printer. As a by-product, you'll also generally get higher speed printing in both draft and quality mode.

Again, your Mac choices are limited. The ImageWriter LQ is the standard, at about $1,100, discounted.

My favorite twenty-four pin printer over the past few years has been the Epson LQ-800 and its successor, the LQ-850. I've had a chance to see them in action on the desks of several friends and I've been impressed. These machines are about as fast as my old Toshiba, but cost a cheap computer less. And their slick letter-quality print is a big improvement on the adequate but rather blocky type I remember from the original Epson LQ-1500. There are good printers out there from lots of other manufacturers, too—Alps, Brother, C. Itoh, NEC and Okidata are just the most familiar names—but you can use the LQ-850 as a guide when you're shopping in the $700 (discounted) price range.

Another interesting recent twenty-four pin entry is the Toshiba ExpressWriter 311, which weighs only eleven pounds and comes with a carrying handle. It's not a machine you'd want to carry around the world, but it's a nice light load to truck back and forth from the main office occasionally.

The difference in price between nine-pin printers and their twenty-four-pin cousins is narrowing. Epson now offers the LQ-500, which threatens that magic $500 list-price barrier, and other manufacturers will certainly be following suit. While these less expensive machines will probably offer you top-notch print quality, if you buy one soon you'll most likely be sacrificing speed and certain convenience features that more expensive models offer. But prices and capabilities have been improving so rapidly in the dot matrix printer market that this may not be true for long.

Paper tiger

Just about every printer ever made would work slick as a whistle if it didn't have to use paper. It's this unfortunately necessary stuff that causes the trouble. It can be maddening to load. It's a pain in the neck when you have to switch from fanfold to single sheets. And dealing with envelopes makes these other problems seem like a piece of cake.

When you're shopping for a printer, don't just look for a good price and pretty type. Keep your eye on what's called "paper handling," which most manufacturers have improved dramatically in recent models. A few basic points to consider:

- How does the printer load the kind of paper you'll be using most often? Favor—heavily—those that handle the process automatically at the touch of a button.
- If you're a user of fanfold paper, does the machine include a pin or tractor mechanism that centers the paper and draws it through the machine? Many don't, and you wind up paying extra for one. If there is a tractor feed, is it bi-directional—that is, can you reverse paper out of the platen if you want to?

- How does the printer make you handle the switch from fanfold paper to single sheets? Do you have to remove the fanfold altogether, and then reload it when you're done, or is there a bypass system of some kind? My old Toshiba had no bypass. I had to roll my fanfold paper out, run my letters, then go through the finicky routine of loading the fanfold paper again. This is not exactly hard work, but it *is* exactly the kind of mindless, time-wasting annoyance you want to avoid when you invest in high-tech contraptions.
- How does the printer handle individual envelopes? The IBM Proprinter a managerial friend of mine uses has a special slot you can feed envelopes into even when the machine is loaded with fanfold paper. Good stuff.
- If you expect to be using single sheets exclusively, does the manufacturer offer a sheet feed mechanism? Is it grotesquely expensive? Are there good third-party mechanisms available for less?

By the way, there's no rule that says you have to use fanfold paper for your drafts and in-house work, then switch to single sheets for outside communications. You can run cheap paper through a sheet feeder and avoid the annoyances definite drawbacks of fanfold paper altogether. Sheet feed mechanisms usually cost at least a few hundred dollars, and they can make your high-tech printer look like a nineteenth century gadget for shelling peas, but they also make most paper handling chores less onerous. Buying one may be worth it to you over the long haul.

Noise

My old Toshiba is built like a Mack truck—and it's just about as quiet. In my nook of an office, the operating printer acoustically took over the space. I couldn't concentrate on other work and I sure couldn't talk on the phone. This was no big deal if I was just printing out a letter, but when I was running a document more than two or three pages long, the only reasonable thing for me to do was to leave the room.

Most newer dot matrix printers seem to be a bit less assertive than my 1351, but they are anything but silent. Some sound like machine guns, some mimic ripping upholstery, some whine like a small animal in distress. One exception is the IBM Quietwriter, which is a *thermal transfer* dot matrix printer. Its pins are electrodes which heat up and actually melt the ribbon's ink onto your paper. The result is astonishing near-silence. Unfortunately, the Quietwriter lists for about $1,700, and finding good discounts on IBM products can be tough.

Other quiet options include *ink jet* dot matrix printers from Diconix, Hewlett-Packard, Canon and—for the Mac—GCC Technologies. In these machines, ink is fired from a group of tiny nozzles onto your paper to form letters. The Diconix machines are small as well as quiet—the Model 150 has become the standard portable printer of globe-trotting, laptopping journalists. The GCC WriteMove (under

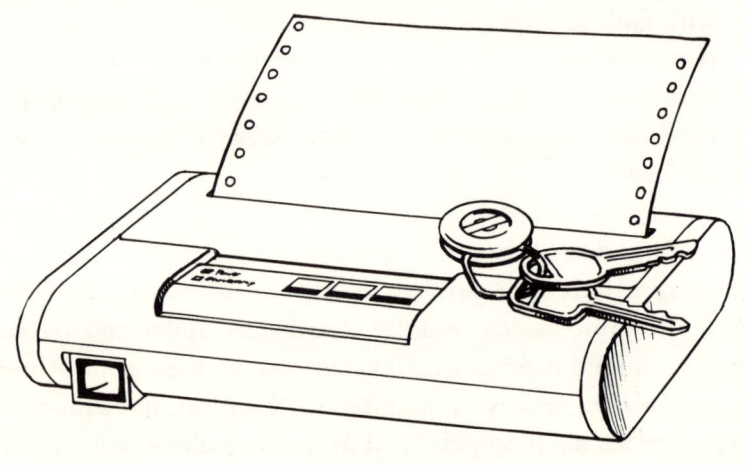

Diconix 150

$600) functions similarly for Mac types, while yielding output that is considerably better than that you'd get from an ImageWriter. The Hewlett-Packard DeskJet, which lists for about $1,000, but is often available for about $700, is being touted as a low-cost alternative to laser printers. This may not be the best way to look at this machine, but the DeskJet is certainly a capable, reasonably priced and quiet printer. A new version, called the DeskWriter, brings the same capabilities to Mac users.

How fast is fast enough?

Compared to typing something by hand, virtually all dot matrix printers are lightning fast (at least compared to the way *I* type things by hadn, er, hand). But just as with the operations of computers themselves, in the world of printers there's fast, and there's *fast*.

Most home office workers don't need supreme speed, especially if they produce mostly short documents on an irregular basis (the normal pattern). A printer with the performance specs of the Panasonic KX-P1091i (about a hundred characters per second in draft mode, about thirty in NLQ) is more than adequate for a lot of people.

But if, like me, you need to run frequent long drafts, or if you have giant database reports to get out, you'll be happier paying a premium for a printer that can really zip through them. Machines like the Epson LQ-850 are about a third faster than the Panasonic machine in draft mode and over twice as fast in letter quality. More expensive units are even quicker—some pressing 300 cps draft and a hundred LQ.

A rough rule of thumb: the more you use your printer, the more you'll care about speed. Especially if you expect to be doing true volume printing—frequent runs of mass mailings, for example—quickness may be your second most important consideration—right there behind reliability.

Bigger's not always better

I've already implied that my dot matrix printer is big and heavy. That's partly because of what seems to be a Toshiba bias in favor of sheer mass, and partly because I bought the printer version of a long-bed pickup truck. Most printers come with a carriage wide enough to accept standard-sized fanfold paper—the kind that tears down to 8-1/2 by 11. My printer's carriage, though, is wide enough to handle what some people call "printout paper"—the industrial-strength 14-7/8 by 11 stuff that often comes with green bars across it to help your eye track along rows of numbers.

I paid extra for a wide carriage for reasons that look weak to me now. Because of a system established at the magazine I worked for, I was used to editing copy on oversized paper. I liked the idea of having plenty of room to the right of the margin in which I could jot notes and make revisions. I soon discovered, though, what I should have realized before I laid out all that cash—that my future work and my past work actually had little in common. The author I'd be editing most often from now on was going to be myself, and if I needed vast amounts of white space on the page to tune up copy that I'd already rewritten on the screen, I soon wouldn't be needing any printer at all. For me—as I suspect it would be for most of us working at home—a wide-carriage printer was an expensive luxury, not a necessity. These machines, which are typically $200 to $300 more expensive than their standard-sized counterparts, do make sense, though, if you're going to be doing certain kinds of work, especially running moderate-sized spreadsheets or long lists culled from big databases.

I understand that Epson is offering a sort of half-way machine, the Epson LQ-950, which was designed to accept regular 8-1/2 by 11 paper turned sideways. If you've been dreaming of this feature, you can now get it without moving all the way up to a wide-body machine.

A wide carriage forces you to pay another premium: extra weight. My 1351 weighs in at a serious forty-two pounds—over forty-five with its tractor feed mechanism attached. In comparison, the Panasonic KX-P1091i weighs about fifteen pounds and the Epson LQ-850 about twenty. Even if you need a wide carriage, you can choose the lightweight path—the wide-carriage Epson LQ-1050 presses the scales at only about twenty seven pounds. As a rule, consider going for similar lightweight options. Being able to move your printer around without courting a slipped disk is just another form of that versatility that's so important in home offices.

Simple size is a similar consideration. Again, my Toshiba is a space-eating monster—twenty-three inches long by fifteen inches deep. By comparison the KX-P1091i, at mere sixteen inches by twelve, consumes not much more than half the desk space. Such small "footprints" can be a big benefit in many tight home offices. It's not a bad idea to make simple paper cutouts of the footprints of the machines you're considering. This way, you can actually see which printers will best fit the space you've got available.

Of course, if you got money to burn, you can throw all this information out the window and consider a more glamorous option.

LASER PRINTERS

When I first heard about laser printers, I had visions of a futuristic unit perking away on a desk somewhere, maybe smoking a little, as it somehow *burned* letters onto sheets of paper. The reality is a little less exciting: laser printers have more in common with photocopiers than with starwars zapblasters. It's nifty technology, but you won't be able to shoot down any spy satellites with it.

The three essential elements of most laser printers are a so-called laser diode, a highly-polished rotating photosensitive drum, and toner, a sort of magnetized dust. Reacting to signals from your computer, the diode directs tiny, precise beams of light to charge the drum with electrostatic patterns. The drum, in turn, charges the paper rolled against it. And the charged paper attracts toner in the pattern of the charges. Heat fuses the toner to the paper. Unlike other types of printers, lasers handle printing a page at a time, not character by character. As a result, they are sometimes called "page printers." Most laser printers can produce six to eight pages per minute (ppm), creating patterns of letters or pictures on command.

Laser printers commonly produce these characters at 300 dots per inch (dpi)—a resolution short of what you'd find in a magazine or book, but high enough to produce good-looking print in any number of type styles. With a laser printer, you can get into desktop publishing in style.

Not surprisingly, lasers have captured the top end of the printer market. But they *are* expensive. A few are available for a street price of $1,000 or so, but most are closer to twice that price, and many cost much more, even at a discount. The Apple LaserWriter, long the laser of choice for Mac users, is about the most expensive of all. Even so, it's

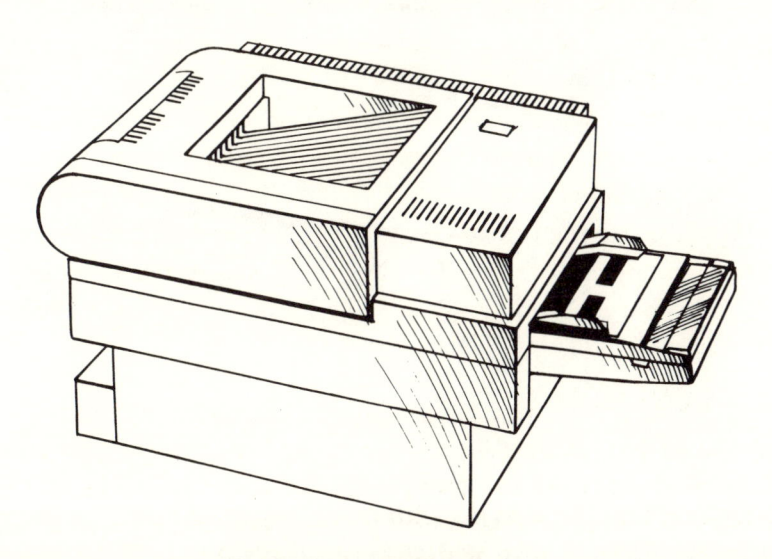

Apple LaserWriter II

popular even among IBM and clone users who are serious about desktop publishing because of its implementation of the PostScript page-description language (see the box opposite).

There are a number of less-costly, non-PostScript laser printers made for DOS computers, but most people think that only expensive PostScript machines exist for Macs. This isn't so. GCC Technologies offers their PLP (Personal Laser Printer) at a list price of about $1,700.

Even so, I'd hesitate to recommend a laser to someone—either a Mac partisan or an IBM aficionado—working at home on a budget. On the other hand, in early 1987, I blew my own budget by retiring my still-vigorous Toshiba in favor of a Hewlett-Packard LaserJet II, then the king of the business laser printer market. Why? Well, I wanted to experiment with a few desktop publishing projects. And while the LaserJet II isn't a PostScript machine—I couldn't afford one—I would be able to download "soft fonts" from disks in my computer to create fairly sophisticated documents.

As it turns out, I do simple, non-professional desktop publishing quite often for friends and local groups, but I love my laser printer for

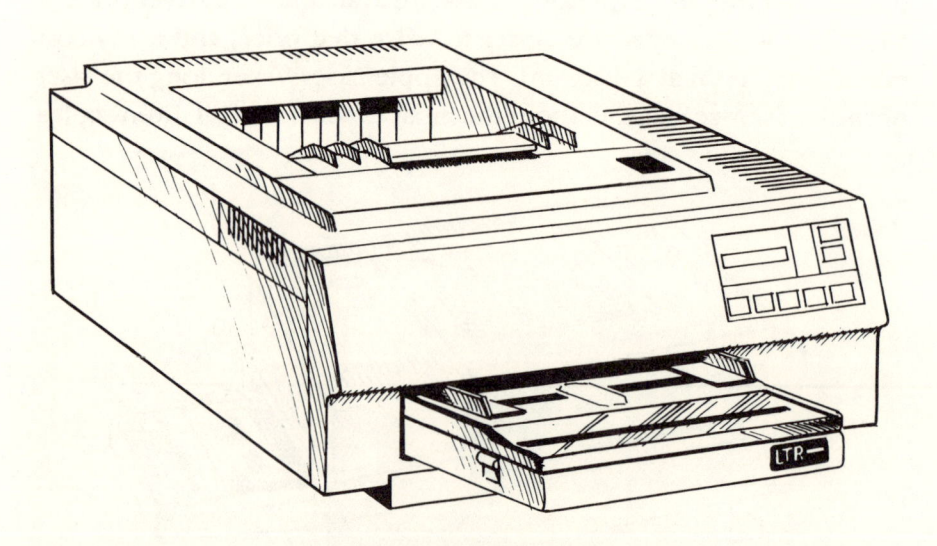

Hewlett-Packard LaserJet II

reasons that have little to do with it's ability to spit out Garamond or Univers typefaces. I love it first because it's quiet. When it's on, it

PostScript™

A few laser printers—those best suited for high-end desktop publishing—incorporate something called PostScript (Adobe Systems).

PostScript isn't a program. It's a *page description language* (PDL), a so-called "higher-level language" that replaces the normal, dot by dot communication of data from computer to paper. Basically, PDLs instruct the printer how to construct the pattern of an entire page, rather than telling it to go through a series of individual operations. They provide a terrifically efficient way to convey instructions for complex pages combining characters of different size, various type styles and graphic designs of virtually every possible type.

PostScript printers are very expensive, at close to $4,000 at the bottom end, but they are awfully attractive to a lot of computer users. As typified by the Apple LaserWriter, their most obvious special feature is their built-in, or "resident" typefaces—Courier, Helvetica, Times Roman, Palatino, Bookman, Avant Garde, New Century Schoolbook, Symbol (mostly Greek letters) and ITC Zapf Dingbats (printers' and graphics symbols). You can use any (or all) of these type styles, in virtually any size and in various styles (bold, italic and so forth). This can be lots of fun, and if you're working on serious

to page 142

publishing projects, it can be helpful or necessary. But you can achieve a similar affect with "soft fonts" downloaded into the memory of a non-postscript laser printer like the Hewlett Packard LaserJet II. This book, for example, was set and proofed using downloadable Bitstream *Fontware* fonts.

The greatest advantage of PostScript is that it is what's called "device independent." You don't actually have to print out your document on a laser printer, with it's fine but limited 300 dots-per-inch resolution. You can send it out to any one of a number of other PostScript output devices, including a true typesetter like the Allied Linotronic 100. This means that you can create a manuscript on your computer, proof it exactly by printing it out on your PostScript laser printer, then hand the disk over to a type house PostScript typesetter. (Keep in mind, though, that I was able to do essentially the same thing with this book using non-PostScript soft fonts. But few type houses are set up to handle the sort of package I created.)

Most home workers don't need PostScript or a PostScript printer, as marvelous and tempting as they are. But, just in case, there's a way to hedge. You can add PostScript capabilities to a Hewlett Packard LaserJet II through an add-on card that fits into a slot within the printer. The QMS JetScript lists for about $2,500 and gives

to page 143

your HP II the ability to operate as a PostScript printer while still letting you operate it as a standard LaserJet if you want to. (This is important, because a lot of DOS programs really don't properly support PostScript). If you're in the market for a laser printer, consider starting with a much less expensive non-PostScript machine. If you come to realize that you require PostScript's capabilities, you can always plunge for the JetScript.

Recently, PostScript clones have been arriving on the market. And Apple and Microsoft have announced that they will jointly be developing their own page description language. By the time you read this, there may be true competition in this field.

•

sounds just like a computer—you hear its cooling fan and that's about all. I love it second because it's fast—at least the equivalent of a 200 cps dot matrix machine—and it never drops into an ugly "draft" mode. That's the third reason I love the thing—even when you want a quick look at a long, unedited document, you get to read it in superb, 300 dpi type.

None of this is necessary. All of it is addictive. Would I spend the $1,700 again? You bet.

(Late note: Hewlett-Packard now offers the LaserJet IIP. "P" for "personal." It lists at $1,495, but will almost certainly give you LaserJet capabilities for under $1,000, street price. And the new LaserJet III will be priced about $300 cheaper than the LaserJet II it's slated to replace. Finally, Hewlett-Packard is coming out with a Postscript cartridge and an AppleTalk interface kit that will make newer-model H-P printers fully compatible with Macs.)

Lest you get carried away by my enthusiasm, though, consider some of the very definite drawbacks to laser printers for many home office uses.

In the first place, lasers aren't impact printers, so you won't be able to run carbon invoice forms, for example. If your operation depends on this sort of thing, you should steer clear of a laser unless you're willing to spring for two printers.

Second, lasers can manage legal-sized paper, but don't expect to run anything larger. The over-sized stuff wide-carriage dot matrix printers were designed to deal with? Forget it.

Third, lasers get hot, and this means trouble with sticky things like labels and envelopes. If you want to run labels on a laser printer, make sure you buy the ones manufactured specially to stand up to the heat.

Fourth, sticky flaps aren't the only problem you'll run into with envelopes. A laser printer normally prints in what's called "portrait" mode, so that text comes out oriented normally on a vertical 8-1/2 by 11 inch piece of stationery. But envelopes are loaded into these printers lengthwise, and portrait mode printing types across them rather than along their length. So you have to instruct the laser to print out in what's called "landscape" mode—appropriate to the horizontally-oriented envelope.

This isn't really a big deal. But then you have to somehow tell the printer where to put the address. With a dot matrix printer you can simply roll the platen until the envelope is properly placed, but there is no platen in a laser printer, which works a page at a time, not line by line. The result is that lots of letters printed on these marvels of technology wind up being mailed in hand-addressed envelopes.

I've developed a fairly complex macro to handle all of this for me, and a number of companies offer little address utilities that you can buy. The problem's not insurmountable, but it is a pain in the neck to have to coddle such an advanced machine. Setting up my laser printer to handle all the jobs my dot matrix machine managed simply took a long and frustrating day. You'll have to fiddle around a lot with yours, too, if you buy one. Just be ready for it.

Fifth, laser printers are big. They take up a good chunk of desk space, and they weight too much to be horsed around very often.

Finally, laser printers cost a lot to run. Rather than buying a $10 ribbon once in a while, you'll be plunging for a $100 cartridge.

The toner cartridge

The Hewlett-Packard machine and most other laser printers these days are based on what's called the Canon LBP-SX engine. This system includes a removable, disposable or reusable cartridge that contains both the photosensitive drum and a supply of toner. It's similar to the

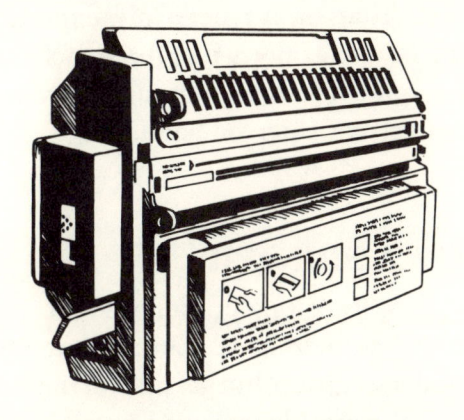

Canon-engine toner cartridge

guts for many of the personal copiers out there today. (But it's not the same. Printer toner is different from copier toner.)

There are other engines—the Ricoh dual-cartridge system is the best known competitor—but the Canon is the standard, and it's the only one I've ever had experience with. The system is convenient. You can change cartridges in less time than it takes to swap most ribbons—and with less mess, too. I give my printer what I'd consider moderately heavy individual use, and I run through perhaps two and a half cartridges a year.

Actually, I've been using the same two cartridges for a while, because I've been having my used-up units *recharged* for about $50 a pop. This can be a little dicey. Many companies are in the recharging business, but not all are reputable. Your best bet is to ask around among other cartridge users for the names of rechargers who have provided good service. Once you find a company you trust, you can keep two cartridges in circulation for a long time, since each can be recharged up to five times. I've been lucky. My recharged cartridges have been working fine.

(Late note: My last recharge didn't work out so well. I didn't get the rich black tones I want. And the replacement I demanded was no better. So I may be heading back to new, full-price cartridges.)

One of the things rechargers should *not* do is drill a hole in your cartridge—they should disassemble it so they can clean and inspect it before they refill it. Neither Canon nor the two best-known companies that use the Canon cartridges like you to recharge. They claim you get an inferior product. That hasn't been my experience (generally, anyway). But if you'll be using only two or three each year, maybe you'd have greater peace of mind if you simply bought new ones. And remember—always have a fresh cartridge on hand.

SHOPPING FOR A PRINTER

I wouldn't even begin to look for a printer without studying a copy of *PC Magazine*'s annual printer issue. Check your library, bug your friends, call your local user group, but get hold of the most recent issue. Use it to help identify the machines that do best what you need done. And use the knowledge you gain to check out the expertise and honesty of the salespeople you deal with, if you decide to shop retail.

If you already know what you want, printers are as available through mail-order as any other computer-related items. I've ordered both my printers that way. One deal went smoothly, the other, as I've mentioned, was something of a mess.

MODEMS

A printer may be your most important peripheral—or maybe not. For some home workers, the ability to communicate with other computers in other places is the key to success. For this, you need a modem. A modem's job is twofold. It has to convert your digital data into analog form so that it can be transmitted over the phone lines, and it has to convert incoming analog data into the digital form your computer can handle. In technical terms, it "modulates" and "demodulates." And it gets its very name from compressing those two words into one.

(Pronunciation gets shifted in the process. "Modem" rhymes with "throw dem.")

Modems sit (figuratively, at least,) between your computer and your telephone, literally plugged into both PC and phone line. Even if you never expect to send digital data by phone, you may want a modem anyway. None of the great phone dialing programs available will do their stuff without one.

The first thing to look for in a modem is whether or not it is "Hayes compatible." Hayes is the best known company in the modem field, and the computer commands (issued by or through your communications software) that make its units work have become the standards in the field. Most modems on the market today respond to the Hayes command set, but there are the occasional mavericks. This is one case where you don't want to fall in with the underdog. Don't go looking for trouble and complications when you shop for a modem. Make sure the one you buy is Hayes compatible.

The next thing to consider is speed. Digital data is passed in binary form—everything is reduced to a series of zeros and ones. Each of those zeros and ones is a single *bit* of digital data. Modems are rated according to how many bits they can handle per second.

(This speed measurement is often incorrectly called a modem's *baud rate*. Baud is a measurement, not of digital bits, but of shifts in the analog carrier signal. In slow modems, like the 300 bits per second

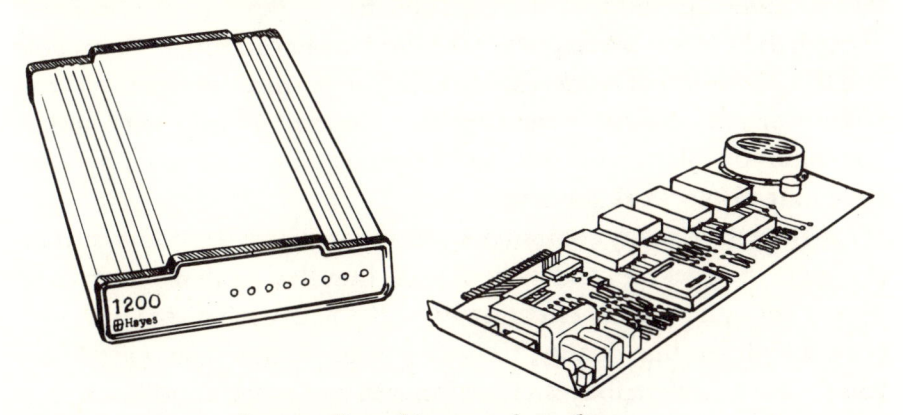

External and internal modems

(bps) model I started out with, the baud rate and the number of bits per second were essentially the same. For technical reasons I'm not going into because I don't fully understand them, this is not true of faster modems. Nonetheless, you'll often hear people talking about baud rate when they really mean bits per second. Now you can play the game, too.)

The current speed standard for modems is 1,200 bps, but 2,400 bps units have been around for a long time and many models are now quite reasonably priced. It's common to see good 1,200 bps internal modems listed for under $100, and good 2,400 bps internals for well under $200. Faster modems are out there, but they still cost an arm and a leg, and are still the domain of the large company with specific high-powered needs.

My modem is a 1,200 bps Zoom Telephonics model. The company offers an add-on 2,400 bps upgrade, but I haven't felt the need to speed up my operation. I'd save on phone bills if I could transmit copy faster, but most of the people I work with have 1,200 bps modems and couldn't handle 2,400 bps data transfers.

Some modems are external, while some slip right into your computer in the form of cards. These are handy, because they keep your desk free of clutter. But if you expect to be using more than one computer, an external model can work with both. And, of course, if you don't have an extra slot in your computer (or don't want to use up the ones you have), external is the way to go.

My Zoom modem is an internal card. But I also have a small external modem, called a WorldPort 1200, for my laptop Toshiba. Small enough to fit in my breast pocket (where I *never* carry it), it's a capable and flexible unit that works as well as any other modem I've used. You might want to consider such a "pocket modem" as your main unit if you think you might eventually add a laptop computer to your desktop system. It would work for both.

These days, many computer systems come with a modem card included in the package. And most of these bundled modems seem to be decent enough for most circumstances. If you live in an area with very poor telephone line quality, though, (usually defined as noisy lines) you'll want a modem that can function well under bad conditions. One way to overcome bad line conditions is to use your modem at other than its top speed—many 2,400 bps modems, for example, are great at handling noisy lines if you use them at 1,200 bps.

SCANNERS

We enter into Magicland here. Even if you yawn at the power of personal computers and shrug at what laser printers roll out, your eyes will widen when you see what a good scanner—with good software—can do.

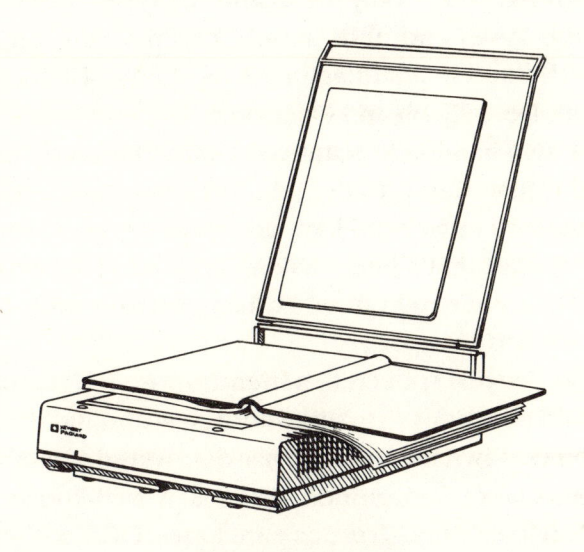

Flat-bed scanner

In a way, these machines are the opposite of printers. Instead of taking what's on your screen or disk and displaying it on paper, the scanner takes what's on paper and feeds it into your computer.

With what's called an "image scanner," you can scan a drawing, for example, store it on a disk in digital form, fiddle with it on screen with a drawing program if you want, blip it cross-country over the phone lines for a collaborator to look at or fiddle with, receive it again, and then drop it into a document you're preparing. Needless to say, scanners are great favorites of people involved in desktop publishing.

But some scanners can do more than simply convert graphics into electronic data. More and more scanners can actually "read" typed and typeset print and store whole documents, not as visual images, but as text files. This optical character recognition (OCR) is largely a function of software written to spot individual letters. It's easiest for these programs to do good work on the simplest kinds of documents—normal typed pages—and hardest for them to operate successfully on complex, typeset pages with columns and headlines.

The king of the OCR scanners—the Kurzweil K-5000—runs about $16,000. But many other scanners—terrific for graphics and often pretty good for OCR work as well, compete in cost with laser printers. Especially if you think you'll only be scanning typed copy into your computer, these lower-end units should be fine. You can find them from such well-known manufacturers as AT&T, Hewlett-Packard, Canon, Chinon, Dest, Ricoh and Panasonic.

There are also hand-held scanners. I owned an early model—for about a week. It just didn't do the job. But newer models, especially those from Saba and Mitsubishi have gotten pretty good reviews.

This is a market that's been making great strides lately. Unless I really needed a scanner right now, I'd hang on and wait. Things will get even better—and cheaper.

(Late note: I've just spoken to a friend whose job requires him to keep up with and check out virtually every new scanning device or technology that comes down the road. He has discovered something called *TrueScan*, from Calera Recognition Systems, a well-known high-end scanning system company. *TrueScan* includes OCR software and a board that you pop into your computer. For about $2,500, it turns a relatively inexpensive scanner into a terrific OCR machine. For $5,000 or less, the functional equivalent of the Kurzweil. My friend's assessment: "Amazing." Hang on. There's surely more to come.)

POWER PROBLEMS

If you have a computer, you should also have a *surge suppressor*. A sudden jolt of extra electrical power—from a lightning strike, glitches in the main line or big machinery starting up nearby—can fry your expensive equipment. These little gizmos, running from about $25 up to $100 or so, are inexpensive insurance. Most of them offer you more than one outlet, and many act as fancy extension cords as well.

More expensive versions, like the *Power Director* from Computer Accessories Corp., are meant to be not only surge suppressors, but a control center for all your electrical equipment. Typically, these book-shaped units sit on top of your power supply and beneath your monitor. You plug all of your equipment (computer, monitor, printer, etc.) into outlets at the rear of the unit, and buttons at the front let you turn things on and off without stretching and reaching. Handy.

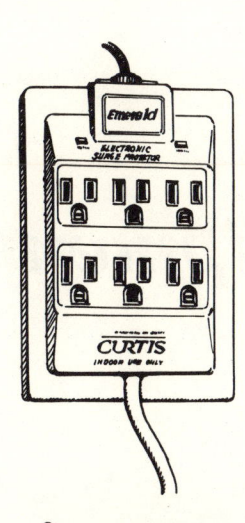

Surge suppressors are *not* power supplies. If the electricity goes off, they don't keep your equipment on. But backup power supplies are available. These come in two types—uninterruptible power systems (UPS) and standby power supplies (SPS). An SPS senses a power failure and in a fraction of a second switches you over to its backup battery supply. A UPS, on the other hand, becomes part of your computer's power system. When external power fails, the UPS doesn't have to switch to battery power, because its battery, constantly topped up by outside electricity, is already on the job. UPS units operate as surge suppressors, too, while SPS backups don't. But SPS units are cheaper.

Surge supressor

And that's the problem with backup power supplies. Even the less expensive SPS units cost a lot—well over $500. UPS units can run well over $1,000. A bit steep. That's why, while I *do* have a surge suppressor, the best I can say is that I *should* have a backup power supply.

(Late note: prices seem to be plummeting. Emerson Computer Power, for example, is now offering UPS units for as little as $200. Other manufacturers will certainly have to compete. At this price, a backup power supply becomes realistic even for us impecunious home office workers.)

7

Electronic Equipment

Depending on your work, good electronic equipment can extend your reach and let you do the work of many. These are the tools—some quite standard, some still fairly exotic—that can help make home offices efficient and profitable. The modern home office can encompass all of these wonderful devices, but it absolutely *requires* only one. Let's start there.

PHONES

The affordable business computer may have created the home office boom, but to many of us working at home, the phone is our most important tool, bar none. The telecommunications system is the home office worker's lifeline—the way we keep in touch with clients, colleagues and contacts.

Over the last few years, phones have gotten so fancy, and related products have multiplied so fast, that the big problem in choosing and setting up your system is integrating the possibilities wisely.

Common features

The phone itself is at the center of your system. There are a set of more or less standard "fancy phone" features: auto-dial, hold, redial and, often, speaker capabilities.

Auto-dial

There was a time when I would have given up chocolate for a week to get an auto-dial phone. I thought that being able to push one or two buttons rather than seven or eleven would be a great convenience. And, of course, it is—to a point. If the person you want to call is among the dozen or two whose number you've programmed into your phone, you're in business. But a programmed phone doesn't replace a phone book. If the number's not programmed, you still have to go through the standard drill of manually looking up the number and dialing.

Feature phone

That's why I soon established a computerized personal phone book and began calling from the keyboard. At first, I handled this through my word-processing program. I kept my computerized list of names active in one of my word processor's nine windows, switched to that file when I needed to make a call, ran a quick search for the right name and number, tapped a single keystroke, and *boom*, I was on the line. When *Hot Line*, with its huge, useful directories and record-keeping capabilities came along, things got even better. Today, I use my phone's auto dialer only for a few personal, non-business numbers—the kind that I might want to call during hours when my computer's not turned on. It sure wouldn't be worth my while to pay extra for expanded auto-dial capabilities on any new phone I buy.

Hold and mute

I don't use the hold function much, either, because I'm blessed with a quiet space in which to work. But I think it might come in very handy in many home offices. It lets you keep a person on the line but cut him off from the sounds of your workspace while you search for a file or consult some research. Especially handy if those sounds include a hungry baby or a snoring husband.

A mute button is a sort of half-hold. When you push it, you can still hear your caller, but she can't hear you—or your background accompaniment. Perfect for the parent on duty.

Redial

Another feature I once coveted is redial. In its most basic form, it lets you touch a single button to try once more the most recent number you've called. In it's most amazingly wonderful form, it automatically redials that number until it gets through. This is terrific when you're jousting with a busy signal—you just go on with your work while your phone, immune to frustration or tired fingers, dials until it finally gets through.

This is another of those functions that I now operate through *Hot Line* in my computer, but I have a friend in the magazine business who is a frequent, dedicated and grateful user of his phone's sophisticated redial function. When he gets a busy signal on a number he's got to get through to, he hits the redial button and goes back to work. His phone dials once every thirty seconds, and when it finally gets through, my friend can hear the other party answer over his phone's speaker. He can either pick up his hand set or act like Mr. Big, lean back, put his feet up, clasp his hands behind his head and take advantage of the speaker phone function.

Phone Features: Hardware Or Software?

Your phone company offers certain telephonic features that you may want to consider. Mine, for example, offers what it calls Phone Plus, which includes call waiting, conferencing, auto dialing, and call forwarding. The charge is $2.75 per month for a residential phone, and $5.50 for a business.

This sort of package might be a life-saver for anyone operating through a single phone line. I know a number of home workers who claim, for example, that they simply couldn't function without call waiting, which alerts them while they're making a call to the fact that another party is trying to reach them.

I've never really liked call waiting, because I've never really liked being put on hold while the person I've been talking to checks his other call. On the other hand, though, I'm sympathetic. Many people operating out of a home office with a single phone line just can't afford to miss many calls, which frequently mean business and often are call-backs that might not come through again. Call waiting may be an inelegant solution, but it does the job. (Another line, with a two-line TAD hooked up, would solve the problem—at considerable expense.)

to page 157

Speaker

Actually, he almost always uses his hand set, and for several good reasons. First, the person talking into a speaker phone always sounds at the other end as if he or she is at the bottom of a well. Second—and much more important—one-sided speaker use strikes a lot of people as a rude and arrogant move—a power play in which one party is essentially saying to the other that he just can't be bothered to hold up the hand set while he talks.

Except for mutually-understood situations, my feeling is that talking over a speaker phone is appropriate only when there is a group at one end or the other sharing the same instrument. By all means check out a speaker phone, but consider using it mainly for free-hand dialing and listening for the other phone to be answered. Talking over it may influence people, but it probably won't win you many friends.

Pulse/tone and volume controls

There are two more features you might like to look for on a phone. A pulse/tone switch lets you use the instrument in areas that haven't yet converted to touch-tone dialing. And volume controls allow you to change the loudness of rings, speakers and sometimes the sound coming over the hand set, as well. This last is a nice touch if you have a hearing problem or a bad connection to Finland.

Speaking of hearing problems, some phones are "hearing aid compatible." This means that their receivers generate a strong magnetic field, which in turn can "drive" a hearing aid. Some models make this claim in sales literature or in their instruction booklets. But if you wear a hearing aid—or have any kind of hearing problem—you should probably search out one with volume control. Even then, you should use a phone before you buy it to make sure it's suitable for you.

The handset

Finally, think about the weight and shape of a phone's handset. I have found that the old-fashioned hand set—a relatively narrow grip between the two somewhat bulbous "business" ends of the thing, is a lot more comfortable during long conversations than the flatter sort of hand set that usually, but not always, includes the dialing keypad. I don't really know if it's a matter of balance or weight or pure shape, but the traditional configuration seems to be more comfortable—not

One serious drawback to call waiting comes up if you also use that line for faxing or computer telecommunications. If the call waiting signal intrudes on these transmissions, it can cause data errors. In some parts of the country, you can—theoretically at least—temporarily cancel call waiting by touching a sequence of buttons on your phone. Friends in different cities tell me that cancellation doesn't always take. In other areas, cancellation isn't even an option. Check this out carefully with your phone company.

Certain feature phones and line arrangements can supply physically what the phone company can offer you electronically. A two-line phone with a "hunting" line, for example, makes call waiting redundant. Most two-liners do the same to conferencing. Many phones offer auto-dialing. And a few even let you program in a forwarding number. This is an area where you need to do your homework. Given your phone company's offerings, your needs and your budget, is it better for you to solve your problems through software (phone company features) or hardware (phones with specific features, and maybe extra lines)? Offerings vary around the country, and so, of course, do individual needs in each home office. Just be aware that there is a choice.

•

comfortable, mind you, just *more* comfortable—when you tuck it under your chin. And the old-style hand sets accept those special shoulder rests, too. (For another option during long chats, see below). Oh, and get a good long cord for your phone. In your one-person home office, you'll probably have to wander around from bookshelf to file cabinet searching for information as you talk.

Phones are manufactured by a whole host of familiar names—AT&T, GTE, Panasonic, GE, ITT, Uniden, Radio Shack, the divested Baby Bells, and others. It's a highly competitive market, and you can get a solid, recognizably-branded phone with most or all of the features I've mentioned, for less than $100 from aggressive discount houses.

But there's another possibility to consider. Will you be using

One line or two—or more?

I've heard a lot of people recently make the flat statement that a home office should have two phone lines. This is a nice idea, for sure, but it's not always necessary.

I've gotten along very well for four years with a single line—the same one that serves the whole house. In my office I have one phone—connected to the computer and dialed through *Hot Line*—and one answering machine (more on this topic later). That's it. Not exactly high tech, but it works fine for me, because I'm home alone all day and don't have to compete for the single line. And—importantly—I'm in a line of work in which my business message on the answering machine needs to be no different from my personal spiel—no corporate name, no product to mention, no slogan to recite.

(This brings up an interesting point. Bringing in a "personal" second line is usually much cheaper than bringing in a "business" second line. In my area, a personal line would cost me about $40 to have installed and about $14 per month in basic charges. Comparable costs for a business line are about $60 and about $30. I am told that I would qualify for a personal line because the phone book listing would be under my own name, whereas if I wanted to be listed under a business or corporate name, I'd have to pay the higher rates. Costs in your area are probably different, and your phone company's concept of "business" may be too.)

Actually, although I haven't invested in one, I'd like to have a second line to use for all outgoing calls. Others would still call me at

Phone Strategies: How Should I Set This Thing Up?

If you're operating with only a single line, your phone system is fairly simple: everything—normal phone calls, fax transmissions, modem communications—goes over that line, and your answering machine sits there capturing everything that comes in while you're out. You may consider call waiting or call forwarding or a speaker phone or a headset, but basically, your options are limited. This can be good. Simplicity is cheap, easy and comfortable.

But your needs may overwhelm your simple one-line system. And when you install a second line, things can get a little complicated. There are a number of ways to deploy those two phone lines.

- Use one (usually, but not always, the original) as your residential number, and do all business calling on the other, where you could use call waiting. This is the cleanest split from your family phone, but it essentially limits you again to a single office line.
- Give one number out for incoming calls and use the other for outgoing calls. For example, you could give clients and colleagues your "residential" number, which you could set up to "hunt" for

to page 160

your second line if necessary (see p. 162). The key, though, is that you'd make all of your outgoing calls (the ones you have to pay for) on the second line. This way, you'll have a clean record of your business phone costs when the two bills come out.

- Use one line for all voice communications and dedicate the other to fax or modem transmissions. Remember, though, that if you truly dedicate that second line, you leave yourself only a single line to handle incoming phone calls unless your fax machine offers automatic switching between fax and voice communications. There's another problem, too. Software telephone dialers like *Hot Line* only work on lines with a modem plugged in. In this system, your modem will be on the dedicated line, while you'll want to be making your calls on the other.

A variation on the last two arrangements is pretty common. Use one line for outgoing calls and the other for incoming calls—except fax and modem transmissions. Hook your faxphone up to that second line, but don't keep it on auto-receive. Give people that number only when they need to send you a fax or data communication, and ask them to alert you before transmit-

to page 161

> ting. This system works well if you use a software dialer, because your modem will already be plugged into this outgoing line, and so can get directly to work when you want to initiate an electronic file transfer.
>
> Of course, another option is to install a *third* line. A number of busy home office types have done just that. The most common arrangement seems to be two lines for voice communication—the first of which will roll over to the second in case of a busy signal—and one dedicated to the fax machine.
>
> •

the same old number, but I'd have a simpler, cleaner record of my own outgoing work-related phone use.

There are, of course, lots of situations in which a second line would be a great boon, if not an absolute necessity. Your rule of thumb should be very simple: a second line is worth the expense if a single line doesn't adequately serve you. Some examples:

- If it's important for you to present a professional image and your house line is often answered by a five-year-old, a second line is a must.
- If your fifteen-year-old asserts his right to unending telephonic communications during your business hours, go for a second line.
- If incoming calls for other family members are driving you crazy, get that second line and turn off the ring in your office for line one.
- If you frequently send or receive information by either modem or fax, you can keep a second line clear for these transmissions. In fact, I know some home office workers who have two

lines for phone calls plus a *third* line dedicated to fax or modem use.
- If you simply can't afford to miss calls, a second line with an answering machine can take messages for you while you're talking on line one. The phone company can hook up your second line as a "hunter", so that calls coming in on a busy line one hunt for and "roll over" to line two automatically.
- If your business requires frequent conference calls, most two-line phones let you connect a caller on line one with a caller on line two. You bypass the phone company's conference call service, control everything yourself and feel like a hotshot all at the same time. By all means, go for it!

You're smart enough to figure all this out. You certainly shouldn't feel guilty for needing that second line. But don't be buffaloed by a lot of hype into paying for something you don't need.

If you do go for a second line, your most obvious move is to buy a two-line phone. For my money, there are three vital elements a two-liner should have beyond whatever set of features you'd want in a single-line instrument.

- *Line-status lights.* These let you know which line you're on and whether you've got anyone holding on the other. Especially if you're not used to having two lines or to managing your own multiple calls, you'll invariably forget that you've asked someone to hang on for a moment.
- *Different-sounding rings for each line.* When I use these things I push the wrong button a lot anyway and wind up talking to dead air, but distinctive rings can keep me from feeling silly too often.
- *An excellent conferencing capability.*

Luckily, most two-line phones offer all three of these features. Some offer a lot more. An especially interesting two-line concept is AT&T's relatively new System 2000, which gives you access to a second line from anywhere in the house even if only your office has been wired for two lines. You plug a "master phone" into both lines there, then around the house, you can plug up to five "extension phones" into existing jacks. With no additional wiring, they all become two-line phones. Each unit is also an intercom, so you can communicate from one room to another. The system also offers a lockout feature that keeps family members who pick up in anther room from interrupting your conversation.

The problem with this terrific setup is cost. System 2000 master phones list at about $350. Extensions are priced at about $220. And as with IBM equipment, it's hard to find AT&T phone gear deeply discounted. But it *is* possible.

The System 2000 and its inevitable competitors are overkill for me. But for many home office workers, they would be just the ticket. This isn't surprising. AT&T specifically targeted the home office market when they developed their new system. See how important we are?

Actually, if I were to go to a second line, I'd simply add a second phone—a heavy old desk set that I already own. I don't need features, because my computer handles most of the fancy stuff. And with a separate phone I'd never mistakenly make business calls on the personal line, which I'd be sure to do if I had to push a line-button on a two-line phone. A second phone isn't a slick solution, and it would take up more space on the desk, but there are situations like mine where slick isn't best.

Up on the roof

A few years ago, I was on the phone with Paul Edwards, one of the gurus of working at home. As we spoke, he left the room he was in, went downstairs, answered the door, accepted a package from the UPS driver and returned to where he'd started from. He was, of course, using a cordless phone. And if he hadn't told me, I wouldn't have known he wasn't sitting in a big leather chair behind a huge mahogany desk in front of a gigantic picture window with a spectacular view of the sun setting into the Pacific.

Almost all of us working at home have chores to do. Almost none of us has a secretary. But a good cordless phone can ease the strain of those two facts of life. You can take calls at the mailbox, near the washing machine, over the changing table (risky!), on the roof fiddling with some skylight flashing or (don't tell anybody) while you're lounging in the porch hammock with a glass of lemonade and a good book.

The problem, though, is that a lot of cordless phones aren't really all that good. They hiss and crackle like an old radio. That's not too surprising, since cordless phones send and receive messages to and from their base stations over the air by way of channels specifically set

AT&T Readyline: An 800 Number At Home

AT&T's target with this service is businesses that expect to receive less than 100 hours of these incoming 800-number calls per month. Readyline is meant to solve a problem faced by some small and home businesses that want to offer free calls to clients or customers, but whose volume didn't justify a standard 800 number. With Readyline service, you can receive 800 calls on a home line, without dedicating that line to free calls only—you keep your regular number for standard calls.

Readyline is *not* a WATTS line—you still pay for your own outgoing toll calls. It's meant to encourage incoming business calls and provide a strong professional image for you. You'll pay about $100 to start up the service. Then you'll pay a flat $20 surcharge on your phone bill each month, along with charges based on the distance and duration of each incoming 800 call. As with purely domestic rates, calls are twenty-five to forty percent lower in the evening, late at night and on weekends and holidays. You also get a ten percent reduction on charges over $100 per month.

With Readyline, you can choose what area codes you want to take free calls from, and you can adjust this area when you like—a big help

to page 165

> for certain types of targeted marketing or during holidays when you might want to broaden your scope. A new feature called "One Number Calling" lets you use the same 800 number for both inter- and intra-state calling.
>
> Regional phone companies offer their own versions of special 800 service. Check them out.
>
> •

aside by the FCC. Sometimes the channel you're using receives messages meant for another phone. Sometimes it picks up other background noise from our high-frequency culture. If this happens with some cordless models, you're stuck—they only function on a single channel. Others, though, let you switch to another channel or one of several other channels if you're having problems.

The best-sounding cordless phone I've ever used—in my purely subjective and absolutely non-exhaustive tests—was an AT&T Model 5310, which is the absolute, expensive ($220 list), top of their line. AT&T offers Models 5300 and 5200 with essentially the same qualities but fewer features for less money. The *niftiest* cordless on the market right now is the slick black Panasonic KX-T3000, which folds up like Captain Kirk's communicator and fits in a shirt pocket. It offers a number of fancy features, too, although the current version doesn't allow you to switch channels. Good cordless phones are made by Cobra, Uniden, GE, Sony, Radio Shack and others. Most offer several models over a wide price range. Unfortunately, you're probably going to require one at the high end. You're looking for a model that allows little background noise and that sounds virtually identical to a phone plugged into a jack. You'll probably also want a model that lets you switch channels—or switches automatically—in case the one you're on starts to get noisy. You may want memory dialing or two-line operation. And, of course, you're going to want one with a long enough range to handle your needs.

Don't believe the ranges the manufacturers supply. These are like EPA gas mileage ratings—good for relative guidance, maybe, but sub-

Panasonic KX-T3000 cordless

ject to wide variations in the real world. Simply using a cordless inside cuts its range down substantially.

The only way to be really sure that a particular cordless phone will work the way you want it to in the location where you need it is to try it out there. In my limited experience, there's a big difference in the performances of various companies' cordless phones—and even in the performance of cordless models in a single company's line. You may have to try several models before you're happy with sound quality and range. But the increased flexibility a good cordless gives you makes the effort worthwhile for many home workers.

Tools for long talks

As a contributing editor to *Home* magazine, I've been asked to write a number of articles on topics I knew little about before I started—chemical pesticides, wood stove emissions standards, co-housing and all kinds of arcane stuff. Like most journalists, I got the information I needed over the phone—call after call, hour after hour—tracking down the right people and nailing down my facts. There were days when I took bathroom breaks and an hour for lunch, but spent the rest of my time with my phone's hand set tucked under my chin. The result? Accurate articles—along with a stiff neck and a raw ear. For a while, I considered using a speaker phone to get around this problem, but my objections to this mode of operation (see p. 156) were too strong. I finished the articles the old-fashioned way before I discovered telephone headsets.

Actually, I wore a headset years ago when, as a very young and very green newspaper reporter, I was assigned to sit at a desk every evening and take obituary information from the funeral homes that would call in. But those old dome-grabbers were heavy, awkward and uncomfortable—they gave me a sore cranium instead of a cramped neck. Their only redeeming feature was that they kept both of my hands free so I could type.

These days, good headsets are so light that you can forget you've got them on. The one I've used is an especially fancy model made by Plantronics and called the LiteSet. It's essentially a cordless phone with a headset instead of a hand set (an ear set, actually—the little ear plug

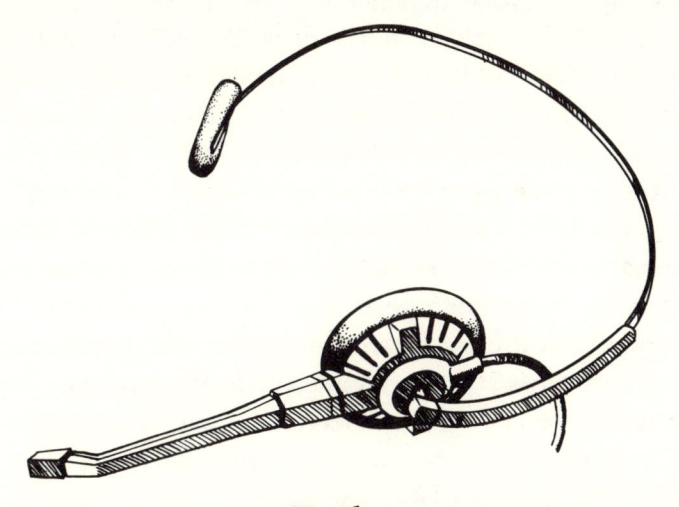

Headset

holds the whole thing on). The LiteSet was apparently a bomb on the market because not too many home users were willing to pay over $200 for such a gizmo. As I write this, the DAK discount house is selling Lite-Sets for about $100. Even this is a bit steep if all you want is a decent, light headset. On the other hand, how much is an uncricked neck worth to you?

Plantronics makes less expensive headsets than the LiteSet. You can get units from the company's SP series for from about $60 to about $90 at the moment. Radio Shack carries a good model for about $60. And Panasonic markets its WM TH10 headset for about $70. If you're on the phone a lot, consider a good, light headset.

ANSWERING MACHINES

It wasn't long ago that these things were uncommon and unloved. Few of us had them and fewer of us liked talking to them. These days, they've become standard equipment not just in home offices but in purely domestic households as well, and most of us have adjusted to talking to machines.

Like a lot of other home office workers, I simply couldn't function without what the industry calls a telephone answering device (and abbreviates TAD). As a one-man band, I'm not always home to answer my phone. But my livelihood depends to a considerable extent on calls from editors and call-backs from contacts. The editors might remember to try again if nobody picks up, but many of the others are doing me a favor to return a call in the first place. To expect them to phone two or three times before they reach me is to expect too much. The machine at least lets me continue the game of telephone tag.

Early TADs were a bit clunky. One of their worst faults was that they made people nervous because they'd typically give you only thirty seconds to leave your message. (Actually, thirty seconds is more than adequate for all but the most garrulous caller, but the *idea* of a time limit rattled lots of us.) These days, virtually all answering machines offer voice activation (VOX), which lets callers talk as long as they want. The machine senses when they stop and only then shuts down.

Current machines also offer another vital feature: remote access. If you're on the road, you can call your own number, beep a code at your TAD and have it play back your messages. This feature is a necessity to any home office worker who travels much. Most remotes also let you turn the answering machine on if you forgot to do that before you left—or you can change your message if you want to.

Some remote systems still require you to carry a beeper that replicates touch-tone frequencies. With most, though, you can simply use a phone's touch pad to send your beeps down the line. This means one less thing to cart around with you, but it can be a problem if you find yourself in West Laryngitis, where the local phone company hasn't yet committed to tone dialing. These areas are fewer all the time in the U.S., but if you travel less-populated areas, you may need to carry an auxiliary beeper.

All TADs have call indicators—some system of lights or numbers that tells you there are calls waiting for you. Mine has a little red light that blinks once for each message on the tape. This is fine at night, when it shows up like a beacon before I flip on the lights, but it's not really adequate during the day. If I wander into my office with something else on my mind, I often don't notice the small red blink. A better system is a big, bright digital readout. My previous TAD used this system, and I never failed to notice it. Some machines these days *two* digital readouts. One tells you how many people called and the other gives you the number who actually left messages. For me, this feature would just satisfy idle curiosity, but you might want to use it to test the effectiveness of different greetings (other wise known as "OGMs"—outgoing messages).

TAD features

Many answering machines offer a list of features:
- *Memo,* which lets you leave messages in person for others in your household.
- *Recording,* which lets you tape a conversation. Some supply a beep that lets your caller know he or she's being recorded. Some don't, so the responsibility for warning the other party rests with you.
- *Dictation,* which lets you use the TAD as a dictating machine.
- *Toll-saver,* which is really just a setting that lets the phone ring four times when there are no messages already on tape, but only two times when you've had calls. This way, when you call in from a remote location, you don't have to make a connection to find out if anyone has left any messages for you. If the phone rings more than twice, you know there's nothing on

the machine, and you can hang up without having incurred the expense of a toll call.

- *Time-stamping*, which tells you—by way of a digitized voice—what time a call came in. This is surprisingly handy information, especially if you've been away from the office for a few hours or if you've been away overnight and haven't called in by way of the remote. My current answering machine doesn't offer date-stamping, but I've seen it in operation enough times to know that my next machine will.

Cassettes and chips

TADs have typically used standard cassettes to record messages. Some, like mine require special "endless loop" cassettes for outgoing messages. More answering machines these days are using micro cassettes, which means the TAD itself can be smaller—a bonus in home offices. Recently, some units have been offered that don't use tapes at all. Messages are recorded digitally directly to a microchip in the machine. This gives you great sound quality (think of a CD), but because the chip can't handle as much information as a cassette, it limits the length and number of incoming messages. A good solution, which appears to be the wave of the future (temporarily, at least) is a digital outgoing message, for crisp and realistic sound, and micro cassette recording for the incoming calls.

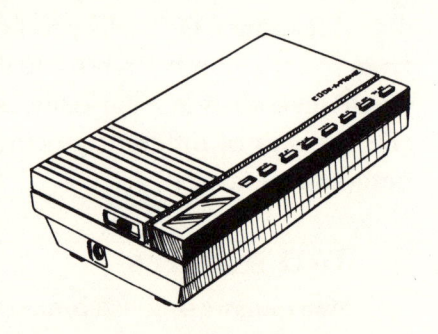

Telephone answering device

Integration

Another established trend in TADs is the answering machine integrated with a telephone. I must say that my basic philosophy is to isolate different functions in separate pieces of equipment. I always worry, for example, that if my answering machine breaks and it's part of my phone, my whole system has to be pulled off the desk and I'm in even deeper trouble than I would otherwise be.

Having said that, though, I have to admit that I use a phone-answering machine combination—a Panasonic KX-T2420—and I've been pretty happy with it. The phone is fine, and while the answering machine is clunky (*Beep. Shhhhh. Clunk. Clunk. Shhhh, clunk. Clunk.*), it's been reliable.

I've also owned a Code-A-Phone 3530 stand-alone TAD, a small unit with bright red digital readouts and a very *un*clunky micro cassette system (*Sss-click*). The 3530 stopped functioning one day, though, and while Code-a-Phone replaced it promptly and politely, I'd

Integrated TAD

already bought the replacement Panasonic (no, I couldn't operate for even a week without an answering machine), and I haven't hooked the new Code-a-Phone back up.

Both of these configurations have worked for me—an integrated system and a separate phone and (small) answering machine. But despite my natural prejudices, I think I'd incline toward a combination unit for most home offices. Desk space is at a premium, and price counts, too. You can almost certainly get a fine integrated unit for less than you'd pay for a good feature phone and a good separate answering machine. And by moving toward integrated equipment, you avoid the redundancy that becomes almost inevitable as you gradually add equipment to your office.

A further example of this sort of integration is the two-line TAD. Most answering machines handle only one line. If you wanted two lines covered, you had to buy two units. Now you can buy a single unit—

usually integrated with a phone—that will answer both lines. These machines will cover the other line if you're talking on one, or monitor both lines—simultaneously, if necessary—if you're out or unavailable. By and large, they otherwise offer the same range of features available on single-line machines.

PhoneMate was the first company to really push two-line TADs, but is being joined now by many of the other well-known names in the phone and answering machine businesses. Units are fairly expensive—many run over $200, even on discount. Depending on your business and style of work, though, that may be money well spent.

The new wave

An intriguing alternative to the traditional answering machine is what's known as "voice mail."

The two best-known voice mail systems that are suitable to home office users are *Watson* (Natural Microsystems) and *The Complete Answering Machine* (The Complete PC Inc.), but I notice that *PC Magazine* awarded an "Editor's Choice" flag to a third program: *BigmOuth* (Talking Technologies Inc.). All three list for less than $400 (*Watson* includes a 1200-bps modem). All three packages run on IBM-compatible computers only, at the moment, but I'm sure similar programs for the Mac can't be far behind.

The three systems are similar in that they all combine a card that pops into your computer with software that runs the system. Each offers itself as either a traditional, if digital, answering machine, or as a more sophisticated system with multiple "mailboxes" in which you can leave and pick up specific messages for and from particular clients or contacts. They will also, if you like, call you at another number to alert you that a message has just been received in a specific mailbox.

Now that even large companies have decided it's too much trouble to have an actual person answer your call, home businesses can use voice mail to convey a very corporate image. You can set them up with one of those voices that tells callers to press buttons for a certain kinds of information or connections. You can even assign regular clients their own codes to let them retrieve and deposit personalized messages in their mailboxes.

If all you really need is an answering machine, you should probably stick with a traditional TAD. But if your business would be served by more advanced capabilities, then voice mail may be just the ticket for you. Remember, though, that if you commit to voice mail, you have to leave your computer running while you're out of your office. (This won't hurt the computer any, but I've known people who equate leaving the computer on with forgetting to turn off the stove).

FAX MACHINES

The first time I ever saw the word "facsimile" was on the back of a Classics Comic—James Fenimore Cooper's "The Pathfinder", I think. To order copies of "The Man in the Iron Mask" or "The Red Badge of Courage" I was told to send in the order blank or the proverbial reasonable facsimile. I asked my Mom what this new word meant, this FAXy-mile.

At least I had the first syllable right. These days, that's almost all that counts: fax is hot. "I'll fax it to you" has become almost as common a closer to business conversations as "Let's have lunch."

My favorite fax story was told to me by a Toshiba executive who claimed that a new user called Toshiba's technical support line complaining that her fax wasn't functioning properly. When the technician asked her what the problem was, she said, "I keep trying to send a document, but it never works. I push the button, insert the page and watch it roll into the machine. But then the machine doesn't send it. It's still right here."

That was a few years ago, and by now all of us sophisticates know that a faxed document is supposed to stay "right here." Only a copy is transmitted to New York or Paris or Tokyo. Very simply, a fax machine lets you send visual images over the phone lines. Drawings, photos, documents with signatures and marginal scribbles in tact—all these can be transmitted across the country or around the world about as simply as making a telephone call.

The same Toshiba executive told me that the biggest reason for the fax boom is...the fax boom. Everyone seems to agree that the market has achieved critical mass. Sales are doubling every year. Business people are beginning to assume that other business people will have fax capabilities, so many companies and individuals are faxing up their offices to present a professional image, to stay competitive—or simply to avoid the embarrassment of admitting they aren't geared up.

Three things got the fax boom started. First, useful machines dipped under $1,000, an important price point. Second, fax—unlike direct digital communication with modems and software—is easy to use and relatively foolproof. Fax machines are not intimidating or counter-intuitive or prone to bizarre behavior. *Anybody*, with a flip through the manual or a few seconds of coaching, can perform the technological miracle of sending a detailed drawing across the country and receiving a corrected copy from the other end. Third, and most obvious, fax is a quick and inexpensive way to send letters and other documents. FedEx can get it there tomorrow for fourteen bucks. A fax machine gets it there *now* for the cost of a call (and a piece of the cost of the machine, but that's just a quibble).

There's another thing about faxes which people often don't realize until after they've hooked one up. More than any other piece of technology—even the phone or the networked computer—a facsimile machine can make someone working at home for a larger organization feel as if he or she is still in the loop. There's something about receiving true copies of memos, notes, drawings, drafts, spreadsheets, letters, calculations, layouts, designs—and even (maybe especially) things like office cartoons—with all their scribbles, cross-outs, corrections and marginalia, that ties you in with the culture back at the main office and keeps you feeling like one of the group.

A quick look at the flip side

There's no doubt that fax is here to stay and that most of us will eventually incorporate a facsimile capability of one kind or another into our home offices. But there are some drawbacks—philosophical, not technical—that we should all watch out for. Because fax *allows* instant visual communication, it virtually *demands* it. I've seen lawyers, instead of ruminating on a letter overnight, zap angry epistles back and forth in the heat of the moment, escalating disputes rather than calming them. I've seen editors, confusing work time with delivery time, shorten deadlines that previously had been measured in weeks, to days—or even hours.

In short, I've seen fax machines drive people nuts. They are the perfect tools for the compulsive, A-type personalities who seem to set the rules of American business. For many in the work force—at home or in a high rise—they make the frenetic pace of business even more driven, more demanding, more frenzied. With a fax machine, there's no automatic breather while you wait for the mails or even Federal Express to process and deliver your communications. After you get over treating your fax like a new toy and using it all the time for everything, you may find that you need to consciously slow down a bit if you're going to give matters the thought they deserve—and retain your own peace of mind.

What to look for

The fax machines that are selling like crazy today are all "Group 3 machines." They meet certain standards set by the Consultative Committee on International Telephony and Telegraphy (CCITT), and they can talk to other Group 3 machines anywhere in the world. Some can communicate with earlier Group 2 and Group 1 machines, too, but this "backward compatibility" isn't vital. Almost nobody's using those old machines anymore.

Phone

As with advanced telephones and TADs, there is a short list of features you should know about before you go shopping for facsimile machines. The first is pretty straightforward: a phone. Most fax machines these days come with a hand set. In many home offices, the fax is also the phone—or at least one of the phones. This makes a lot of sense. Since the machine uses the phone lines anyway, you might as well be able to talk over it, too.

Three-in-one

Most fax phones don't offer all the advanced features of a standalone or integrated TAD unit, but many offer auto-dialing capabilities. If your fax is going to be your phone too, be sure you can get one with the kind of phone features you want and need.

Actually, many faxes are marketed as "three in one" devices. They offer the fax, the phone—and a copier, too. They can all run a document through their systems and produce a thermal-paper copy. This feature won't compete with a true plain-paper photo copier, but it's a pleasant "free" benefit of the technology that is all many home office workers need.

Gray scale

Some machines can distinguish among eight or sixteen tones of gray, while others see just black or white. The ability to distinguish a "gray scale" is important if you're going to be transmitting photographs regularly, less important if you work exclusively with letters and other typed or printed documents.

Auto-feed

On less expensive fax units, you feed documents by hand, one page at a time. More expensive machines offer an automatic feed, usually for up to five documents, but sometimes for as many as ten or twen-

Fax phone

ty-five or thirty. I like this feature because when I use a fax I'm often sending a manuscript rather than a one-page letter. Besides, when I feed by hand, I'm always getting things lined up crooked.

Page-cutting

On the receiving end, some units offer automatic page cutting, which nicely separates the transmitted documents into discreet sheets rather than leaving you to deal with a long scroll. If you mostly transmit, this isn't a big deal, but if you receive a lot of multi-page documents, a page cutter can be very handy.

Speed

Most fax machines are designed to transmit at 9,600 bps, although a few low-end models run at only 4,800. The actual speed of a facsimile transmission depends largely on the quality of your phone lines. If a fax recognizes a poor line, with lots of distracting and error-producing background noise, it will automatically slow down to reduce errors. Faxes are also slower to handle complex graphics or blocks of very fine print than they are to manage letters, memos and other standard typed documents.

Another thing that effects fax speed is the mode in which you choose to transmit. The standard resolution of facsimile transmission is a slightly fuzzy 100 dots per inch (DPI) by about 200 DPI. Most fax units let you select a "fine mode," which slows transmission down considerably, but boosts resolution to about 200 by 200 DPI. A few even offer a "super-fine" 200 by 400 DPI mode, at a further reduction in transmission speed.

In my experience with several models and brands, most pages roll through a fax unit in under thirty seconds each. Some take a good bit less time, and a few seem to take forever—maybe a minute or so. Manufacturer's rated speeds, usually twenty seconds per page or less, are—surprise!—based on optimum conditions.

Polling and broadcasting

"Polling" is a unit's ability to call a sequence of numbers to receive transmissions from various specific locations. "Delayed polling" lets you set the machine to poll at a specific time (usually late at night, when phone rates are at their lowest). Certain home office consultants or entrepreneurs with clients scattered around the country might find this feature helpful. And it's not expensive—even most low-cost units include a polling feature.

The reverse of polling is "broadcasting"—the ability of a fax unit to call a series of numbers to transmit, rather than to receive. At its worst, this results in the dreaded "fax junk mail" that is beginning to clutter systems left on automatic. At its best, though, broadcasting can let you send vital information to a list of clients or colleagues almost simultaneously. Unlike polling, broadcasting is usually available only on more expensive units, although the sleek black Canon Faxphone

20 that I used for several months (discounted price $1,200 or lower) offers it.

Faxing and talking

A feature that I miss on fax machines that don't have it is a "voice request" or "voice confirmation request" function. Basically, this is some means of signalling the other party that you want to talk after the fax has done its job. This voice request is especially handy for the home office worker, because it means you don't have to place another phone call to discuss the document you've just sent or received. This voice request is usually a button that lights up, but some machines include LCD readouts that alert you to the other party's desire for a chat. I'm told that voice request works best when used between units made by the same manufacturer, but I've never run into any problems trying this with disparate machines.

What's going on here?

Two more features that I like are "terminal identification" and what's usually called something like "activity reporting." A unit that offers terminal identification lets you set the time and date and punch in your name and phone number—all to be included in small print at the top of each page that you transmit. When you transmit by fax, you should always use a standard cover sheet with your name (or your company's), address, phone number and the name of the person or organization you're sending to. But this automatic identification on each page can keep individual sheets from getting lost.

"Activity reporting" is simply the automatic keeping of a list of your fax transmissions. I like this for the same reason I like the phone list that *Hot Line* keeps for me—it lets me check my phone bill, and it helps me separate business use from personal.

Automatic switching

Contrary to what you will hear people tell you, you definitely do *not* have to dedicate a phone line to your fax machine. But if you don't, you might want to consider investing in a "smart box" like Dragoon's Faxmate 168, which plugs in between your fax phone and the wall jack and automatically differentiates between an incoming call from another facsimile machine and one from someone who actually wants to exchange words with you.

Without this sort of automatic switching (or a dedicated line), you have two choices: either leave the unit set to automatically receive facsimile transmissions and subject anyone calling you to talk on that line to the shrill tone of an eager fax unit, or leave the unit in manual mode and pick up often to hear the same lovely tone drilling into your own ear. With a box like the Faxmate on the job, you never have to hear that fax whine on the line, although your callers still have to put up with a five-second burst before the box switches over. Not perfect by any means, but possibly helpful when you're using a single line for both fax and phone.

A drawback with the Faxmate is that it doesn't get along well with all answering machines. For electronic reasons that are probably transparently obvious to everyone but me, it can't be counted upon to switch calls reliably between TAD and fax. If you're interested, contact Dragoon for more information on this issue.

The answering machine angle *is* covered by a new hybrid that's beginning to appear—the fully integrated fax-phone-TAD. On units like the Panasonic KX-F120 Fax + system, for example ($1,695 list, under $1,000, discounted), people can even call while you're out, leave a message on your answering machine, *and* transmit a fax. That's a fair amount of power to be able to set on the corner of your desk, and such machines are targeted directly at us working at home. NEC was first with this sort of full court press of integration, I believe, and I've looked at a very nice Toshiba as well. There will, no doubt, be plenty of competition in this area before long. Keep your eyes peeled.

Fax Pricing

For home office workers, fax machines break—very roughly—into two categories: those that list for less than $1,000 and those that cost more. The basic, sub-$1,000 models, are exemplified by the groundbreaking Murata 1200, which is available as I write for between $700 and $800. They generally offer a phone hand set (but few if any advanced phone features like auto-dial), automatic and manual fax settings and a high-resolution mode. Many offer polling capabilities. Some include terminal identification and activity reporting.

If you want the other features—auto-dial, automatic feed, broadcasting, voice request and so on—you're in another league: figure on at least $1,200 (discounted), although prices are still coming down, and by the time you read this, you might well be able to do better.

The nice thing about shopping for fax machines is that virtually all the recognizable names in the field—brands like Brother, Canon, Fujitsu, Hitachi, Mitsubishi, Murata, NEC, Panasonic, Pitney-Bowes, Ricoh, Sharp, Toshiba and Xerox—make good units that do pretty much the same thing in pretty much the same way with pretty much the same quality. You can list your needs and then shop on price alone.

So what fax unit have I chosen? Well, none. I've borrowed faxes from time to time, and I've used them often. They are terrific, seductive, inevitable. But for what I do as a writer, a fax is an expense I can't yet justify. People often want to fax me things, but when I tell them I can't accommodate them, they seem happy to pop whatever it is in the mail or shoot it to me via Federal Express. I'm almost never in such a hurry that tomorrow is too late. In the other direction, most of my business "transmissions" still tend to be in the form of diskettes traveling by mail or FedEx to magazines or publishers who then pop them into their computer systems without having to re-keyboard my immortal prose. They wouldn't be happy at all with a dozen faxed pages of a hard-copy manuscript.

There is a way, though, to make a direct connection between fax and computer. It's intriguing, and it's coming on strong.

Fax boards

These represent one of those great ideas that hasn't made it yet, but surely will. Fax boards (available for from less than $400 to more than $1,000) pop into your computer and, with their software, let you transmit data on your screen to your correspondent's fax machine— or to her computer fax board, for that matter. Talk about integration! You don't need a separate unit, and you can fax documents without even printing them out!

But there is a flaw that too many articles on the subject don't mention until the last few paragraphs. If the document you want to transmit already exists in hard copy form, you need a scanner to read it into your computer before it can be sent by fax. The fax board plus the scanner will cost you more than a very good, multi-featured faxphone.

There's another problem, too. The process of sending a fax, so simple in stand-alone units, begins to get complicated with fax boards. Here's the process: Create a file or otherwise import it into your computer. Convert your file into a format the fax can deal with (usually ASCII for text and graphics standard like *PC Paintbrush*, *Publisher's Paintbrush* or *Dr. Halo* for graphics). Load the fax software. Tell the fax software which file you want to send. Tell the software when you want to send it. And so on.

This process isn't opaque, but it isn't automatic, either. Fiddling with a computer and software menus removes one of fax's great attributes—simplicity.

For most home office workers, fax boards just aren't the ticket yet. But say you're broadcasting or polling requirements outstrip the capabilities of most faxphone units. Maybe, for example, you regularly need to contact hundreds of numbers instead of a dozen or two. Then you should definitely be looking into a fax board.

Regardless, keep your eyes on this technology. The convenient mating of computer, phone and fax is certain to happen eventually, and there may well come a day when a fax unit sitting on your desk takes on the nostalgic glow of a manual Underwood.

COPIERS

Until you start to work significant hours at home, you don't realize how often and how automatically you rely on the corporate photocopier. After a year of flying trips to use the local public library's copier, and frustrated Sunday afternoons and late evenings when I couldn't get at it, I made a personal copier my first, gulping, post-computer, extravagant equipment purchase. It remains one of my favorite and most frequently used tools.

Canon is the King Kong of personal copiers, all based on the sort of convenient, no-mess single-cartridge system that's familiar to laser printer users. (Canon calls this a "dry monocomponent toner projection system.") Other companies—Sharp, Ricoh and more—are muscling in on the territory, but the Canon line remains the best-known and most visible in small businesses, bank branches and home offices, so it makes a good example.

The smallest and cheapest Canons are small and cheap indeed. The PC-3, for example, weighs only twenty-five pounds and costs less than $500, discounted. It's also pretty basic: you feed it yourself, one sheet at a time, it neither reduces nor enlarges, and it won't handle legal-sized paper. But think what it *does* do—in a tiny, versatile, portable package, it handles ninety percent, maybe more, of most home office copying chores. Which keeps you from hustling off to the library or the copy center in the middle of the day, wasting twenty minutes or more on a ten-second chore.

Bigger and more expensive copiers—from Canon and other makers—do more. My writing often requires a lot of research. I need

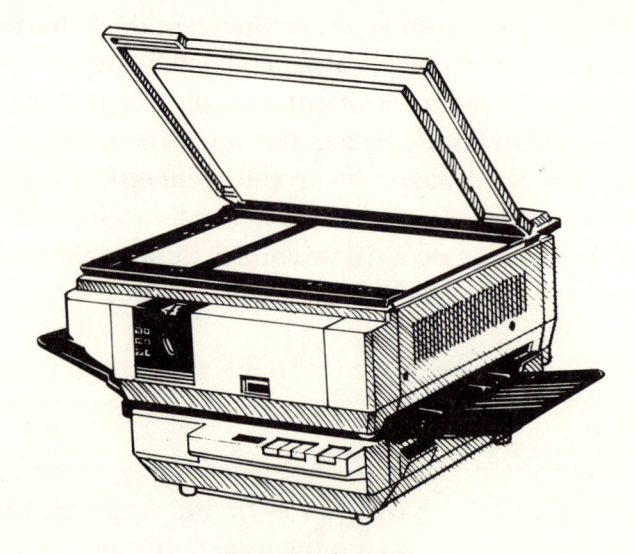

Personal copier

to be able to handle legal-sized paper and to reduce large pages to manageable size. As a result, I finally wound up with a PC-25, which was Canon's top of the line model at the time. It does all of this and also offers an automatic sheet feeder and multiple copies.

Small copier technology keeps getting better. My PC-25, for example reduces and enlarges to specific ratios: 67 percent, 78 percent and 120 percent. It also has a slightly inconvenient sliding copy board. Canon's new top model, the PC-7, reduces and enlarges to *any* ratio between 70 percent and 122 percent, and it has a stationary copy board that won't knock over that nearby stack of papers.

You should keep in mind, though, that even the best of the personal copiers are no competition to the big Xeroxes you may be used to in the corporate world. Quality is fine, but speed is low and feeding, sorting and other special, automatic features scanty. I've had corporate types laugh condescendingly at my little beauty—while they were waiting for "emergency" copies it was churning out for them. And while I bless my copier daily, I must confess myself to getting impatient sometimes watching it labor away at eight copies per minute. Isn't human nature something?

As with most hardware, software, peripherals and equipment, you should shop hard when you enter the market for a copier. It pays off.

When I settled on the Canon PC-25—which at the time listed for $1,795—I began to check real prices. The best I could find were in ads published by several of the big volume discount houses in New York City. From them, I could buy the machine for $795 (which should tell you a little about margins in this business). Before unlimbering my credit card, though, I called a local office machine company that specializes in copiers.

"I'm interested in buying a Canon PC-25," I told the salesman on the other end of the phone. "What's your price?"

"We can let you have one of those for $1695."

"Well, I'm looking at a price in *The New York Times* here of $795."

"Oh. Well, we can't match prices with those guys." Pause. I began reaching for the old Visa. "But I can sell it to you for $895, and we service all our copiers within twenty-four hours of when you call."

Sold.

DO YOU REALLY NEED THIS STUFF?

There are really two basic rules for buying equipment for your home office. The first is obvious, but often ignored: Buy only the tools you really need. A computer? Basic to the modern home office. A phone? Of course. A fax or a copier? Tempting, for sure, but maybe not really necessary. My rule of thumb is that I need a piece of equipment if and only if I've been *repeatedly* and *significantly* inconvenienced by not owning it.

The second basic rule is what I think of as "The Principle of Obsolescent Technology." It incorporates doing your homework so you know what's available out there and what's likely to come down the pike in the near future. But its main element is a very boring one: Try to buy only products that are (1) thoroughly debugged, and (2) reduced in price. In other words, don't get sliced by that dangerous cutting edge of technology. A desk top fax unit qualifies, for example. A fax board probably doesn't. But pay attention—it probably will.

This attention—doing your homework—is vital. Know what you need. Know the lowest price around for it. Shop hard. And remember that the absolute rock-bottom price isn't always the best deal for you. Service, convenience and good vibes count. Only you can decide how much.

8

Designing Your Home Office

The most important thing about your home office isn't that it's at home. Or even that it's an office. The most important thing about it is that it's *yours*.

I once worked in a place where I wasn't allowed to remove a handsome but superfluous bookcase that was attached to the wall over my desk. I wanted to free that space so I could hang up a chart to help me track work I was responsible for managing. But the bookcase matched others in the office and my employers were more concerned with the look of the place than with how efficiently things got done there. This sort of thing may be dumb, but it's the absolute prerogative of employers. Ultimately, all you can do is shrug your shoulders and make the best of it.

At home, though, you don't have to put up with this kind of nonsense. You can plan your office layout to suit the jobs you do and the way you do them. In fact, designing a home office—whether you're going to be working there full time or only occasionally—should be a healthy and liberating exercise in pleasing yourself. But if it's going to bear fruit, this exercise, like most good things, takes time, concentration, and an organized approach.

DEVELOPING A PROGRAM
Some standards

There are a few needs we all share, no matter what sort of office we work it. To do good work, every one of us needs to be able to concentrate. So we need a certain level of privacy, good lighting, adequate comfort and safety, and convenient access to the tools and data our jobs require.

There are standards for certain office elements, and although you'll eventually want to factor yourself into the equation, they make good starting points.

Computer monitor. It should be from 16 to 28 inches from your face, and it should be set below your eye level, so that you look down ten to twenty degrees when you're reading from it. You'd probably want a nine-inch monitor at the close end of this range. If you use a big, oversized monitor, you probably want it beyond the far end. My monitor is a standard twelve-inch number, and its comfortable for me at about twenty-six or twenty-seven inches.

Copy holder. Keep it in the same plane as your monitor, so that your eyes won't have to work hard when they move from screen to paper and back.

Work surface depth. Should be at least 22 inches deep, according to the books, but this is inadequate for many computer users. A computer (if you keep it on your desk) and its keyboard can easily combine to be better than two-feet deep. Even with my computer under my desk, I prefer my main work surface to be a full, luxurious, three feet deep.

Work surface height. The standard height of a work surface is 29-1/2 inches, if you're going to be writing on it by hand. Standard typing height is 26-1/2 inches, which happens to be exactly right for me. If you are building your work surface in, or if you're using an adjustable-height table or desk, determine your own best height by sitting in your chair and "walking through" your work motions. The proper typing height is the one at which your elbows are bent at a ninety degree angle.

Work surface space. At least 18 inches of workspace to the left or right of your keyboard. More is better. More on both sides is better yet.

But we're all different. We do different work. We live in different spaces. We have different habits. We are different physical types. A well-designed home office meets our universal requirements with particular solutions. So you want to think carefully about

How Ya Do the Things Ya Do.

The key to a good home office design is analyzing carefully what it is you'll be working at and what your working style is. The obvious place to start is with your body. Are you left or right handed? Are you tall or small? Are you disabled in any way?

These considerations will help you figure out the best placement for things like your printer, your phone, your file cabinets and your book shelves. They'll indicate how much space you need for certain activities. They'll tell you if you have to spend much time or money on style, as opposed to function. There are other personal considerations, too. For example, I'm deaf in my left ear. Therefore, I want my phone to my right. And to take advantage of what is usually a drawback, I want all my biggest noisemakers—computer, printer, copier—over to my left, where I can't hear their cooling fans, power sources or mechanisms laboring away.

This is very straightforward, but it's also very personal. My set-up wouldn't suit you if you're a normal right-hander. You probably prefer to answer the phone with your left hand and push printer buttons with your right. This is *your* office. Take the trouble to analyze *your* physical requirements.

Along the same lines, this is also the time to consider your work habits, the jobs you'll be doing and—generally at least—what kinds of equipment you'll be using. For example, do you habitually spread papers around you, or do you work more neatly from files or individual documents? Do you like to get up and prowl around as you think over knotty problems? Will you be working mainly on your keyboard, or will you be doing a lot of hand work? Do you need a second work station—a drafting table, maybe, or a light table to check slides? What office equipment will you install right away and how much room will it take up? Do you expect to be buying more soon? Will you be receiving clients? If so, how many at a time?

This sort of detailed self-analysis is vital. Without it, you approach your potential home office space with only the vaguest notion of how to arrange it. With it, you've got what architects call a "program"—a list of carefully considered personal priorities that you can apply to that space to create the best possible home office *for you*. Unless you're building a whole new room, you won't be able to accommodate every element of your program, but even if you have to do some serious compromising, you should be able to address your major concerns.

For example, when I put together my first full time home office, I was simply unable to carve out space to my left for my oversized printer. And since the printer took up so much room to my right, the phone had to go to my left. Bass ackwards, as my grandfather would have said. But by not forcing the phone into limited space near the printer, I did reserve plenty of desk space for note-taking, book-propping and occasional sketching. And none of this affected my 26-1/2-in. high work surface. I couldn't salvage some fairly important elements of my program, but the real core of my work habits wasn't affected.

FUNCTION AND STYLE

Function is the key to a successful home office. Style is entirely optional if you don't entertain clients. It has no value except to make you feel comfortable, energetic and secure.

If you just want a few touches to soften or offset the utilitarianism of file cabinets and electronic gadgetry, you're right in the mainstream—most home-office workers don't get too fancy. But if you enjoy interior design, and can afford its cost, terrific. On the other hand, if all you care about is the biggest possible space to spread out your work in, go for it.

The point is that a home office is personal space, where every single element should be considered in the light of *your* comfort and convenience. Forget fashion. Forget status. Suit yourself.

Comfort, of course, is an individual issue, but most home offices, not surprisingly, have a distinctly casual feel. Decoration tends toward things like family photos, kids' drawings, souvenirs and personal icons of one kind or another. For me, at least, things like this help most during difficult times. They trigger a smile and lend a little strenth. One of my favorites is a photo I've got of the young Casey Stengel, in his New York Giants baseball uniform and spikes shaking hands with a bowler-hatted and be-spatted King George V during a 1920's European baseball tour. The contrast between wild baseball royalty and the proper blue-blooded kind makes me chuckle every time, no matter how anxious I am about meeting a deadline or wrestling with a difficult project.

Of course, there are a few areas where style can directly affect function. The ones that come up most often are:

Colors. Warm neutrals keep things calm and don't change drastically with shifting natural light. They also obscure the light layer of dust that builds up on the rear and corners of desktops and tables.

Carpets. These are a good idea for several reasons. They absorb sound, they're easy on the legs, they can help set your workspace off from the rest of the room. And they can add some color and pattern to all those warm neutrals.

Drapes. In most home offices, good drapes or shades are necessary to control natural light. More about this in the next chapter. In certain circumstances, drapes can act as sound-deadening barriers. And they, also, can be colorful enough to brighten up an otherwise dull room.

View. If you're lucky, a pleasant view to the outside can be as calming as a favorite poster or photograph. On the other hand, some views are so magnificent—or so depressing—that they are permanent disruptions. A little minor landscaping can often work wonders outside home office windows.

Plants. It's not that I hate green, growing things, it's just that I always wind up killing them. The poor few plants I've experimented with have always shrivelled and died within weeks—sometimes days—of when I brought them home. Crumbling brown tendrils drooping forlornly out of dusty pots aren't especially uplifting. But if you have a reasonably green thumb, the presence of living, oxygen-producing plants can be both beautiful and comforting. Just be sure to put them someplace where you'll run no risk of dousing the machinery when you make your rounds with the watering can.

BASIC DESIGNS

Okay. You found your space with the help of Chapter 2, and now you've developed your program and become reconciled to the inevitability of compromise. Let's take a look at the four standard layouts: the strip, the L, the galley and the U. Each of them can be interpreted in a number of different ways.

The strip, for example, can be based on a long, kitchen-like counter, or it can be made up of a straight-line sequence of components and discreet pieces of furniture—a computer rack, say, next to a small work table, near a bookshelf or filing cabinet. Obviously, if you've got a lot of equipment or need much storage space, your wall has to be pretty long, and not everything will be within easy reach. A simple strip office can work fine, especially if you don't expect to accumulate much fancy equipment, but it's probably the least desirable of the basic designs.

In an L-shaped layout, the second leg can be something as simple as a typing return or as grand as a duplicate workspace. Ls are more common than strips, partly because corners are often wasted space that home office hunters can put to good use, and partly because they're simply more convenient. Many small home offices qualify as Ls because their owners have discovered that the computer printer is the joker in the deck. It just won't fit on the average primary work surface. So it's

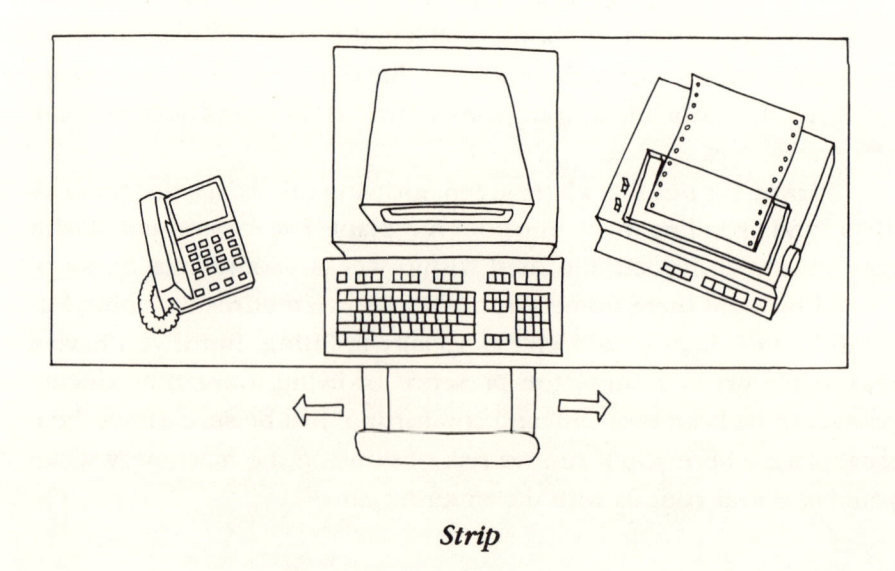

Strip

often set on a small table or desk placed off to one side or the other and rotated ninety degrees for ease of use. Sometimes what looks like a strip office is converted into an L every time its owner sits down to work. That's when the printer (or the computer, in some cases) is pivoted out on its stand or rack.

What If You Have Clients?

Most home offices aren't established to impress—or even accommodate—anybody but the person working in them. Efficiency is the main point, closely trailed in most cases by economy.

But if you expect to receive clients in your office, all that changes. You have to take other people—often people you know only slightly, if at all—into account. There are clients and clients, of course. Some are very buttoned up and self-consciously businesslike, while others are casual types who may be working out of their own homes. But it's safe to assume that your dealings with them will benefit from two things: comfort and privacy—an environment in which they'll feel at ease doing business.

This lets shared bedroom space out, as well as lofts reachable only by ladder or tossed-together areas with nowhere to sit. It may also exclude an adjournment to even the most elegant living room, if the family's around and your clients feel as if they're speaking to your entire household.

Three simple observations I've picked up from my travels:
- A separate entrance is great if you can swing it. You can keep clients out of your family space altogether, thereby keeping both them and your family

to page 192

more comfortable. If you live in a small town, you've probably seen doctors, and maybe lawyers, set up highly professional offices this way. Garage offices lend themselves especially well to this sort of separation—in mine, the separate doors open off of the necessary New England mudroom.

- A good inexpensive way to impress clients is with a small "conversational" grouping: couch, chair, rug, coffee table, lamps. If you have enough space, you can establish this arrangement permanently in your office (it's also a pleasant place for you to sit alone when your work doesn't require the keyboard or the drafting table). Or you could consider a temporary rearrangement of livingroom furniture to cut down on the unsettling openness of a family room. You can speak softly in such comfortably cozy set-ups, so privacy concerns are reduced.
- If you must meet clients in an office that's simply part of another room, think carefully about screening it off from family space—at least when you expect clients to be present. Spatial privacy may not guarantee aural privacy, but, like the conversation grouping, it

to page 193

implies it. A simple dressing screen can work, as can tall pieces of furniture: bookcases, armoires, highboys.

Actually, my favorite solution to this whole problem is to meet clients at their place. Most appreciate the convenience, and as long as you don't moan about how unsuitable your office is to receive guests, they'll think you're providing a great service. When I was scripting industrial videos and writing for companies and small corporations, I *never* attempted to do business with a client or potential client in my home office. I *always* went to them. It worked out fine.

A similar solution is to meet on a neutral site—usually a restaurant for lunch. This is fine for initial conferences, but is not so hot for later technical discussions involving papers, drafts, drawings or plans. A useful variation might be a local club that offers meals and conference rooms. Remember, though, that if you suggest lunch, your clients will expect you to pay for it. Even though that's a write-off, if you're just getting started it may put too much of a strain on your home-office budget.

•

A galley is basically two strip arrangements back to back, but it doesn't really have to be a narrow space lined with two long parallel counters. A more common arrangement puts the office chair between a wall with a work surface and a standard desk facing the other way. In the age of computers this has become a common layout in executive offices all over the world. The computer, in these set-ups, is usually set up on the work surface behind the desk, which is generally used for hand work, reading and phone calls. In these corporate circumstan-

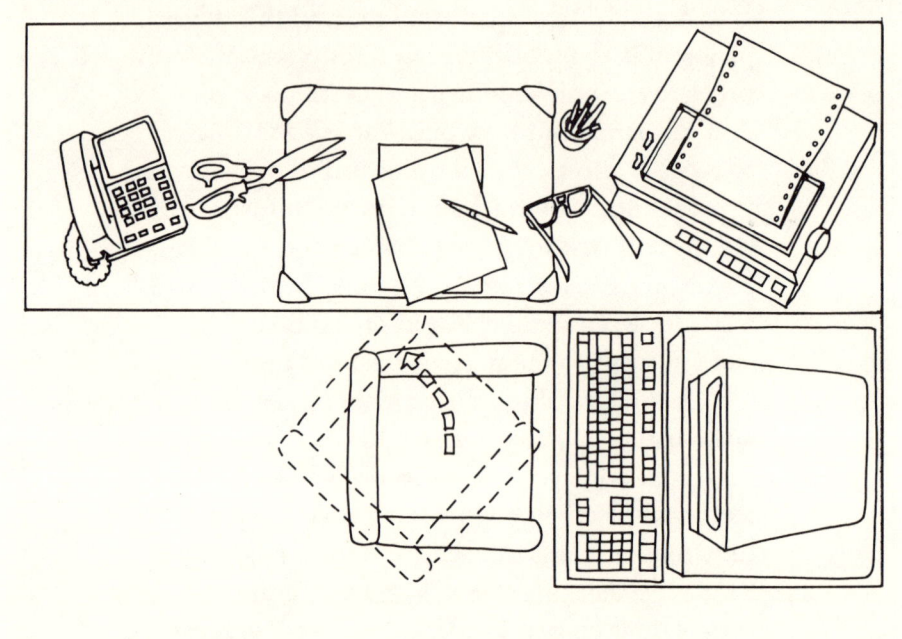

L

ces, there's often a small seating area out front for conferences with clients and colleagues. All this executive stuff aside, I've always liked galley layouts. It's quick and slick to just swivel your chair if you want to move from computer to hand work or phone.

A U can be thought of either as a galley with a connecting leg or an L with another angle. It incorporates the convenience and easy access of both. My new office is a classic U: three work surfaces set against three walls. But I've happily worked in U arrangements in which only one or two walls came into play, and in many corporate offices, U-shaped layouts don't rely on walls at all. A U really gives you the sense of sitting at your own personal control center—everything important is usually within easy reach.

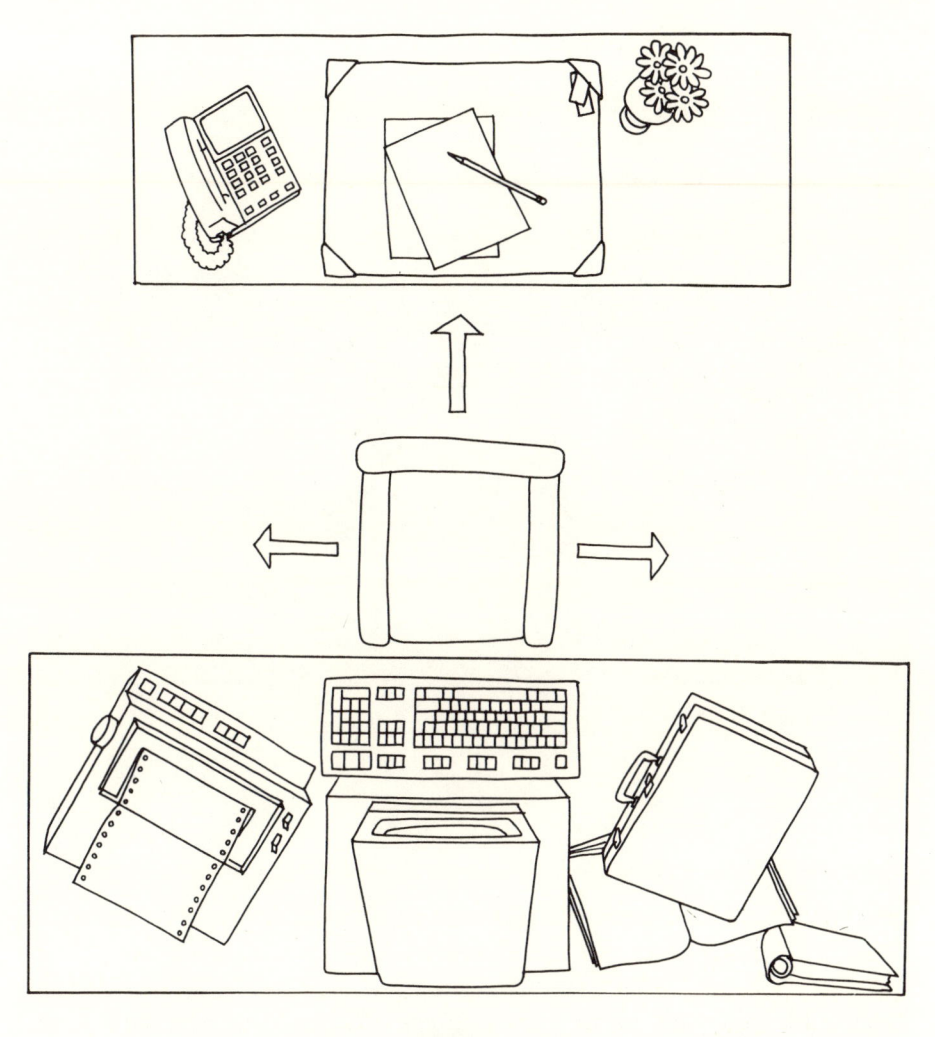

Galley

Your space will probably suggest some version of one of these basic layouts. Don't try to squeeze an inappropriate plan into a space, but *do* keep poking and prodding at the arrangement you come up with. The best plan isn't always the most obvious one. And even if your basic idea is sound, you can almost always think of ways to improve it. The best time to ponder the possibilities is when you actually settle down to draw your plans on paper. First, though, there's a vital consideration to explore that's all too often given short shrift.

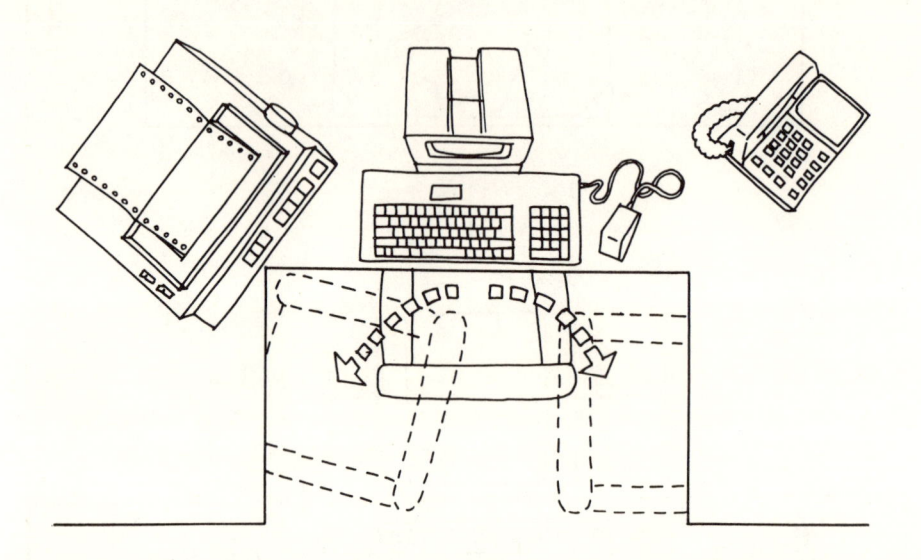

U

GETTING IT ON PAPER

Having located your home's most likely office space, identified your personal program and pondered standard layouts, it's time to sit down and get to work with a pencil and some paper to create a floorplan (overhead view) and some elevations (walls).

This paperwork doesn't have to be architect-quality, but it shouldn't be mere quick sketches, either. It has to be drawn to scale. This may seem basic to you, but I don't know how many thumbnail plans I've seen that were totally impractical because unscaled elements wouldn't really fit the space.

Finding More Space In Your Space

Space is usually at a premium in home offices. Most of us need a lot more of it than we've really got, and we have to be creative about finding it where it's not evident.

- One way is to put your computer on the floor to open up a useful and otherwise obscured sweep of desktop (see *Tilt!*, on page 37).
- Another is to create vertical slots under or next to table tops for large flats. Masonite™ dividers held apart by a simple pine frame work great.
- If you work with oversized drawings or plans, you can roll them up and pop them in an umbrella stand, wastebasket or trash bin.
- Consider stacking boxes or other containers to create a group of cubby holes.
- File cabinets can often be squeezed into otherwise dead corners. They also squeeze nicely into the back of closets. And there's frequently room under a window for a lateral file, which can do double service as a lamp table.
- Dead files (and even those that are barely alive) should be boxed up and moved out to basement, attic or garage loft.

to page 198

> You don't want to waste space on stuff you may never look at again.
> - Hallways often offer lots of wall space for bookshelves, or at least a stretch of low bookcases.
> - You can cork whole walls if you want to. And you can paint the cork tiles white. This is a great way to create space for schedules, lists and calendars, not to mention humanizing elements like posters, cartoons and your favorite Yogi Berra quotations.
>
> Your ideas will be at least as good as mine—better, because you'll be looking at the space in question. The point is: Use your imagination and don't waste an inch.
>
> •

Creating scaled drawings is easy. It requires neither training nor artistic ability; simply the ability to read a tape measure, note your readings and draw straight lines on graph paper. Believe me, if I can do it, so can you.

Start with a temporary rough sketch of your space's floorplan. Include doors, windows, built-ins you intend to leave in place, and other obvious features. As you measure the area, you will transfer your results to this sheet. (As you move around the walls, you may find that you have to modify your sketch because you've left out a small nook or subtle jog.)

For my money, the best measuring tool for this job is a good twenty-five-foot builder's tape. My faithful Stanley Powerlock II is long enough to handle virtually any home office space, and its inch-wide tape is fairly rigid, so I can extend it six or more feet before it flops to the floor. That's really handy if there's no one to hold the other end. On the other hand, I can also bend the tape contractor-style to get a measurement in a corner or against the floor.

Depending on your space, you may have to measure an entire room, one end of a larger space, a corner or just a single stretch with two or three feet of its adjacent walls. Regardless, it's usually easiest to start in a corner and measure from one obvious point to another. Measure to the *outside* of door and window frames.

I always find that it's best to go around several times, first for the major measurements, then for the locations of things like electrical and lighting outlets and phone jacks (assuming I'm not going to rip them out and start over).

When you're done, your rough sketch should look like a doodle-sheet from math class. It will be covered with numbers, many of them

Rough sketch

fractions. Look the sheet over carefully. Make sure you know exactly what number represents exactly which distance. Remeasure if necessary, and draw arrows if you have to. Then repeat the whole procedure for whatever elevations (wall plans) your space requires. (Remember that you can simply transfer many measurements from the floorplan.)

With all your measurements at hand, you're ready to create a set of scaled drawings. Architects commonly use a scale of 1/4 inch to 1 foot, but there's no reason in the world why you have to. Especially if you're dealing with a fairly small space, a scale of 1/2 inch to 1 foot might be more helpful. The easiest way to proceed is to use graph paper printed in 1/4-inch squares. With a 1/4-inch scale, one square equals a foot. With a 1/2-inch scale, two squares equals a foot. Pretty simple either way.

Architects use a simple tool that makes it even easier. Called an architect's scale, it's essentially a three-sided ruler marked off in a dozen or so typical scales, half reading right to left and half reading left to right. Instead of having to count off half-inches on a regular ruler, for example, you can flip to the half-inch scale and just count feet: one, two, three. This makes your job a little quicker, and intermediate markings let you translate odd fractions pretty accurately. You can get architect's scales in most stationery stores and art supply shops. Mine cost a couple of dollars twelve years ago. I've seen them these days from less than $4 to more than $13. A cheap one should do you.

Your scaled drawings will look quite different from your rough sketches. They won't just be neater, but because your subjective perceptions will have been supplanted by accurate measurements, their proportions will almost certainly be different. Finish up your floor plan

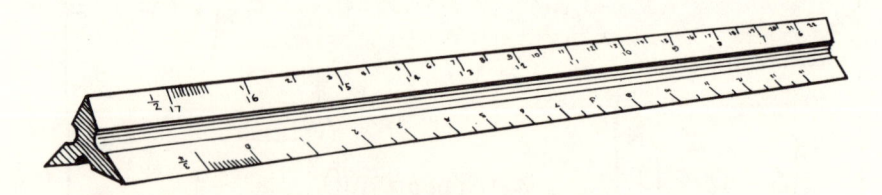

Architect's scale

by noting switches, fixtures and jacks, and by using a compass to turn the arc of each door's swing. Note the positions of these elements on your elevations, too.

Now comes the part that some people feel silly with. Scale your furniture, potential furniture and equipment just as you scaled your space. Transfer the measurements to colored paper (construction paper's great) and make yourself some cutouts. Make furniture one color, equipment another, and remember that you'll probably need separate sets for your floorplan and elevations.

The idea is simple: use your cutouts to try different layouts. With your program firmly in mind, shift these little representations around.

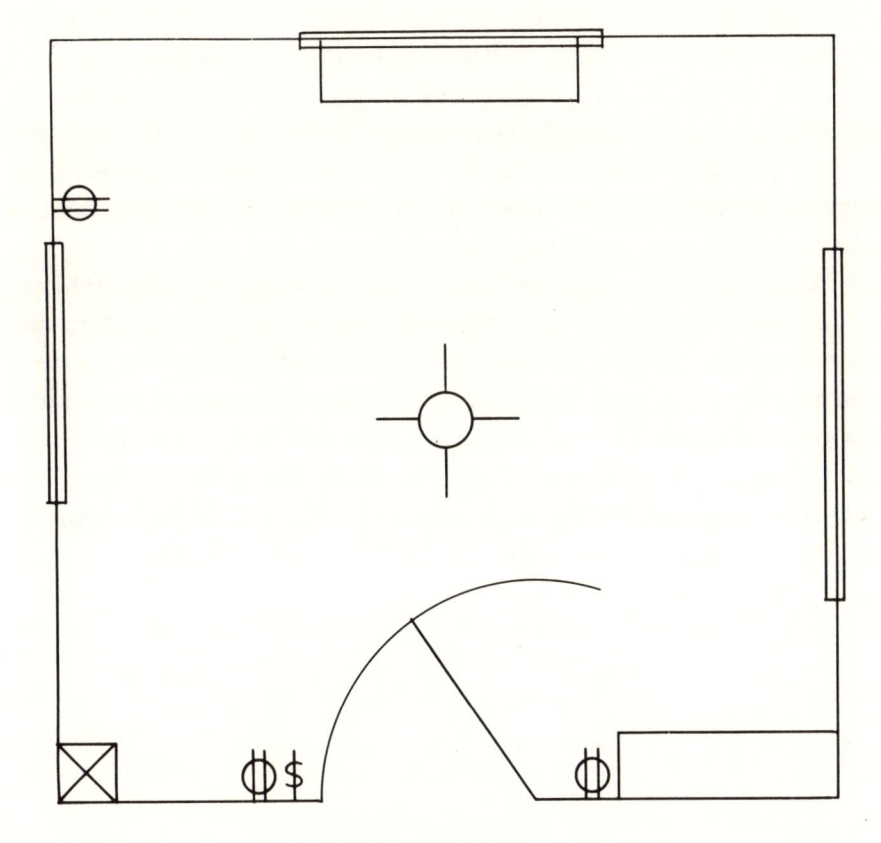

Scaled drawing

For the floor plan, you'll be working in some places with two layers: equipment over furniture—good thing you cut them out of different colored paper. As you work through the puzzle, you'll probably arrive at several workable designs. Your personal priorities will dictate which will serve you best.

Once you've decided on a design—or think you have—test it one more time by "walking through" your work routines. If you can actually set up your furniture or mock-ups, fine, but I've found it almost as helpful to sit down in front of the plans and partly imagine my way through this procedure. It's important, though, that you physically go through the motions of reaching, turning, and working. Is everything smooth? Are locations convenient? Do relative positions make sense? Have you covered all your needs? Lighting? Work surfaces? Filing and storage space? Bookshelves? Equipment?

If you're like me, you'll run into at least a few problems. Once, I discovered that a file cabinet tucked under my main work surface kept me from scooting far enough to my left to conveniently operate my printer. So I modified the design to move the file cabinet. The last time around, I realized that I'd certainly kick my computer if I just set it on edge under my desk, so I designed in another desk support behind which the machine could operate in safety.

You can, of course, avoid much of this labor by paying an architect or designer to plan your office for you. But even if you plan to go this route, consider working through at least most of this process yourself. And even if you've paid dearly for a professional design, subject it to a rigorous walk-through, just as you would a plan of your own. After all, you know yourself and your work better than anyone else. And remember, the *most* important thing about your home office is that it's *yours*.

9

Lighting

Good lighting designers have all kinds of theoretical and practical experience, know surprising facts about lighting levels and intensities, take room size, shape, use and color into account and, of course, carry around an encyclopedic knowledge of available lamps, fixtures, and electric and electronic gizmos. Most decent lighting appliance stores either have a designer on staff (whose services may or may not be free) or can put you in touch with one (who services will definitely *not* be free). Once they understand your space and what you want to do in it, these experts can really be a big help.

But I know that most people setting up a home office aren't going to search out professional assistance. Besides, it doesn't hurt to work things out for yourself, even if you intend to consult with a designer eventually. So here's a collection of advice, opinion and experience—minus any pro talk about "footcandles" or "luminescence"—that should help you put together a decent lighting system for your home office, whatever its size, shape or layout.

A year or so ago, I was talking to a lighting designer about his job. We chatted about clients and fee structures and great solutions to interesting problems. Explaining one of his more straightforward schemes, he casually mentioned something that was clearly obvious to him, but was a revelation to me. "Lighting," he shrugged, "is angles."

Pow! This short little sentence, tossed off in passing, brought into focus for me all the worst problems I was worried about in specifying lighting for my new garage office.

In the age of computers, the great enemy of comfort and efficiency is glare, which can make working in front of your monitor a true, splitting headache. Glare obscures characters under bright puddles of reflected light, and you wind up leaning forward, tensing your neck muscles and squinting to make out what you're doing. If you've used computers at all, you've probably bobbed through this unpleasant little dance yourself, and you've experienced the painful result.

Glare, as any dedicated television watcher can tell you, is caused by light bouncing off the glass surface of your screen. And now you see why "lighting is angles," unlike most of the good advice I've received over the years, didn't simply enter one ear and exit the other, but lodged firmly in my mind.

Put simply, you can eliminate glare by making sure that no light sources have the angle on you. With electric lights, this means either locating them where their beams won't reflect into your screen or fitting them with diffusers that soften their glow or lenses or louvers that direct their beams in another direction. With natural light, it means taking the location of windows into account and making sure you can screen off or redirect their light when necessary.

NATURAL LIGHT

The best light is sunlight. But only sometimes. Dependably diffuse north light has been the artist's favorite for centuries, and it's terrific office light, too. But not all our windows face north, and even those that do can give us problems.

I've been in corporate offices where whole departments are working with makeshift screens (usually sheets of 8-1/2 by 11 paper that have been turned black by being run through an unloaded photocopier) taped to the sides of their monitors to ward off the glaring sunshine streaming through nearby window walls.

Luckily, this sort of thing is usually pretty easy to control at home. Your first inclination might be to simply hang blackout curtains. But

Getting wired

You can't, of course, have lights without electricity. And unless you've got the juice you might have a bit of trouble with your computer, printer, answering machine, fax and copier, too.

Although many home office workers don't bother, it's a great idea to run individual dedicated circuits, using 12-gauge wiring, for your computer, your printer and other large pieces of electrically-powered equipment (a scanner, for example, or a photocopier). If that sounds like overkill to you, at least consider running a dedicated circuit to your computer.

Even when you're fixing up an existing space to be your office, new circuits can usually be added without tearing the walls apart. Talk to your electrician about coming up through the basement or down through the attic. He or she can usually fish wire through top or bottom plates and into the appropriate wall cavity.

Depending on your circumstances, a "sub feeder" in basement or attic can accept a run of wire or cable from your main electrical service panel, then let you run circuits from there into your office space. This is a good system because it makes future upgrades to your office space easier. It also lets you protect each circuit with two fuses or breakers—one at the sub feeder and one back at the main panel.

to page 207

there are times of day and types of working situations when daylight is a positive boon to your efforts and your attitudes. A better solution is a blind system that can be easily adjusted and modified. I'm quite happy with normal, horizontal mini-blinds, but vertical blinds are theoretically superior because they let you better adjust the angle at which light will be admitted into your space.

Windows behind you can present a glare problem too. In my new office, I've got two of them about twenty feet back (where the garage doors used to be), and if I don't close the blinds, they show up quite clearly as reflections in my screen. Originally, even closing the blinds didn't entirely ease my eyes, because several of my overhead track units played on the metal and caused another type of glaring reflection. I simply adjusted the lighting, but I could have avoided this problem altogether by installing fabric blinds.

A different sort of problem crops up when you've got a window directly behind your computer's monitor. You don't get direct glare into your screen, but you do get terrific contrast between the bright sunlight and the darker screen it surrounds. Your eyes keep having to adjust and readjust to the extreme differences in intensity, and the result is eyestrain, headache and, researchers have found, depression.

As if this weren't enough, this sort of set-up often also gives you a sort of "bounce-back," or indirect glare in your screen. The bright window-light floods in, bounces off your shirt or blouse or jewelry or face, which in turn reflects back to you from your screen.

The best solution to this problem is to avoid it entirely if you can. But don't reject an otherwise good location just because a window is staring you in the face. You can always install blinds or a shade. Or you can simply, as I did in my old nook office, cover the window with a big bulletin board. This is one place where adjustability isn't too important, because even good, diffuse light coming through a window behind your monitor will cause too much contrast and overtax your eyes.

ARTIFICIAL LIGHT

Broadly speaking, there are two kinds of artificial lighting that you'll need in your work space. First, you'll want to make sure that the area is adequately illuminated for safety and comfort. This

If you're planning new electrical outlets, be sure to plan their locations carefully. These days, the rule in new construction calls for an outlet every six feet. You may, in fact, want even more than that. If the walls are open, now's the time to install them. Even if you're only adding one or two outlets, though, you may want them in special locations—at counter-height, say, instead of down near the floor. Decide *before* the electrician arrives to do the job, and make sure you communicate your needs clearly.

If you can't run new dedicated circuits into your home office space, at least make sure that your computer, especially, is not plugged into the same circuit as other big electrical appliances. You don't want your PC power supply straining and surging with your refrigerator's compressor or the on-off cycles of the dishwasher or the washing machine.

And take care with your other office equipment, too. For example, running a laser printer and a photocopier simultaneously can draw 2,000 watts. If the same circuit supplies other heavy-drawing appliances, the combination could blow a fuse.

Speaking of fuses, make sure you're using the appropriate fuses or breakers for the circuit in question. It's sometimes tempting to use, say, a 20 amp fuse to keep an overloaded 15 amp circuit from blowing, but that undercuts the whole

to page 209

Ambient lighting

is often provided by the lights you flick on when you walk into a room—the ceiling fixtures and table or floor lamps that keep you from walking into furniture at night and banish the more extreme shadows during the day. If you're setting up in a space that already gets regular use as a living space, the room will already have some form of ambient lighting. But the chances are that this existing arrangement probably isn't really suitable—too many bad angles.

You can check this by performing what's called "the mirror test." Hold up a mirror (or anything reflective) in the space where you plan to set up your monitor. The hot spots that hit you in the eye will turn up as glare on your screen. (Be careful here to make sure that you hold your reflective surface at the same angle your monitor's screen will assume when it's in place. Few screens are actually vertical. Most lean back anywhere from ten to thirty degrees, thereby bringing ceiling lights into play.)

What can you do about these hot spots? Well, in many corporate offices, you'd simply be issued a mesh screen to fit over your monitor. It diffuses glare somewhat and makes it harder to read your work. In your home office, you control the situation, so you have other, more effective options.

In some cases, you can change the angle by simply moving the offending fixture. Shift that table lamp across the room or put that floor lamp at the other end of the couch. In other cases, you can direct the illumination elsewhere. Track lighting can be pivoted, and lenses or louvers can be added to recessed fixtures. In extreme cases—a big, central, overhead fixture, for example—you might have to remove bulbs or even rewire switches.

If you're starting from scratch or can install new ambient lighting in your office area, think in terms of indirect lighting right off the bat. Most of the artificial ambient lighting in my new office comes from three groups of track lights, all fitted with flood (as opposed to spot) lamps. I spent a lot of time up on a ladder aiming each individual can toward a specific target. Some wash walls. Others illuminated bookshelves. A few are pointed upward to brighten parts of the ceiling. The effect is gentle and calming, not brassy-bright. And the angles are right.

This idea of bouncing light off your walls or ceiling is pretty effective much of the time. It's not a cure-all, though. A strong spotlight purpose of fuses—to protect you against unsafe electrical situations.

Each piece of equipment you work with in your home office has its own on-off switch. It can get to be a workout bending and stretching to reach all of them. I prefer to take my exercise outside the house, so in my new office, I've duplicated in a more sophisticated way a setup I evolved in my old cubby. I've grouped switches that control my computer, my printer and my desk lamps in a cluster under my table within arm's reach.

In my earlier office, this was a matter of plugging machines and lamps into a strip of switched outlets, which in turn was plugged into the wall. Not the greatest solution. But the nook only had a single circuit anyway, and I at least achieved great convenience. Now I have a set of switches, each one of which controls a different outlet, which in turn lies on a different circuit. Terrific.

A short summary of electrical considerations:

- Consider new, dedicated circuits for computer, printer, copier and other major electrical draws.
- Don't rely on extension cords.
- Use surge protectors for all major equipment.

to page 210

- Be sure your circuits are protected by properly rated breakers or fuses. Don't use a 20 amp fuse for a 15 amp circuit.
- For convenience's sake, consider grouping switches for computer, printer and a lamp or two within reach of your seat.
- If you're having new electrical wiring installed, consider appropriate outlet locations carefully. Your needs may not coincide with standard placements.
- Don't fool around with electrical work. Hire a licensed electrician to install new circuits, sub panels and boxes.

•

directed at your wall, for example, can create a harsh point of light that's easily strong enough to create glare in your screen. Diffusion is as important as indirection.

Of course, you don't have to use track lighting. Any decent lighting salesperson will be able to show you a whole range of track, recessed and surface-mounted fluorescent systems using diffusers, louvers and shields to control both the brightness and direction of the light they produce.

Task lighting

The other sort of lighting you need to consider is the kind you'll need close to your work. This *task* lighting can be anything from an old-fashioned desk lamp to a custom designed combination of sophisticated fixtures. It gets fairly tricky around computers, because you need no task lighting focused on your monitor, only a little directed at your keyboard, but probably a fair amount merely inches away to illuminate documents, drafts, notes, files or drawings, not to mention your Rolodex™, your phone, your printer and any other equipment or supplies you normally work with.

When I went looking for task lighting I was shown a $400 fixture specifically made to throw gentle, diffused light down onto a computer keyboard. A nice idea. It wouldn't overload the monitor, it would properly illuminate the keys and it would at least help light nearby work. But the price was way too high for me, and, besides, I couldn't figure out a reasonable way to suspend it from my very high ceiling. So I looked at lots of other possibilities: spotlights on a track, regular table lamps, a standard fluorescent desk unit, a system of lamps fixed beneath my bookshelves. None really cut the mustard.

I eventually bought two standard architect's lamps (Ledu C10D, $110 each). Each accepts a 60-watt incandescent bulb, surrounded by a circular, warm white fluorescent. I put one to the right of my keyboard, covering the phone and the area where I jot notes, and the other to the left, near my printer. They are almost infinitely adjustable.

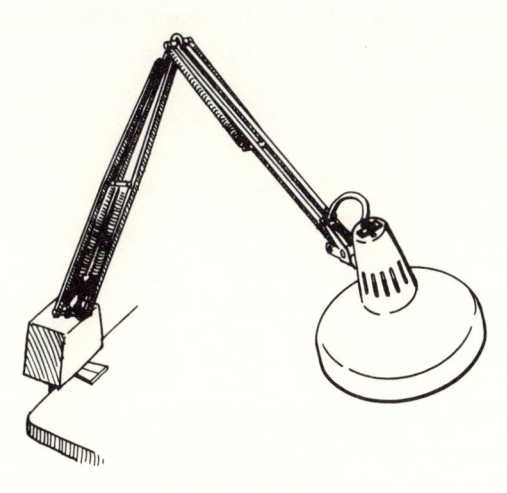

Architect's lamp

I can twist, rotate and pivot them any way I want them. I can direct them down at my work for bright light or away at the wall for gentle reflectance. I can use the incandescent, the fluorescent, or both together. They are, by many people's lights, ugly, and I've heard more than one aesthetically-minded designer sneer at them for their stalky utilitarianism. But to me, they're beautiful, because they do what I need done: they cover all the angles.

A few more points to consider when you're thinking about artificial light:

- Think carefully about the color of your walls and ceiling. A flat, white or off-white coat, for example, makes a great, diffusing reflector for indirect lighting fixtures.
- Stay away from reflective work surfaces. Neither black nor white is especially good, and any plastic laminate should be matte. Stay away from high-gloss wood surfaces, too, although the neutral or medium tone of much wood furniture is great. One of the reasons I liked my old, un-varnished Masonite™ work surface was that it was easy on the eyes.
- Consider indirect, under-counter lighting as part of your ambient lighting system. I checked it out as a form of task lighting, for which it's not really suited. But if you have bookshelves above your work surface, a system of properly designed lamps artfully hidden beneath them can eliminate the shadows that tend to surround equipment, file trays and the like.

10

Using Your Home Office

Ultimately, the way you approach work in your home office will be the result of personal style and individual circumstances. But it's important to get off on the right foot. Even grizzled old corporate Type A's get out of sync when they shift to working at home. And that idea of a disrupted rhythm or pattern is a key to three common problems faced by new home office workers. Some habitually—almost obsessively—avoid work. Others zone out everything else and work around the clock. And most, at one time or another, get lonely.

DISCIPLINE AND THE RHYTHMS OF WORK

The comment I hear most when people learn that I work at home is this one: "Oh, I know I could never do that. I just wouldn't ever have enough discipline."

I preen, naturally, lording it over these poor weaklings who need bosses frowning over their shoulders to get their work done. Actually, of course, I realize that I'm no stronger or better disciplined than they are—I've just developed a different set of habits. My working day is triggered in a different way from theirs.

There's no law of nature that says productive work has to include a commute, a foam cup of bad coffee and an office full of white noise and colleagues—or a demanding boss cracking the whip. After all, housewives have gotten their work done day after day year after year for centuries. So have farmers. So have all sorts of small businesspeople. It only takes a moment of thought to remember that the tradition of working at home is much older than the now common practice of working away from it.

What housewives and farmers and small businesspeople—and successful home office workers—have had going for them is a rhythm of some kind, a sort of schedule. It might have been the rising and setting of the sun or the passing of the seasons or the expectations of the buying public or a private little ritual. I firmly believe that self-discipline in a home office has a lot more to do with habit and pattern than with steely resolve and iron will. People used to working outside of the house instinctively understand that if they work at home, they may wind up running on home rhythms rather than work rhythms. And they have a point. But to correct this, they only have to change their habits, not their characters.

At first, you may have to manufacture a new working pattern at home. Many of us are used to getting in the car, driving to the office, sitting down at our desks and—good day or bad, happy or sad—getting to work. That's a rhythm—a set of habitual actions that work us through the transition from rest to labor. Those of us who work regularly at home need a routine way to make that transition, too. At first, our new pattern may seem artificial and unnecessary, but if we stick with it, it becomes automatic—a habit that stands us in good stead on those days when our will is wavering.

There are all sorts of stories about the consultants and businesswomen who start their days at home just as they did when they commuted: they rise early, take their shower, don their suits, brew their coffee, square their shoulders and carry their briefcases across the room and into their home offices. Most of us have established some less compulsive sequence to trigger our workday every morning. I know a man who can't work before the 8:25 weather report—and seemingly can't *not* work after it. Before the current temperature, he might as well be on vacation. After the three-day forecast, he's all business. A retired friend of a friend, who uses his home office in the afternoon only, gets to work right after his mail is delivered and he performs a strange little dance that involves disposing of junk mail and shaking the blow-in cards out of magazines. I also know a woman who's hardly had to change her habits at all. Her day starts at 8:30, when she can expect to begin taking calls from clients. She really doesn't need to be a self-starter, lucky her.

My ritual is probably fairly typical. I see my daughter off to school at about 8:45, then I finish both my tea and the chapter in the book I'm reading. When I'm done with the chapter, I head for my office, putting the book on a kitchen stool on the way (superstitious nonsense with no practical import), sit down and switch on the computer. By then, I'm "at work." The rhythms made me do it.

But how about distractions? When you work at home, there are all kinds, no matter how well you've designed your workspace and ordered your day. Some you have no control over—the UPS driver knocking at your door, a child falling off a stool, your next door neighbor revving up his chainsaw. You deal with these active distractions as best you can (I know of one man who wears a Walkman at his desk to screen out neighborhood noise) and get back to work.

Often, though, it's the distractions you *can* control that really take a toll. And there are plenty of them when you work at home: housework, yardwork, the beckoning refrigerator. It's no secret to any of us that these passive distractions are really internal avoidance mechanisms. When things aren't going well at the keyboard or drafting table, it's all too easy to wander off to pull weeds, make beds or have a snack. As a writer who has his share of bad days facing a blank screen (or even worse, one I've filled with dreck), I'm all too aware of the magnetic pull of passive household distractions.

I solved some of these problems by giving in to them. Sure I'll stop for a snack—but only to spend a half hour with my daughter when she gets home from school. Yes, I'll wash the dishes—but only if I get to them right after lunch. I made my most potent avoidance mechanisms part of my rhythm, and they've by and large stopped being problems.

But this is only a temporary or occasional solution. It doesn't get to the root cause of much avoidance: Panic.

DEALING WITH FEAR

Over a decade ago, a friend of mine decided he wanted to go into the video business, running it out of his home. He knew his way around a camera, had a business degree and some management experience, and had done enough informal market research to believe that the particular niche he wanted to fill would be profitable. He secured a line of credit, designed business stationery, bought his equipment—and promptly sank like a stone. He made only the feeblest attempts to develop his business and spent most of his time brainstorming new ideas with anyone who'd listen. It took me a while to realize he was simply paralyzed by fear.

His mental process was simple. (1) He really wanted to make a go of his business. (2) He'd burned his bridges and committed all his resources to this idea. (3) If it was a failure, he'd be devastated. (4) If he didn't really put his idea to the test, it couldn't fail. (5) If his idea didn't fail, he could preserve his dream of success. (6) Therefore, he wouldn't really try to make a go of his business.

This isn't entirely rational, but it's a string of thoughts and emotions we've all experienced in one form or another. Of course, on a practical level, my friend, like all of us, should have made sure that he'd developed some business before he made his leap into a home office.

Having a job to do is a key—and not just financially. In my experience, the people who have real trouble getting down to business in a home office are people who don't yet have a real business to get down to—folks who are just starting something or who aren't yet making much of a living from home and are afraid that they might never really get going. For these people, there is no outside rhythm at all—no meetings or schedules or presentations or projects. They have to make it all up, establishing new patterns and habits out of thin air. Under these circumstances, fear can really start gnawing at you. Washing the dishes looks like a pretty good way to spend some time.

The only real remedy for this sort of panic is work. By all means, bring some into the home with you if you can, but even if you can't, dig some up as quickly as you can. Even if it's not quite what you had in mind. Even if it's not profitable. What you want are commitments, responsibilities, schedules to meet. You want to be too *busy* to be scared of the new course you're charting.

For me, at least, the very best spur to getting down to brass tacks is deadline pressure. I'm in front of the keyboard virtually every day, but like a lot of other writers (and others, no doubt), I tend to ease along when I've got time in hand. I dither. I wait (faint hope) for inspiration to strike. But I can really crank it out on deadline.

Even this is a form of rhythm, isn't it? Instead of the regularity of seasons or daily needs, I tune into the beat of periodic stress. And that's important for all of us. The freedom of working at home is freedom from commuting, maybe freedom from an obnoxious boss, but it's not freedom from responsibility. The last thing you want to be free of is pressure to perform. Just as it is for housewives and farmers, a vital part of our home-office rhythm is good, honest stress.

Most home office workers face some fear. Most indulge, at one time or another, in some form of avoidance. But most avoid the extremes exemplified by my friend. In fact, many more home workers may face another problem altogether.

WORKING TOO HARD

People who work at home put in an average of 62.4 hours a week. A recent study showed that a third of them rank working too hard as the biggest drawback to working at home. I have no idea what my weekly average is, but I know that I work a lot harder and longer at home than I did as an editor in an office. This is counter to the bizarre yet popular image of a home worker cheerfully fitting his or her job into spare time, but it makes perfectly good sense. Many of us are working for ourselves. We have no guaranteed salary, no sick leave, no paid vacations. It's no wonder we get a little intense when we think about car payments or groceries or the mortgage.

Even those of us still on someone else's payroll are working in comfort with (probably) fewer distractions and twenty-four-hour, seven-day-a-week access to our computers and related equipment. It would be surprising if we *didn't* regularly break the forty-hour barrier.

Of course, those of us bringing work home from a corporate office are stretching what is already probably a long week.

And the moonlighters among us may work a solid forty hours at a salaried job, and then double that at home, working evenings and weekends to get something else going.

Frankly, I don't see much wrong with this. Hard work is neither a crime nor—except at the far extreme—a health hazard. But remember, just like the novice home worker who has no ritual to trigger his or her working day, you may have no pattern to end yours.

Especially if you work at home full time—without commutes, without distractions and without regular hours—you can, if you want to, squeeze work out of every minute you're not sleeping or eating. Even a part-time home worker can easily slide into overwork unconsciously. With all the facilities at hand it's all to easy to pop into the office for a few minutes of work after supper—and not emerge until bedtime. Or to take a few minutes to run a calculation on Saturday morning—and disappear until dark.

We all need to put in long hours occasionally, and some of us thrive on a regular diet of twelve or fourteen hour days. But, especially if there's a family involved, we need at least to acknowledge the difference between a normal day's work and overtime. We should have a habitual close to the day's work. This can be a specific time (the standard 5:00, say), or a regular event (like the kids getting home from school), or another responsibility we have to take care of (cooking supper, walking the dog). At the very least, this sort of schedule gives us time to lift up our heads and take a deep breath. If there are kids or a spouse or roommates, it gives us time to hear about their days and talk about our own. We can always go back to work later if we really have to, but if we think of this as overtime, putting our noses back to the grindstone takes a conscious decision, a pondering of the priorities.

So how much work is too much? I wouldn't presume to say. Everybody's needs, situation, stamina and rhythms are different. But *do* give yourself a standard close to your work-at-home day. This way, you'll at least have to *choose* to work like a dog.

LONELINESS

For many of us, the central fact of working in a home office is solitude. No problem—most of us like it. Working alone means no distractions, so we can concentrate harder and longer. Theoretically, at least, we produce better work, and more of it. Solitude is wonderful.

But there are things most of us miss from the wider world of work, too. Simple camaraderie, for one thing. The odd chat or swap of gos-

Here's Looking At You, Kid

Today I'm on deadline—two deadlines, actually, on two different projects—and I'm concentrating hard, working in that barely controlled frenzy so familiar to writers with a time limit. But my daughter keeps running in, playing a game in which she is the postman, dropping off letters and packages.

Sometimes, working at home can be no different from working as part of a team in a big office. You do your job. You collect your money. You go back for more. And sometimes this feels great. After all, you're making a living more or less on your own terms. On the other hand, I don't want my work at home to become like any other job. I'm not here because I couldn't hack law school or weave through the corporate maze. I'm here because those other paths looked stultifying to me.

Under these circumstances, writers on deadline are like dogs at their dinner. Bother them and they snap at you. But these letters are love letters ("Dear Daddy I Love You Love Hilary") and the packages are "presents" wrapped 5-year-old-fashion in leftover Christmas paper and lots of cellophane tape. So I don't snap. But I'm annoyed.

Usually, I'm ruthless about my time. Ruthless with myself, first. My schedule may have be-

to page 221

sip. The things I miss most are the interrelated feelings of teamwork and competition that I enjoyed when I worked regularly with others.

So sometimes our treasured solitude slips over the line into loneliness. It's not crippling, as a rule, but it can get to be a little depressing after a while. It can unbalance us, dry us up, fuzz us out, dull us down.

I don't actually get very lonely, but I do sometimes feel as if I'm turning too sharply inward. So I make a special effort almost every day to get out and about for at least a little while. Nothing fancy. I wander down to the post office every morning, where I can always get in a short chat with my friends behind the counter—and often a longer one with a neighbor who's also popped in. At noon, I often go out for lunch. No three martinis here, just a sandwich and the chance to exchange a few words with waitresses or cooks or lunching acquaintances. I also stop by the library a couple of times a week, to rummage through the stacks and talk about books and town affairs with the wonderful staff or whoever else happens to be around.

It may sound as though I'm not home enough to get any work done, but if I did all three of these things in a single day (which I often do), they might take up an hour. That leaves me plenty of time at the keyboard—and it's good, fresh, *un-lonely* time.

Of course, my business is essentially individual. Yours may not be. For you, as Paul and Sarah Edwards and others have suggested, it may be more accurate to think of working *from* home rather than *at* home. You may be out meeting clients or customers regularly. Or you may at least be keeping in touch with the outside world by phone. Many home workers, in fact, are in virtually constant contact with company, clients or colleagues, either by voice communication or by computer or fax. This sort of electronic connection will certainly leave you with less need for social regeneration—although I've found that while I may be anything but lonely after a long day on the phone, I usually *do* need to get out and find a dog to kick.

If you're a telecommuter or a part-time home worker, your loneliness may well be tinged with apprehension over whether your work arrangement will cause you to miss a few rungs on the corporate ladder. After all, being out of sight may mean being out of mind, and we all know that what you do and how well you do it isn't always what you're judged and promoted on. Most telecommuters get in to their come mostly habit, but if I don't stick to it, I'm in for a rough day. I have to sit down to write between nine and nine-fifteen in the morning, or my psyche declares a holiday and I spend the whole day beating the resentful little slacker back into line.

Ruthless next with others. A surprising number of people still think that if you're at home all day, you're not working. A more enlightened class understands that you're working, but they call and say things like, "I thought you might like to take a break." You bet I'd like to take a break. I'd like to spend the winter skiing at Jackson Hole, too, but I have to make a living.

So I've had these ground rules from the first day I started working at home: I had to be stern with myself and firm with—sometimes even rude to—others. What was that I said back there about stultifying?

The mail keeps coming, one piece at a time, and I open little gifts and cards and envelopes (she's found a stash of her mother's stationery, and I don't want to know). Part of the game is that, as each piece of mail arrives, I call her up and tell her how much I like it. "Ring ring," I call into the other room, and she smiles and twinkles and says "HEL-loooo," in her special silly voice, putting one hand near her mouth and the other to her ear. A soprano Big Bopper communicating with Eliot Ness. We have a

to page 223

central offices once or twice a week, and this is a very good idea if you don't want to get hung out to dry.

At some point, though, you'll be forced to make a basic decision. Do you want to continue to work largely at home, or do you want to move up to higher levels in your company? The fact is that, except in extremely rare situations, you can't expect to have both. This is where priorities once again come into play, and it's also where thoughts of full time self employment at home get seriously examined.

So much for the three great *subjective* difficulties faced by many home office workers. But there are a lot of practical and particular problems that we face, too. The first is very practical and particular indeed.

REGULATIONS AGAINST HOME OFFICES

By and large people using the kind of home offices we've been talking about in this book are virtually invisible. In fact, they are exemplary neighbors because they have a special interest in a quiet, safe neighborhood or apartment building. Nonetheless, some cities make life tough for the honest home-worker. Chicago for example, has an infamous regulation that essentially bans home offices if they are your primary workplace. Washington, D.C., on the other hand, permits them, but requires home workers to get a free home occupation permit. D.C.'s regulations may set the tone for new rules in many cities across the country. Here are some of their basic elements:

- A home worker must get a free home occupation permit.
- A home office business may not occupy more than 25 percent of the house
- A business run out of a home may not attract more than eight clients or customers in any eight-hour day
- Limits on the number of employees who don't live in the house, the kind of sign that can be erected, and the number of business-related delivery trips that can be made to and from the house in an eight-hour day.

Most of these regulations were put into effect for two pretty good reasons: to preserve residential neighborhoods from the noise, traffic, dirt and danger of many businesses, and to erect a barrier against the kind of piecework sweatshop conditions some employers imposed on *short conversation, then she goes back to writing notes. ("Dear Daddy I Love You And Thank You For The Trip To New Yoek Love Hilary.")*

To make it at home, you don't just have to do your job; you have to sell your *ability* to do it. On many days, I spend more time marketing my ideas and myself than I do putting phosphor to screen. I've geared up and gotten pushy. Just as if I *had* gone to law school or joined a big company. Along the way, I've learned that tension is the central fact of life when you're not on somebody's payroll. Stress is the freelancer's constant companion.

That's not necessarily a bad thing, but every once in a while, all this sternness and firmness and rudeness and pushiness and pressure and tension begins to turn me into, shall we say, a not very pleasant person. I indulge in angst. I occasionally rant. I sometimes pout, which at least has the merit of being silent. And I don't just snap when I'm bothered on deadline; I bite.

But today I'm getting love letters and making happily goofy phone calls. My concentration is being spoiled and my time is being wasted, and I gradually realize that I don't care. My daughter forestalls my wrath and gains my complicity with her innocent, absolute, vulnerable belief in the transcendence of love—especially when its expression can be turned into a game.

to page 225

their workers. The lawmakers didn't envision the kind of electronic revolution that made the modern home office possible, but that doesn't make their rules any less the law.

If your town or city has regulations limiting or banning home offices, you'd better know about it. Call City Hall and find out. What you *do* about it is up to you. There seem to be three standard responses. Some people simply obey the law and decide not to establish an office at home. (At least I assume some people do this—these are the ones you don't hear about.) Most people simply ignore the rule, go ahead with their home offices and home-office work, and never hear anything about it. More and more folks are going public in an attempt to get outmoded regulations modified or dropped. If you decide to follow this course, you might get help and support from a couple of organizations: The National Association for the Cottage Industry (NACI), P.O. Box 14460, Chicago, IL 60614 and the American Home Business Association, 397 Post Road, Darien, CT 06820. You can also find pertinent information on Paul and Sarah Edwards' Work At Home Special Interest Group (SIG) on *CompuServe*.

Even those of us not plagued by working too little or too much, suffering from loneliness or fighting off obnoxious regulations have to deal with another concern that can be equally frustrating.

TAXES

I've been tempted to break this section out and call it Chapter 11, because that's where you deserve to wind up if you get your home office tax information from a book. I'll lay out a few very basic guidelines for you here, but the most important tip is this: Get an accountant—preferably one with experience advising people who work at home. At the very least find one used to working with small businesses.

- To qualify as a home office for tax purposes, your space has to be used "exclusively and regularly" as your *principal place of business*. You can't take the family room just because your desk is in the corner (although you *can* take a portion of a room base on the percentage you use for business).
- If you meet these requirements, the amount of household expenses you may deduct equals the percentage of your house's space that you use as an office. (If, for example, you use 150

> Her notes and presents and chuckles and silly talk remind me of the things that I forget over and over again: that—for me at least—good work has to do not just with concentration and dedication, but with balance and a steady sense of priorities. And with love, too. Unbusinesslike love. Childlike love. Home cookin'.
>
> •

square feet of a 1,500 square-foot house, you can deduct ten percent of most expenses.)
- You can't use a home office to create a tax loss. You may only take deductions up to the amount of profit your business in that space makes.
- Keep complete, detailed, almost obsessive records of *all* business expenses. People who list home office deductions are audited at a higher rate than people who don't.

There's much more to the home office tax dance. The fine art of depreciation. The whole issue of when you can deduct the cost of equipment if you are not self-employed. How much can you deduct of your health insurance payments? These things and others get pretty complicated, and can have a huge effect on your ultimate tax bill. *Please* don't try to get by on magazine articles and friends' advice. Get an accountant—or be sorry.

INSURANCE

The important thing to know here is that your homeowners' policy (or its apartment or condo equivalent) almost certainly does *not* cover most of the equipment and furniture in your office. Nor, in all probability, does it protect you from the liability claims of clients or others who are injured when they come to your house to do business.

Many homeowners' policies cover *nothing* that you use for business. Others cover only depreciated value, and then to a ludicrously low limit—maybe a couple of thousand dollars. What you want is either a rider, an endorsement (a change in your basic policy) or, if necessary, an additional "floater" policy that will cover all your business equipment and furniture at its *replacement* value, less a reasonable deductible. Consider business liability coverage only if you expect to be entertaining clients. Also consider theft insurance, which may require a separate policy.

Talk to your current insurance company about your home office requirements, by all means, but do a little comparison shopping, too. You may well find that you can swing a better deal with another company, folding a new homeowners' policy around your other needs. Keep in mind that a lot of insurance agents work out of home offices. It's not at all a bad idea to search one of these folks out. He or she has probably been through the same calculations, and should have a pretty good idea of what you need and the best way to get it.

IMAGE

For a lot of home workers, presenting a professional image is vital. Your business doesn't just have to supply its product or service professionally—it has to *look* professional to correspondents and *sound* professional to callers.

This is a strange area, and many independent-minded home workers don't feel comfortable treading what they consider a line wavering between illusion and reality. I have a certain sympathy with that point of view, and I don't go to great lengths to disguise the fact that I work at home and not in a fancy corporate office somewhere. I do, though, want people to think I'm good at what I do. And in this imperfect world, style is often perceived as an element—or at least an indicator—of substance. So I've gone to some trouble to make sure that, within certain boundaries that I talk about below, I present a crisp, competent front to the business world in those areas where I most often come into contact with it. Specifically, I've taken some pains with my stationery, my business cards and my phone manners.

Stationery

I'm always surprised at how many home-office workers try to slide by on cheap typing paper. Take it from someone used to working with eccentric writers of all kinds and anything but stuffy about these matters—nothing is more likely to get your message ignored than to dispatch it looking as if it were a preliminary draft of a high school history paper. Erasable bond just doesn't cut it.

Even if your printer puts out ugly type, your epistles will be taken more seriously if they appear on decent letterhead stationery. Select good watermarked paper and include your name (or your business's), address and phone number. Use your business logo by all means, if you've got one, but steer clear of too much glitz. You want to present a businesslike impression—not the impression of someone compensating for *not* being businesslike.

You can order standardized stationery from virtually any business supply store or catalogue, choosing from among different paper styles and dozens of pre-designed looks. I prefer a more personal approach, and I've designed for myself the two (very simple) styles of stationery that I've used since I began to work at home full time. Custom stationery costs more than the catalogue stuff, but it gives you exactly the look you want, not what some bulk company considers the right effect for an accountant or civil engineer. And although every expense can seem immense when you're just getting started, over the life of a thousand sheets of stationery, the price differential is insignificant.

To create the stationery you want, you'll have to work with a typesetter (to choose type style, size and layout) and a printer (who will give you a reasonable choice among paper weights and qualities and who will take a picture of the "camera-ready" design and then print your stationery for you). You can keep costs and hassles down by finding a printer who offers typesetting on the premises. Or you can add to costs and hassle—but also possibly to the effectiveness of the result—by hiring a graphic artist to design your stationery for you.

Business cards

My approach to business cards is similar. I think it's worth the expense to have your cards custom typeset and printed. Unfortunately, most cheap cards picked out of a quick-print style catalogue look like cheap cards picked out of a quick-print style catalogue. They're fine if you're just trying to get your name around, but they don't much help if you're trying to convey a strong professional image. My cards are very simple. They're printed on a slightly textured creamy stock in a handsome typeface and they convey a quiet, understated impression that I'm comfortable with. Your cards should almost certainly be different, because the image you wish to convey almost certainly will be. Consider the textured, off-white stock, though. Even clean hands quickly smudge the brilliant white stock often used for inexpensive cards, and the effect is inevitably grubby.

Phone manners

For most of us, our phone style is even more important than our stationery or cards. It depends, of course, on the type of business you're doing and on your own sense of self. In many cases, answering with your business's name is the best way to go, and most of my home-office friends do just this. "Biancalana Graphics" is probably a better opener than the mere residential "hello." Some of my journalist acquaintances are, in the honored newsroom tradition, more abrupt, snapping out a crisp "Hugo Pilsudski" or maybe just a gritty "Kravetz." Image is all.

When I first came home full time, I began by answering the phone with my full name—just as I had at my desk as an editor. It made me feel businesslike and professional. It may even have fooled the people who called into *thinking* that I was businesslike and professional. But now that I'm actually making a living as a writer, I've backed off and make no pretense about the fact that I work at home. I now simply answer "hello" even during normal business hours. I'm a writer, after all, not a company—not even, truth to tell, a real businessman.

The final vital image-maker is your answering machine's outgoing message. These greetings, through no fault of the manufacturers, are often the TAD's Achilles heel. I've sat through hundreds of long, dreadful performances, tapping my foot in frustration at not being able to leave my message and hang up. Let me get this off my chest.

I don't want a poem.
I don't want a song.
I don't want a scene from "Casablanca".

I don't want a cute little apology for having to speak to your machine. If you've hooked the thing up, don't say you're sorry.

I want to leave my message and get on to something else, not feel like a captive audience (this is especially annoying if I have to call you often—even if your act is truly clever, hearing it over and over is going to wear it out fast). A professional message is pleasant, precise (if you want special information, say so), and *brief*—ten seconds should be more than enough.

Harrumph.

Your business and personal needs are almost certainly different from mine. The point is that you should think seriously about the image your stationery, cards and phone manners will project. It should make you happy and help your clients, contacts and colleagues feel comfortable with you and your capabilities. Even if you decide to forget all this wonderful advice and communicate through scribbled notes on torn legal sheets, you should do it because you've *decided* to, not just because you haven't considered the effect.

PERSONAL EFFICIENCY

Okay, now that your image is perfect, it's time to deal with reality. My stationery and phone manner might convey the impression that I'm on top of everything, but that still leaves me with the difficult task of actually getting—and holding—my act together.

For me, the worst part of working from home is that I can't afford a secretary to take care of my disorganized, absent-minded self. I manage to muddle along, but I've had to work at it. Here are a few random thoughts based on my own experience and that of many home-working friends.

Efficient messiness

Forget about being neat and efficient at the same time. First, it's simply too much of a drain on your energy in a one-person operation. Why bother to clean off worktops, re-shelve books and return files when what you really need to be doing is focusing on your project? Besides, the chances are you'll need to look at some of that stuff again before you're done. Keep it out and at hand. By all means clean up your space when you're done for the day if you want to, but if you're compulsive about home office neatness during working hours, I bet you're great at avoiding work.

Second, I believe that a certain calculated clutter can actually *improve* your efficiency. For example, I've found that if I neatly stack outgoing mail on the counter near the door, I invariably walk right by it when I head out to run errands with a dozen other things on my mind. So to make sure I *can't* forget the mail, I simply dump outgoing pieces on the floor by the threshold. When I trip over them, I remember them. You can use the same inelegant but effective technique for all sorts of similar purposes. The trick, of course, is that my pile of envelopes is a specific, temporary and *purposeful* mess, unlike my normal disorder, which is the result of pure sloth. The mail never becomes invisible like that pile of old newspapers in the corner.

Keeping track of time

My worst fear as a solo worker is that I'll miss an appointment or a deadline. In my former life, I always had help remembering this stuff—co-workers, a secretary and a boss, not to mention a gigantic, accurately annotated office calendar.

The biggest problem for me is remembering simple daily appointments. At home, I've worked right through any number of lunches and meetings because there's no ebb and flow of co-workers to remind me of the time. Standing up a potential client isn't the best way to demonstrate your competence. Fortunately, the solution is simple—an alarm clock. All you have to do is remember to set it.

Actually, the device I've been using lately isn't simply a clock. It's a tiny computer called a Psion *Organizer II*, which is billed as a pocket-sized replacement for address book, calculator, calendar and a host of other standard business needs. Most important for me, though, is that it lets you load in any number of engagements for specific times that can be days, weeks, even years into the future. At the appropriate hour, it comes alive and warbles electronically. It can even remind you on its little screen just what you're supposed to be doing. Because I have neither a mommy nor a secretary on the premises, I've come to rely on the Psion alarm, and it has saved me a lot of embarrassment.

The *Organizer* is supposed to displace my little pocket engagement calendar, too, but it hasn't. Although I need an alarm to remind me of the time, I still like to keep my actual record of appointments on paper. Several principles come into play here. First, it's easier to see, read, and change entries in a notebook than on a hand-held electronic device, no matter how ingenious. Second, in a notebook you can jot down related notes, addresses, instructions and directions. This is tough, if not impossible, on a computer of any size, let alone a tiny one.

The third principle is related to the first two—you should have all diary and calendar information in a single place. Using two or three devices, notebooks or wall sheets is a recipe for disaster. Since *most* of my info works best in my little pocket appointment book, I try to put *all* of it there. I learned this lesson soon after I began to work at home. Thinking I was being very businesslike, I set up a large wall calendar next to my desk and kept track of many appointments both on it and in my more portable pocket appointment calendar. But inevitably, things started falling through the cracks. Dates I made away from home never seemed to get transferred from notebook to wall. Those I made over the phone often weren't entered in the notebook. It was a mess. Now I keep my appointment book propped open against a document-holder on my desk so I can see it easily, and I use it to keep track of all my appointments, meetings and deadlines. I could, of course, have gone the other way and begun to rely only on a wall calendar. But the small notebook-style appointment calendar is more versatile, and so it won out.

A few more words about the Psion *Organizer*. It's an ingenious little device, but it has three significant flaws. Least serious, but annoying, is the fact that it tells time in the European or military style. Four PM, for example, becomes 16:00. A pain. Second, although it records names, address and phone numbers, it doesn't function as a tone phone dialer. You should be able to call the appropriate number from memory, hold the *Organizer* up to the phone's receiver and push a button to send out the proper beeps. Third and most crippling, its tiny alphabetically-arranged keyboard is almost impossible to use efficiently. Entering a significant amount of data by hand (as opposed to shooting it over from a normal PC by way of a cable) is virtually impossible.

Sharp has now entered this market with its *Wizard*, which shares at least the last of these problems with the Psion. These gizmos are fascinating, but I don't think they'll really reach the mainstream until voice technology improves to the point that we can speak our entries into them. In the meantime, don't forget just how efficient pencil and paper can be.

Buying office supplies

Here's another of those things you simply don't need to think about when you work in a standard company or corporation. Paper, pens, folders and necessary equipment simply *appear*. You don't have to shop for them, and you certainly don't have to pay for them. In a home office though, you're the purchasing agent and the billpayer as well as the user.

I buy virtually all of my standard office supplies from discount mail-order suppliers. I've used Quill, Lyben, Viking and several others, all to my complete satisfaction. I buy in what I think of as "limited bulk"—thirty or forty reams of paper at a time, dozens of roller-ball pens, multiple boxes of Pendaflex files and legal-sized file folders, thousands of paper clips and staples. This isn't big-time purchasing, and it often doesn't even qualify me for special pricing below the basic discounted amount, but it's convenient, competitive and keeps me in supplies for a long time.

The only time I buy supplies from local retail stores is when I need something right away. Recently, for example, I had to have several three-ring binders immediately for a proposal that was already overdue. I got them, but I paid through the nose. You may be able to speak to local suppliers and arrange a discount. Ten percent is fairly standard—but it still won't result in truly competitive prices. There are exceptions. Discount office-supply chains like Staples are beginning to make appearances in larger cities around the country. Check your yellow pages and the business pages of your local paper.

The mail order houses are pretty aggressive in sending out catalogues and updates, and they're always touting specials of one kind or another. I find that flipping through a catalogue without knowing what you want is a good way to wind up spending more money than you need to. Check your needs, make a list and *then* turn to the catalogues—or the discount chains—to compare prices.

You can't do it all

You may work alone, but your success may well rest on your ability *not* to tackle certain tasks. It's one thing to be a generalist in matters of office supply and management, but another to waste time on truly substantive matters that are better handled by others.

For example, I sometimes do taped interviews for articles I'm writing. I used to transcribe these tapes myself as a matter of course. I can type all right, after all, and even though I don't have a proper dictating machine with foot controls, I can manage to enter on the keyboard the pearls of wisdom dropped by my subjects. But it seems to take me *forever*, and I've got other things to do. So now I send the tapes out. It usually costs me around $20. I also farm out things like photography, desktop publishing and traditional paste-up services, when I need them. This is all stuff I *could* do, but not as well or as fast as the pros I choose. Because farming these jobs out frees up my time, I consider the fees of these folks to be money well spent.

Actually, this sort of thing often entails no cash at all. There is a flourishing system of barter among all small businesspeople, and home office workers seem to be among the most enthusiastic practitioners. You offer a service or product that others need. See if you can swap it for what you want. Easy as pie. (But talk to that accountant you hired about the tax ramifications of barter.)

Health

For some reason, working at home makes me feel *creakier* than working in some company's office somewhere. Maybe it's because I walk less when I'm around home. I don't know. But I find I definitely have to take serious steps if I want to keep feeling good and healthy around here.

First, of course, comes that good chair I've already talked about. Spare no expense to avoid backaches.

Second, exercise. I try to get out and run every day. You may prefer bicycling or walking or aerobics or swimming or contorting on one of those exercise machines. You're the boss. Choose your time and choose your poison, but do choose something. Some serious, concentrated physical activity is important. Take a break, get some fresh air, stretch, raise your pulse rate, grab a shower. You'll feel better and you'll work better. You'll also probably work longer. Years longer.

Third, watch your diet. Just because the fridge is only a few feet away doesn't mean you have to raid it. If worse comes to worst, just don't keep any insidiously seductive snacks on hand. I had to ban chocolate ice cream.

Fourth, heed Chapter 9's advice to take care over your lighting. Especially remember to do what you can to avoid glare in your computer's monitor. You simply cannot work with a headache. And you can't be a decent housemate, either.

ON YOUR OWN

Ultimately, of course, you're the one who has to figure out the best way to use your home office. If you've been working there for a while, you've got your own tricks and systems. If you're just starting, you'll develop a personal style in no time. Your approach will depend on your priorities, your domestic arrangements, your space, your equipment, your temperament and your reasons for working at home.

You'll almost certainly come up with quirky, odd and fascinating ways to do the things you need to do. Let me know about them. We may work alone, but we're all in this together.

Mark Alvarez
c/o Goodwood Press
P.O. Box 942
Woodbury, CT 06798

Buyers' Guide

COMPUTERS

Personal computers have become "commodity" items, as the business writers put it. They are being built by dozens of companies all over the world. Many computer stores or chains have their own house brands—some quite good. This list includes most national companies and a few smaller outfits. Check the stores in your area, talk to friends and read the computer press for more names, and—more importantly—opinions on quality and reliability.

Acer Technologies Corp.
4010 Charcot Ave.
San Jose, CA 95131
800-782-1155

Advanced Logic Research Inc.
9401 Jeronimo Rd.
Irvine, CA 92718
800-444-4257

Amdek Corp.
3471 North First St.
San Jose, CA 95134
800-722-6335

American Mitac Corp.
410 E. Plumeria Dr.
San Jose, CA 95134
800-648-2287

Amstrad Inc.
1915 Westridge Dr.
Irving, TX 75038
214-518-0795

Arche Technologies Inc.
48881 Kato Rd.
Fremont, CA 94539
800-422-4674

AST Research Inc.
2121 Alton Ave.
Irvine, CA 92714
714-863-1333

AT&T
1 Speedwell Ave.
Morristown, NJ 07960
201-247-1212

Compaq Computer Corp.
20555 FM 149
Houston, TX 77070
713-370-0670

CompuAdd Corp.
12303 Technology Blvd.
Austin, TX 78727
800-666-1872

Cordata Technologies Inc.
1055 W. Victoria St.
Compton, CA 90220
800-621-6746
In CA 800-331-5867

Core International
6500 East Rogers Circle
Boca Raton, FL 33487
407-997-6044

Dell Computer Corp.
9505 Arboretum Blvd.
Austin, TX 78759-7299
800-426-5150

Epson America Inc.
2780 Lomita Blvd.
Torrance, CA 90505
800-922-8911

Everex Computer Systems
48504 Kato Rd.
Fremont, CA 94538
800-356-4283

FiveStar Computers
1621 West Crosby
Carrollton, TX 75006
800-752-5555

HeadStart Technologies Co.
40 Cutter Mill Road
Great Neck, NY 11021
800-882-1888

Hewlett-Packard Corp.
974 E. Arques Ave.
P.O. Box 486
Sunnyvale, CA 94086
800-752-0900

HiTech International Inc.
712 Charcot Ave.
San Jose, CA 95131
408-435-8827

IBM Corp.
Old Orchard Rd.
Armonk, NY 10504
800-447-4700

Kaypro Corp.
533 Stevens Ave.
Solana Beach, CA 92075
800-452-9776

Leading Edge Hardware Products Inc.
225 Turnpike St.
Canton, MA 02021
800-343-6833

Memorex Telex Corp.
4343 S. 118th E. Ave.
Tulsa, OK 74146-4066
800-331-2623

Mitsubishi Electronics America Inc.
991 Knox St.
Torrance, CA 90502
800-556-1234
800-441-2345

NCR Corp.
1601 S. Main St.
Dayton, OH 45479
800-544-3333

NEC Information Systems Inc.
1414 Massachusetts Ave.
Boxborough, MA 01719
508-264-8000

Northgate Computer Systems
13895 Industrial Park Blvd. #110
Plymouth, MN 55441
612-553-0111
612-553-0631

Olivetti USA
765 U.S. Hwy. 202
Somerville, NJ 08876
201-526-8200

PC Designs Inc.
2500 N. Hemlock Circle
Broken Arrow, OK 74012
800-322-4872

PC Link Corp.
29 W. 38th St.
New York, NY 10018
800-221-0343

Sanyo Business Systems Corp.
Computer Division
52 Joseph St.
Moonachie, NJ 07074
800-524-1021

Tandon Corp.
405 Science Dr.
Moorpark, CA 93021
800-228-8595

Tandy Corp.
1800 One Tandy Center
Fort Worth, TX 76102
817-390-3700

Tatung Company of America Inc.
2850 El Presidio St.
Long Beach, CA 90810
800-421-2929

TeleVideo Systems Inc.
550 E. Brokaw Rd.
P.O. Box 49048
San Jose, CA 95161-9048
408-954-8333

Wang Laboratories Inc.
55 Technology Dr.
Lowell, MA 01851
800-962-4727

Wyse Technology
3571 N. 1st St.
San Jose, CA 95134
800-438-9973

Zenith Data Systems
1000 Milwaukee Ave.
Glenview, IL 60025
800-842-9000

Zeos International Ltd.
530 5th Ave. NW #1000
St. Paul, MN 55112
800-423-5891

PORTABLE COMPUTERS

Many of these companies make desktop models, too, but there are some specialists in this field.

Compaq Computer Corp.
20555 FM 149
Houston, TX 77070
713-370-0670

Data General Corp.
4400 Computer Dr.
Westboro, MA 01581
617-366-8911

Dataview Corp.
One Meca Way
Norcross, GA 30093
404-564-5668

Dolch Computer Systems
2029 O'Toole Ave.
San Jose, CA 95134
800-538-7506

Hewlett-Packard Corp.
974 E. Arques Ave.
P.O. Box 486
Sunnyvale, CA 94086
800-752-0900

IBM
Old Orchard Rd.
Armonk, NY 10504
800-447-4700

NEC Information Systems Inc.
1414 Massachusetts Ave.
Boxborough, MA 01719
508-264-8000

Sharp Electronics Corp.
Sharp Plaza
Mahwah, NJ 07430
201-529-9500

Toshiba America Inc.
Information Systems Division
9740 Irvine Blvd.
Irvine, CA 92718
800-457-7777

Zenith Data Systems
1000 Milwaukee Ave.
Glenview, IL 60025
800-842-9000

COMPUTER KEYBOARDS

If you don't like the keyboard that comes with your computer, there are third-party manufacturers you can turn to.

DataDesk International
7650 Haskell Ave.
Van Nuys, CA 91406
800-826-5398
In CA: 800-592-9602

Key Tronic
P.O. Box 14687
Spokane, WA 99214
800-262-6006

Northgate Computer Systems
13895 Industrial Park Blvd. #110
Plymouth, MN 55441
612-553-0111
612-553-0631

EXPANDED MEMORY BOARDS (LIM)

If you need to break the 640K limit on Random Access Memory in standard DOS machines, these cards will let you do it—if your software's agreeable.

Boca Research, Inc.
6401 Congress Ave.
Boca Raton, FL 33487
407-997-6227

Intel PCEO
Mailstop CO3-07
5200 NE Elam Young Pkwy.
Hillsboro, OR 97124-6497
800-538-3373

Micron Technology Inc.
Systems Group
2805 East Columbia Rd.
Boise, ID 83706
800-642-7661

Newer Technology
1117 South Rock Rd. #4
Wichita, KS 67207
316-685-4904

Orchid Technology
45365 Northport Loop West
Fremont, CA 94538
415-490-8586

TAPE BACKUP SYSTEMS

You fail to backup your hard drive at your peril. Tape systems are the best, if not the cheapest, way to go.

Alloy Computer Products
100 Pennsylvania Ave.
Framingham, MA 01701
617-875-6100

Archive Corp.
1650 Sunflower Ave.
Costa Mesa, CA 92626
714-966-5589

Irwin Magnetics
2102 Commonwealth Blvd.
Ann Arbor, MI 48105
800-222-5871

Jasmine Technologies
1740 Army St.
San Francisco, CA 94124
800-347-3228

Mountain Computer, Inc.
240 Hacienda Ave.
Campbell, CA 95008
408-379-4300

Tallgrass Technologies
11100 West 82nd St.
Overland Park, KS 66214
913-492-6002

PERSONAL COPIERS

These wonderful machines range from small and basic to medium-sized and moderately sophisticated.

Canon USA, Inc.
One Canon Plaza
Lake Success, NY 11042
800-652-2666

Minolta Corp.
101 Williams Srive
Ramsey, NJ 07446
201-825-4000

Mita Copystar America, Inc.
777 Terrace Ave.
Hasbrook Heights, NJ 07604
201-288-6900

Ricoh Corp.
#5 Dedrick Place
West Caldwell, NJ 07006
201-882-2000

Sharp Electronics Corp.
Sharp Plaza
Mahwah, NJ 07430
201-529-8200

Toshiba America, Inc.
9740 Irvine Blvd.
Irvine, CA 92718
714-583-3000

SURGE SUPPRESSORS AND EMERGENCY POWER SUPPLIES

Surge suppressors for sure. And an emergency power supply can save vital data when the lights go out.

Alpha Technologies Inc.
3767 Alpha Way
Bellingham, WA 98226
206-647-2360

American Power Conversion
350 Columbia St.
P.O. Box 3723
Peace Dale, RI 02883
401-789-5735

Applied Research and Technology, Inc.
The Pavilion #201
5770 Powers Ferry Rd., N.W.
Atlanta, GA 30327
404-951-9556

Clary Corp
320 W. Clary Ave.
San Gabriel, CA 91776
818-287-6111

Computer Accessories Corp.
6610 Nancy Ridge Dr.
San Diego, CA 92121
619-457-5500

Curtis Manufacturing Company
305 Union St.
Peterborough, NH 03458
603-924-3823

Emerson Computer Power
15041 Bake Blvd.
Irvine, CA 92718
800-222-5877

Exide Electronics
3201 Spring Forest Rd.
Raleigh, NC 27604
919-872-3020

Kensington Microware, Ltd.
251 Park Ave. South
New York, NY 10010
212-475-5200

MicroSync
15018 Belay Dr.
Dallas, TX 75244
214-788-5198

Para Systems
P.O. Box 815188
Dallas, TX 75381-5188
800-238-7272

Perma Power Electronics, Inc.
5601 W. Howard Ave.
Chicago, IL 60648
312-647-9414

SL Waber Inc.
520 Fellowship Rd., No. 306
Mt. Laurel, NJ 08054
609-866-8888

Taesung Industries, Inc.
2001 Westside Pkwy, Suite 240
Alpharetta, GA 30201
800-874-3160

Tripp Lite
500 N. Orleans
Chicago, IL 60610
312-329-1777

Unison Technologies, Inc.
23456 Madero
Mission Viejo, CA 92691
714-855-8700

Universal Vectors, Corp.
Suite 400
580 Herndon Parkway
Herndon, VA 22070
703-435-2500

FACSIMILE MACHINES

If you're ready to join the boom, these companies can send you information.

AT&T
295 North Maple Ave.
2327 G1
Basking Ridge, NJ 07920
201-221-5290

Brother International Corp.
8 Corporate Place
Piscataway, NJ 08855
201-981-0300

Canon
One Canon Plaza
Lake Success, NJ 11042
516-488-6700

Dragoon Corp. (Faxmate)
1270 Avenida Acaso, Unit F
Camarillo, CA 93010
805-987-4911

Fujitsu
Corporate Dr.
Commerce Park
Danbury, CT 06810
203-796-5400

Hitachi
401 West Artesia Blvd.
Compton, CA 90220
213-537-8383

Mitsubishi Electronics America Inc.
991 Knox St.
Torrance, CA 90502
800-556-1234
800-441-2345

Murata Business Systems
4801 Spring Valley Rd.
Dallas, TX 75244
214-392-1622

NEC
8 Old Sod Farm Rd.
Melville, NY 11747
516-753-7000

OMNIFAX
8700 Bellanca Ave.
Los Angeles, CA 90045-0014
213-641-3690

Panasonic
Two Panasonic Way
Secaucus, NJ 07094
201-348-7000

Pitney-Bowes
Ricoh
5 Dedrick Place
West Caldwell, NJ 07006
201-882-2000

Sharp Electronics Corp.
Sharp Plaza
Mahwah, NJ 07430
201-529-8200

Toshiba America Inc.
9740 Irvine Blvd.
Irvine, CA 92718
800-457-7777

Xerox
100 Clinton Ave. South
Rochester, NY 14644
716-423-5078

FAX BOARDS

Fax meets computer. Not yet the way for most people, but maybe just the ticket for you.

American Data Technology Inc.
44 W. Bellevue Dr., #6
Pasadena, CA 91105
818-578-1339

Brook Trout Technology Inc.
110 Cedar St.
Wellesley Hills, MA 02181
617-235-3026

Brother International Corp.
8 Corporate Plaza
Piscataway, NJ 08855
201-981-0300

The Complete PC
521 Cottonwood Dr.
Milpitas, CA 95035
408-434-0145

DEST Corp.
1201 Cadillac Court
Milpitas, CA 95035
408-946-7100

GammaLink
2452 Embarcadero Way
Palo Alto, CA 94303
415-856-7421

Intel PCEO
Mailstop CO3-07
5200 NE Elam Young Pkwy.
Hillsboro, OR 97124-6497
800-538-3373

Microlink International Inc.
4064 McConnell Dr.
Burnady, B.C.
Canada V5A 3A8
604-420-0366

Omnium Corp.
1911 Curve Crest Blvd.
Stillwater, MN 55082
(P.O. Box 186)
800-328-0223

Pamirs Business International Corp.
550 Lake Site Dr., #2
Sunnyvale, CA 94086
408-736-2583

Panasonic Corp.
Panasonic Industrial Co.
2 Panasonic Way
Secaucus, NJ 07094
201-348-7000

Quadram Limited Partnership
1 Quad Way
Norcross, GA 30093
800-548-3420

Ricoh Corp.
5 Dedrick Place
West Caldwell, NJ 07006
201-882-2000

Xerox Imaging Systems/Datacopy
1215 Terra Bella Ave.
Mountain View, CA 94043
415-965-7900

FURNITURE

Write for information and catalogues, which can be a great source of ideas.

A.M. Loveman Lumber & Box Co.
P.O. Box 90123
Nashville, TN 37209

Acco International
770 S. Acco Plaza
Wheeling, IL 60090

Advance Products Co., Inc.,
P.O. Box 2178
Wichita, KS 67201

All-Steel Inc.
Route 31, Ashland Ave.
Aurora, IL 60507

Alpha
2241 North Main St.
Walnut Creek, CA 94596

Amco Engineering Co.
3801 N. Rose St.
Schiller Park, IL 60176

American Seating Co.
901 Broadway, N.W.
Grand Rapids, MI 49504

Ampersand Inc./Datapro Ltd.
1234 W. Cedar
Denver, CO 80223

Artec
1600 Royal St.
Jasper, IN 47546

Aspen Design & Manufacturing
1295 S. Kalamath St.
Denver, CO 80223

Atlantic Cabinet
P.O. Box 100 - Interstate Industrial Park
Williamsport, MD 21795

Atlantic Data Furniture Products
P.O. Box 151777
Tampa, FL 33684

AVM Data Products
43 Jefferson St.
Ellicottville, NY 14731

Bevis Custom Tables Inc.
P.O. Box 2280
Florence, AL 35630

Branwood Manufacturing
2929 S. 38th St.
Phoenix, AZ 85040

Bretford Manufacturing Inc.
9715 Soreng Ave.
Schiller Park, IL 60176

Bush Industries
One Mason Dr. -- P.O. Box 460
Jamestown, NY 14702-0460

C.A.C. Corp.
4737 Gretna
Dallas, TX 75207

Citadel Data Group, Inc
189 Sunrise Highway
Rockville Center, NY 11570

Computer Furniture & Accessories
515 W. 132nd St.
Gardena, CA 90248

Computer Furniture Corp.
P.O. Box 2663
Chapel Hill, NC 27514

Computer Roomers Inc.
9219 Viscount Row
Dallas, TX 75247

Computerise, Inc.
47-09 30th St.
Long Island City, NY 11101

Custom Computer Furniture
P.O. Box 374
N. San Juan, CA 90248

Dayton Continental
P.O. Box 1318
South Bend, IN 46624

Dennison Monarch Systems Inc.
P.O. Box 4081
New Windsor, NY 12550

Electronic Systems Furniture Co.
17129 S. Kingsview Ave.
Carson, CA 90746

Florida Data Corp.
600D John Rodes Blvd.
Melbourne, FL 32935

Foremost Furniture
(Sauder Woodworking Co.)
502 Middle St.
Archbold, OH 43502

Frontline Products
1915 W. Glenoaks Blvd., Suite 200
Glendale, CA 91201

GF Furniture Systems Inc.
P.O. Box 1108
Youngstown, OH 44501

Gusdorf Corp.
11440 Lackland Rd.
St. Louis, MO 63146

Hamilton Industries
1316 18th St.
Two Rivers, WI 54241

Hamilton-Sorter Co., Inc.
3158 Production Dr., Box 8
Fairfield, OH 45014

Haworth, Inc.
One Haworth Center
Holland, MI 49423

Herman Miller, Inc.
8500 Byron Rd.
Zeeland, MI 49464

HSP Computer Furniture
P.O. Box 5545
Birmingham, AL 35207

Hubbard Scientific
1946 Raymond Dr.
Northbrook, IL 60062

Human Factor Technologies
P.O. Box 235
Londonderry, NH 03053

IBM Corp. Workstation Products
P.O. Box 10
Princeton, NJ 08540

Input-EZ Corp
555 Quivas St.
Denver, CO 80204

John James Inc.
P.O. Box 501321
Houston, TX 77250

Kimball Office Furniture Co.
1600 Royal St.
Jasper, IN 47546

Krueger Inc.
P.O. Box 8100
Green Bay, WI 54308

Lifeline Ltd.
P.O. Box 579
Middale, UT 84047

Luban Inc.
1129 S. Bridge St.
Belding, MI 48809

Luxor Corp.
2245 Delaney Rd.
Waukeegan, IL 60085

M & M Industries
10 Gateway Rd.
Bensonville, IL 60106

Marvel Metal Products
3843 W. 43rd St.
Chicago, IL 60632

National Office Furniture
1600 Royal St.
Jasper, IN 47546

Nordhaus Chairs
7122 N. Clark St.
Chicago, IL 60626

O'Sullivan Industries
19th and Gulf Sts.
Lamar, MO 64759

Omnium Corp.
203 N. Second St.
Stillwater, MN 55082

Once A Tree
3192 Commercial St.
San Diego, CA 92113

Panel Concepts Inc.
P.O. Box C-25100
Santa Ana, CA 92799

PC Mobile Workcenter Inc.
1045 Matheson Blvd.
Mississauga, Ontario
Canada L4W 3P1

Picture House
166 Boynton Blvd.
Daytona Beach, FL 32018

RC Smith Co.
801 E. 79th St.
Minneapolis, MN 55420

Royal Seating Corp.
P.O. Box 753
Cameron TX 76520

Rudd International
1066 31st St.
Washington, D.C. 20007

Sauder Woodworking Co.
(Manufacturer of Foremost Furniture)
502 Middle St.
Archbold, OH 43502

Smith Systems Manufacturiing Co.
P.O. Box 64515
St. Paul, MN 55164

Steelcase, Inc.
1120 36th St., S.E.
Grand Rapids, MI 49501

Storwal International Inc.
One Yonge St.
Toronto, Ontario
Canada M5E 1E5

T & A Diversified Products
1743 Ames Ave.
St. Paul, MN 55106

Tab Products Inc.
P.O. Box 01269
Palo Alto, CA 94303

Techne Design
BCIC Building
North Bennington, VT 05257

Tiffany Stand & Furniture Co.
9666 Olive Blvd., Suite 750
St. Louis, MO 63132

Tri-World Trading Corp.
P.O. Box 65
Campbell, CA 95009

TRMC
5800 Fairfield Ave., Suite 135
Fort Wayne, In 46807

Universal Industries
1561 N. Bonnie Beach Pl.
Los Angeles, CA 90063

Versa Tec Corp.
P.O. Box 2095
Tampa, FL 33601

Vogel Peterson
Route 83 & Madison St.
Elmhurst, IL 60126

Whittier Wood Products
P.O. Box 2827
Eugene, OR 97402

Williams & Foltz
1816 Fourth St.
Berkeley, CA 94710

Wilson Jones Co.
6150 Touhy Ave.
Chicago, IL 60648

Windsor Hardwood Furniture
P.O. Box 430
Windsor, CA 95492

The Wood Works
901 Kentucky St., Suite 304
Lawrence, KS 66044

MAIL ORDER SUPPLIES

Companies that sell furniture and/or office supplies through catalogues. Some sell at a discount, some don't.

Bell Atlantic
456 Creamery Way
Exton, PA 19341-9988
800-523-0552
Fax: 215-524-5738

BrownCor
P.O. Box 290910
Davie, FL 33329-0910
800-327-2278
Fax: 305-370-7160

CompuAdd
12303-G Technology Blvd.
Austin, TX 78727
800-627-1967

Devoke
1500 Martin Ave.
Box 58051
Santa Clara, CA 95052-8051

800-822-3132
Fax: 408-727-4935

Frank Eastern
599 Broadway
New York, NY 10012
800-221-4914
Fax: 212-219-0722

Global
45 South Service Rd.
Plainview, NY 11803
800-845-6225
Fax: 516-845-7712

Inacomp
20717 Kelly Rd.
East Detroit, MI 48021-2702
800-999-9898
Fax: 313-776-7541

Inmac
Fifteen regional centers in the U.S., with different, non-toll-free numbers and fax lines. Corporate headquarters:
2465 Augustine Dr.
P.O. Box 58031
Santa Clara, CA 95052-8031

Lyben
1050 Maple Rd.
Troy, MI 48083
313-589-3440
Fax: 313-589-2112

Misco
P.O. Box 399
Holmdel, NJ 07733
800-631-2227
Fax: 201-264-5955

Moore
P.O. Box 5000
Vernon Hills, IL 60061
800-323-6230
Fax: 312-913-3294

Pryor
224 William St.
Box 1563
Bensenville, IL 60106-8563
800-558-6866
Fax: 312-860-0284

Quill
100 S. Schelter Rd.
P.O. Box 4700
Lincolnshire, IL 60197-4700
312-634-4800
Fax:312-634-5708
    west of the Rockies:
5440 E. Francis St.
P.O. Box 50-050
Ontario, CA 91761-1050
714-988-3200
Fax: 312-634-5708

Source
740 Annoreno Dr.
Addison, IL 60101
800-323-9622

Uarco
121 North Ninth St.
DeKalb, IL 60115
800-435-0713
Fax: 815-756-3219

Visible
3626 Stern Ave.
St. Charles, IL 60174
800-323-0628
Fax: 312-377-1073

ON-LINE SERVICES

If you know how, you can dig up almost any kind of information using your phone and your computer together.

AT&T Mail
AT&T Customer Assistance
P.O. Box 3505
New Brunswick, NJ 08903
800-367-7225

BRS
BRS Information Technologies
1200 Route 7
Latham, NY 12110
800-468-0908

CompuServe
Compuserve
5000 Arlington Centre Blvd.
Columbus, OH 43220
800-848-8199

Delphi
General Videotext Corp.
3 Blackstone St.
Cambridge, MA 02139
800-544-4005

Dialcom
Dialcom, Inc.
1109 Spring St.
Silver Spring, MD 20910
301-588-1572

Dialog
Dialog Information Services, Inc.
3460 Hillview Ave.
Palo Alto, CA 94304
800-334-2564

Dow Jones News/Retrieval
Dow Jones & Company
P.O. Box 300
Princeton, NJ 08540
800-257-5114

EasyLink
Western Union Telegraph Co.
One lake St.
Upper Saddle River, NJ 07458
800-435-7375

GEnie
General Electric Information Services Co.
401 North Washington St.
Rockville, MD 20850
800-638-9636

Infoline
Pergamon Orbit Infoline
8000 Westpark Dr.
McLean, VA 22102
800-421-7229

Infomaster
Western Union Telegraph Co.
One Lake St.
Upper Saddle River, NJ 07458
800-325-6000

Knowledge Index
Dialog Information Services, Inc.
3460 Hillview Ave.
Palo Alto, CA 94304
800-334-2564

Lexis and Nexis
Mead Data Central
9393 Springboro Pike
Dayton, OH 45401
800-922-1015

MCI Mail
MCI
1900 M St., NW
Box 1001
Washington, DC 20036
800-444-6245

NewsNet
NewsNet
945 Haverford Rd.
Bryn Mawr, PA 19010
800-345-1301

Orbit
Pergamon Orbit Infoline
8000 Westpark Dr.
McLean, VA 22102
800-421-7229

Prodigy
Prodigy Services Company
P.O. Box 4064
Woburn, MA 01888-9961
800-822-6922

Vu/Text
Vu/Text Information Services, Inc.
325 Chestnut St.
Suite 1300
Philadelphia, PA 19106
800-323-2940

Wilsonline
H.H. Wilson Company
950 University Ave.
Bronx, NY 10452
800-367-6770
In NY: 800-462-6060

ORGANIZERS
Computerized notebooks, and then some.

Psion Organizer II
Psion Incorporated
320 Sylvan Lake Rd.
Watertown, CT 06779
203-274-7521

Sharp Wizard
Sharp Electronics Corp.
Sharp Plaza
Mahwah, NJ 07430
201-529-9500

ORGANIZATIONS
Of interest to home workers.

National Association for the Cottage Industry (NACI)
P.O. Box 14460
Chicago, IL 60614

American Home Business Association
397 Post Rd.
Darien, CT 06820

American Federation of Small Business
407 S. Dearborn St.
Chicago, IL 60605

Association of Electronic Cottagers
P.O. Box 1738
Davis, CA 95617

Mothers' Home Business Network
P.O. Box 423
East Meadow, NY 11554

National Association of Home Based Businesses
P.O. Box 362
Owings Mills, MD 21117

National Association of Home Business Owners
P.O. Box 423
East Meadow, NY 11554

National Small Business United
1155 15th St. NW
Washington, DC 20005

TELEPHONES AND ANSWERING MACHINES

The heart of even the fanciest home office.

AT&T
295 North Maple Ave.
2327 G1
Basking Ridge, NJ 07920
201-221-5290

Bell South
1155 Peachtree St. NE
Atlanta, GA 30367
800-235-5273

Cobra Electronics Group
6500 West Cortland St.
Chicago, IL 60635
312-889-8870

Code-A-Phone Corp.
P.O. Box 5656
Portland, Or 97228
503-655-8940

Colonial Data Technologies, Inc.
80 Pickett District Rd.
New Milford, CT 06776
203-355-3178

General Electric
3135 Easton Turnpike
Fairfield, CT 06432
203-373-2211

GTE
1 Stamford Forum
Stamford, CT 06904
203-965-2000

ITT
320 Park Ave.
New York, NY 10022
212-752-6000

NorthWestern Bell
9394 West Dodge Rd.
Omaha, NE 68114
800-822-1000

PacTel Products
50 Fremont Ave.
20th Floor
San Francisco, CA 94105
800-426-2372

Panasonic
One Panasonic Way
Secaucus, NJ 07094
201-348-7000

Phone-Mate, Inc.
325 Maple Ave.
Torrance, CA 90503
213-618-9910

Radio Shack
1700 One Tandy Center
Fort Worth, TX 76102
817-390-3300

Record-a-Call
19200 South Laurel Park Rd.
Compton, CA 90220
213-603-9393

Sanyo Business Systems
51 Joseph St.
Moonachie, NJ 07074
201-440-9300

Southwestern Bell
1 Bell Center -- 42nd floor
St. Louis, MO 63101
800-558-7347

Sony
Sony Dr.
Park Ridge, NJ 07656
800-222-7669

Uniden
6345 Castleway Court
Indianapolis, IN
317-842-0280

HEADSETS
Consider these if you're on the phone all day.

DAK Industries, Inc.
8200 Remmet Ave.
Canoga Park, CA 91304
800-325-0800

Panasonic
One Panasonic Way
Secaucus, NJ 07094
201-348-7000

Plantronics
345 Encinal St.
Santa Cruz, CA 95060-2132
800-538-0748
In CA: 800-662-3902

Radio Shack
1700 One Tandy Center
Fort Worth, TX 76102
817-390-3300

VOICE MAIL

Computerized answering and message services.

BigmOuth
Talking Technology Inc.
4383 Piedmont Ave., #B
Oakland, CA 94611
415-652-9600

The Complete Answering Machine
The Complete PC Inc.
521 Cottonwood Dr.
Milpitas, CA 95035
800-634-5558

Watson
Natural Microsystems
8 Erie Dr.
Natick, MA 01760
617-655-0700

MODEMS

You need one of these to use your computer's power over the phone lines.

Cermetek Microelectronics Inc.
1308 Borregas Ave.
Sunnyvale, CA 94088-3565
800-862-6271

General DataComm Inc.
1579 Straits Turnpike
Middlebury, CT 06762-1299
203-574-1118

Hayes Microcomputer Products Inc.
705 Westech Dr.
Norcross, GA 30092
404-449-8791

Migent Inc.
865 Tahoe Blvd.
Incline Village, NV 89450
702-832-3700

Multi-Tech Systems Inc.
82 Second Ave. SE
New Brighton, MN 55112
800-328-9717

Novation Inc.
20409 Prairie St.
Chatsworth, CA 91311
818-996-5060

OmniTel Inc.
5415 Randall Place
Fremont, CA 94538
415-490-220

Prentice Corp.
266 Caspian Dr.
P.O. Box 3544
Sunnyvale, CA 94088
408-734-9855

Prometheus Products Inc.
P.O. Box 4156
Fremont, CA 94539
415-490-2370

Racal-Vadic
1525 McCarthy Blvd.
Milpitas, CA 95035
408-946-2227

U.S. Robotics Inc.
8100 N. McCormick Blvd.
Skokie, IL 60076
312-982-5010

Ven-Tel Inc.
2342 Walsh Ave.
Santa Clara, CA 95051
408-727-5721

WorldPort
Touchbase Systems
160 Laurel Ave.
Northport, NY 11768
800-541-0345

Zoom Telephonics Inc.
207 South St.
Boston, MA 02111
617-423-1072

PRINTERS

The paperless office is not at hand.

Advanced Matrix Technology Inc.
1157 Tourmaline Dr.
Newbury Park, CA 91320
805-499-8747

ALPS America
3553 N. 1st St.
San Jose, CA 95134
408-432-6000

Apple Computer Inc.
20525 Mariana Ave.
Cupertino, CA 95014
408-996-1010

Blaser Industries
8300 E. Raintree Dr.
Scottsdale, AZ 85260
800-322-3399

Camintonn Corp.
2332 McGaw Ave.
Irvine, CA 92714
800-843-8336

Citizen America Corp.
2401 Colorado Ave., #190
Santa Monica, CA 90404
800-824-9921

C. Itoh Electronics Inc.
2505 McCabe Way
Irvine, CA 92714-6297
714-660-1421

Copal USA Inc.
2291 205th St., #105
Torrance, CA 90501
800-441-7763

Dataproducts Corp.
6200 Canoga Ave.
Woodland Hills, CA 91365
818-887-8000

Diconix Inc.
3100 Research Blvd.
P.O. Box 3100
Dayton, OH 45420
513-259-3100

Epson America Inc.
23530 Hawthorne Blvd.
Torrance, CA 90505
213-539-9140

Fujitsu America Inc.
3055 Orchard Dr.
San Jose, CA 95134
408-946-8777

GCC Technologies
580 Winter St.
Waltham, MA 02154
800-422-7777

Hewlett-Packard Corp.
974 E. Arques Ave.
P.O. Box 486
Sunnyvale, CA 94086
800-752-0900

IBM Corp.
900 King Drive
Ryebrookn NY 10573
800-426-2468

Infoscribe
Division of Eurotherm Corp.
11507 Sunset Hills Rd.
Reston, VA 22090
703-689-2805

Jasmine Technologies
1740 Army Street
San Francisco, CA 94124
415-282-1111

Kyocera Unison Inc.
3165 Adeline St.
Berkeley, CA 94703
415-848-6680

LaCie, Ltd.
16285 S.W. 85th, Suite 306
Tigard, OR 97224
503-684-0143

Mannesmann Tally Corp.
8301 S. 180th St.
Kent, WA 98031
206-251-5500

NEC Information Systems Inc.
1414 Massachusetts Ave.
Boxboro, MA 01719
508-264-8000

Office Automation Systems Inc.
9940 Barnes Canyon Rd.
San Diego, CA 92121
619-452-9400

Okidata
532 Fellowship Rd.
Mount Laurel, NJ 08054
800-654-3282

AEG Olympia Inc.
Box 22
Sommerville, NJ 08876
201-231-8300

QMS Inc.
One Magnum Pass
Mobile, AL 36618
205-633-4300

Qume Corp.
500 Yosemite Dr.
Milpitas, CA 95035
800-223-2479

Relisys
320 S. Milpitas Blvd.
Milpitas, CA 95035
800-635-0999

Ricoh Corp.
3001 Orchard Parkway
San Jose, CA 95134
408-432-8800

Seikosha America Inc.
1111 MacArthur Blvd.
Mahwah, NJ 07430
201-529-4655

Star Micronics America Inc.
200 Park Ave.
New York, NY 10166
212-986-6770

Taxan USA Corp.
18005 Cortney Court
City of Industry, CA 91748
800-544-3888

Texas Instruments Inc.
P.O.Box 181153
Austin, TX 78718
800-527-3500

POSTSCRIPT™ BOARDS
Turn your Hewlett-Packard into a PostScript printer.

Conographic Corp.
16802 Aston St.
Irvine, CA 92714
714-474-1188

Custom Applications Inc.
5 Middlesex Technology Center
900 Middlesex Turnpike

Billerica, MA 01821
800-873-4367

Destiny Technology Corp.
300 Montague Expressway
Milpitas, CA 95035
800-874-5553

Eicon Technology Corp.
2196 32nd Ave. (Lachine)
Montreal, Quebec
Canada H8T 3H7
514-631-2592

LaserGo Inc.
9235 Trade Place, Suite A
San Diego, CA 92126
619-530-2400

LaserMaster Corp.
7156 Shady Oak Rd.
Eden Prairie, MN 55344
612-944-6069

Princeton Publishing Labs Inc.
19 Wall St.
Princeton, NJ 08540
609-924-1153

QMS Inc.
1 Magnum Pass
Mobile, AL 36618
205-633-4300

Tall Tree Systems
2585 East Bayshore Rd.
Palo Alto, CA 94303
415-493-1980

SCANNERS

Magic, magic, magic.

Advanced Vision Research Systems Inc.
2201 Qume Dr.
San Jose, CA 95131
408-434-1115

AT&T Audiographic Communication Systems
185 Monmouth Pkwy.
West Long Branch, NJ 07764
800-227-6161

Chinon America Inc.
660 Maple Ave.
Torrance, CA 90503
800-441-0222

CompuScan Inc.
300 Broadacres Dr.
Bloomfield, NJ 07003
201-338-5000

Calera Recognition Systems
2500 Augustine Dr.
Santa Clara, CA 95054
408-986-8006

DEST Corp.
1201 Cadillac Court
Milpitas, CA 95035
408-946-7100

Hewlett-Packard Corp.
974 E. Arques Ave.
P.O. Box 486
Sunnyvale, CA 94086
800-752-0900

Microtek Lab Inc.
680 Knox St.
Torrance, CA 90502
In CA 213-321-2121

Pentax Technologies
880 Interlocken Pkwy.
Broomfield, CO 80020
303-460-1600

Saba Technologies
9300 SW Gemini Dr.
Beaverton, OR 97005
800-654-5274

Shape Inc.
Electronic Instrument Division
P.O. Box 366
Biddeford Industrial Park
Biddeford, ME 04005
800-247-1724
In Me and AK: 207-282-6155

Xerox Imaging Systems
185 Albany St.
Cambridge, MA 02139
617-864-4700

SOFTWARE

This is by no means a listing of every software publisher in the country—there are probably thousands. It doesn't even cover every company I know of. It *does* include all the houses whose packages are mentioned in this book. Computer magazines are full of ads for software, and most run reviews and "what's new" features on all kinds of software packages. Check there for more information, addresses and phone numbers.

Aldus Corp.
Pagemaker
411 First Ave.
Suite 200
Seattle, WA 98104
206-622-5500

American Video Teleconferencing Corp.
In-Sync
110 Bi-County Blvd.
Farmingdale, NY 11735
516-420-8080

Apple Computer Corp.
Hypercard
20525 Mariani Ave.
Cupertino, CA 95014
408-996-1010

Ashton-Tate Corp.
dBase IV
MultiMate Advantage II
Framework
FullWrite Professional
20101 Hamilton Ave.
Torrance, CA 90502
213-329-8000

Black & White International, Inc.
Switch-It
P.O. Box 1040
Planetarium Station
New York, NY 10024
212-787-6633

Borland International
Paradox
Quattro
Sidekick
Sidekick Plus
Sprint
1800 Green Hill Rd.
Scotts Valley, CA 95066
408-438-8400

Justin Boyan
Boyan
9458 Two Hills Ct.
Columbia, MD 21045

Broderbund Software
DTP Advisor
17 Paul Dr.
San Rafael, CA 94903
800-527-6263

Buttonware Inc.
PC-Calc
PC-File
P.O. Box 96058
Bellevue, WA 98009
206-454-0479

Casady and Greene Inc.
Quickdex
P.O. Box 223779
Carmel, CA 93922
408-624-8716

Central Point Software
PC-Tools
9700 SW Capitol Highway
#100
Portland, OR 97219
503-244-5782

Chang Labs
C.A.T.
4300 Stevens Creek Blvd.
San Jose, CA 95129
408-246-8020

Claris Corp.
MacWrite
440 Clyde Ave.
Mountain View, CA 94043
800-334-3535

Conductor Software
ACT!
9208 West Royal Lane
Irving, TX 75063
800-627-3958

Computer Associates International Inc.
SuperCalc
1240 McKay Dr.
San Jose, CA 95131
408-432-1727

DataEase International
DataEase
7 Cambridge Dr.
Trumbull, CT 06611
800-243-5123

Datastorm Technologies, Inc.
ProComm
P.O. Box 1471
Columbia, MO 65205
314-474-8461

DataViz, Inc.
MacLink Plus
35 Corporate Dr.
Trumbull, CT 06611
203-268-0030

DeltaPoint, Inc.
Mindwrite
555C Heritage Harbor
Monterey, CA 93940
800-367-4334

Digital Research
GEM Desktop Publisher
P.O. Box DRI
Monterey, CA 93942
800-443-4200

Dragonfly Software
Nota Bene
285 West Broadway #500
New York, NY 10013
212-334-0445

Dynamic Microprocessor Associates
PC-Anywhere
PC MacTerm
60 East 42nd St.
New York, NY 10165
212-687-7115

Executive Systems
X-Tree
15300 Ventura Blvd. #305
Sherman Oaks, CA 91403
800-634-5545
In CA: 800-551-5353

Fifth Generation Systems, Inc.
Brooklyn Bridge
Fastback
Mace Htest-Hformat
Mace Utilities
11200 Industriplex Blvd.
Baton Rouge, LA 70809-4112
800-225-2775

The Forbin Project
Q-Modem
P.O. Box 702
Cedar Falls, ID 50613
319-232-4516

Fox Software, Inc.
FoxBase
118 W. South Boundary
Perrysburg, OH 43551
419-874-0162

The FreeSoft Company
White Knight (formerly *Red Ryder*)
150 Hickory Dr.
Beaver Falls, PA 15010

FW Corp.
Final Word II
P.O. Box 443
Cambridge, MA 02142
617-489-5078

Roland Gans Software Co.
XWord
350 West 55th St. #2E
New York, NY 10019
212-957-8361

Gazelle Systems
Back-it
42 North University Ave. #10
Provo, UT 84601
800-233-0383

General Information Inc.
Hot Line
401 Parkplace
Kirkland, WA 98033
206-828-4777

Gibson Research Corporation
Spinrite II
P.O. Box 6024
Irvine, CA 92716
714-854-1520

Harmony Technology Associates
Co-Compute
3700 South Sepulveda Blvd. #332
West Los Angeles, CA 90034
800-622-7660
In CA: 213-429-4103

Hayes Microcomputer Products, Inc.
Smartcom III
P.O. Box 105203
Atlanta, GA 30348
404-441-1617

Headlands Press
PC-Talk
P.O. Box 862
Tiburon, CA 94920
415-435-0770

IBM Corp.
DisplayWrite 4
Old Orchard Rd.
Armonk, NY 10504
800-447-4700

Intersecting Concepts
Media Master
4573 Heatherglen Court
Moorpark, CA 93021
805-373-3900

Lifetree Software
Volkswriter Deluxe
411 Pacific St.
Monterey, CA 93940
408-373-4718

Lotus Development Corp.
1-2-3
Agenda
Express
Manuscript
Symphony
55 Cambridge Parkway
Cambridge, MA 02142
617-577-8500

Mastersoft
Word-for-Word
4621 North 16th St. #A-108
Phoenix, AZ 85016
602-277-0900

Meridian Technology Inc.
Carbon Copy Plus
7 Corporate Park
Suite 100
Irvine, CA 92714
714-261-1199

Microlytics, Inc.
Gofer
One Tobey Village Office Park
Pittsford, NY 14534
716-248-9150

MicroPro International
WordStar
33 San Pablo Ave.
San Rafael, CA 94903
800-227-5609

Microrim Inc.
Rbase for Dos
3925 159th Ave. NE
Redmond, WA 98052
206-885-2000

Microsoft Corp.
Excel
Word
Works
16011 N.E. 36th Way
P.O. Box 97017
Redmond, WA 98073-9717
800-426-9400

Microstuf, Inc.
Crosstalk Mk.4
1000 Holcomb Woods Parkway
Roswell, GA 30076
404-998-7798

Peter Norton Computing, Inc.
The Norton Utilities
Norton Commander
2210 Wilshire Blvd.
Santa Monica, CA 90403
213-453-2361

Office Solutions Inc.
Office Writer
2802 Coho St.
Madison, WI 53713
800-228-0747

Paperback Software International
VP-Info
VP-Planner
2830 Ninth St.
Berkeley, CA 95710
415-644-2116

PC/SIG
1030D East Duane Ave.
Sunnyvale, VA 94086
800-245-6717
In CA: 800-222-2996

PowerBase Systems
PowerBase
32100 Telegraph Rd.
Birmingham, MI 48010
800-292-7432

Prime Solutions, Inc.
Disk Technician
1940 Garnet Ave.
San Diego, CA 92109
619-274-5000

Quicksoft, Inc.
PC-Write
219 First N. #224
Seattle, WA 98109
800-888-8088

Relay Communications, Inc.
Relay Gold
Relay Silver
41 Kenosia Ave.
Danbury, CT 06810
800-847-3529

SoftLogic Solutions, Inc.
Software Carousel
One Perimeter Rd.
Manchester, NH 03103
800-272-9900

Software Publishing Corp.
PFS:First Choice
PFS:Professional Write
PFS Professional File
PFS:First Publisher
1901 Landings Dr.
Mountain View, CA 94043
415-962-8910

Software Ventures
Microphone II
2907 Claremont Ave.
Berkeley, CA 94705
415-644-3232

Springboard Software
Newsroom Pro
7808 Creekbridge Circle
Minneapolis, MN 55435
612-944-3915

Symantec Corp.
Grandview
Q&A
Q&A Write
Symantec Utilities
10201 Torre Ave.
Cupertino, CA 95014
408-253-9600

System Compatibility
Software Bridge
One East Wacker Dr. #1320
Chicago, IL 60601
312-329-0700

Ten Point O
Focal Point
3885 Bohannon Dr.
Menlo Park, CA 94025
415-329-0500

Timeworks
Hyperworks Organizer
444 Lake Cook Rd.
Deerfield, IL 60015
312-948-9200

T/Maker Co.
WriteNow
1390 Villa St.
Mountain View, CA 94041
415-962-0195

Traveling Software
LapLink
LapLink Mac
North Creek Corporate Center
19310 North Creek Parkway
Bothell, WA 98011
800-343-8080

Triton Technologies, Inc.
Co/Session
146 Maple Ave.
Red Bank, NJ 07701
201-741-3232

Valor Software
Info-XL
2005 Hamilton Ave.
San Jose, CA 95125
800-648-2567
In CA: 408-559-1100

WordPerfect Corp.
WordPerfect
288 West Center St.
Orem, UT 84057
801-225-5000

Xerox Corp.
Ventura Publisher
101 Continental Blvd.
El Segundo, CA 90245
800-822-8221

XyQuest
XyWrite III Plus
44 Manning Rd.
Billerica, MA 01821
617-671-0888

Index

A

accountant, 224 - 225
address book, 230
Adobe Systems, **141**
alarm clock, 230
Aldus, 112
Allen wrench, 22
Alps, 134
ambient lighting, 208-210
The American Home Business Association, 224
American Video Teleconferencing, 110
Amstrad, 70
angst, **223**
answering machines, 168-172
    outgoing message for, 228 - 229
    two-line, 172
Anthro Corporation, 29
AnthroCart, 29
Apple, 114, 117, 129, 139, **141**
Apple II, 101
appointments, daily, 230
architects, 18
    to plan office for you, 202
    working with, 17
Archive, 124
articulating arm for monitor, **37**
artificial light, 212
   See also ambient lighting
   See also task lighting
ASCII, 181
Ashton-Tate, 84 - 85, 94

AST, 69
AT clones, 56 - 59
AT&T, 149, 158
    System 2000, 162
Atkinson, Bill, **118**
Atlantic, 34
Atlantic "System Four"
   See desks

B

baby
   hear it cry, 10
   when it arrives, 12
Baby Bells, 158
backup, 123, 124, **125**
   Back-it, 124
   DC200 cartridge, 124
   Fastback, 124
Bad Space, 5, 14-16
Balans chair, 20
barter, 233
bedrooms, as too good, 12
Berra, Yogi, 198
Big Bopper, **221**
big moves, 16-17
Bigger Is Better, 5
binders, three-ring, 232
Bitstream, **142**
Black & White International, 121
blinds
   See natural light
bookcases, 4, 13, 198
Borland, 94, 103, 105, 115 - 116

Index

boss, demanding, 214
boundaries, symbolic, 5
boxes for storage, 4, 44
Boyan, 97, 108
Bretford, 28, 32
Brightbill-Roberts, 119
Broderbund, 114
Brother, 129, 134, 180
BrownCor, 44
builders, working with, 17
Building
   Massive Urban Traffic Jam and Paper-Shuffle, 14 - 15
building permit, 17
building regulations, 17
built-ins, 8, 38-40
business cards, 227-228
businesspeople, small, 214
businesswomen, 214
Buttonware, 104, 106

C

C. Itoh, 134
cable extensions, 41
calculator, 230
calendar, 230
   pocket, 231
Calera Recognition Systems, 150
camaraderie, 218
Canon, 136, 149, 180, 182
cartridges
   copier, 4, 181
   printer, 144
   recharging, 145
   See also laser printers
"Casablanca", 228
Casady and Greene Inc., 117
central filing system, none, 5
Central Point Software, 122
chair mats, 24
chairs, 20-24
Chang Labs, 118 - 119
Chinon, 149
choices, 18
Claris, 94
Classics Comics, 173
clients, 44, 191-193, 226
   See also designing a home office
clipboards, 36
clutter, 5
   calculated, 230
co-housing, 167
Cobra, 165

coffee, bad, 214
collar, tight, 15
colleagues, 214
communications, 106
   Boyan, 108
   Crosstalk MK. 4, 108
   Microphone II, 108
   ProComm, 108
   ProComm Plus, 108
   Q-Modem, 108
   Red Ryder, 108
   Relay Gold, 108
   Relay Silver, 108
   Smartcom III, 108
   See also electronic mail
   See also remote computing
Compaq, 69
competition, 219 - 220
The Complete PC Inc., 172
Compucart, 31
CompuServe, 224
Computer Accessories Corp., 150
Computer Associates International, Inc., 101
computer bulletin boards, 95
computer cabinets, 30-31
Computer Currents, 83
computers
   Apple II, 48
   buying, 76
   buying, mail order, 79
   buying, retail stores, 76
   buying, rules for, 77
   buying, rules for mail order, 81
   character based, 51
   clock, 66
   Commodore 64, 48
   connections, 66
   consistent user interface, 50
   cost of Macs vs. IBM compatibles, 49
   dedicated circuit for, 205
   DOS (IBM compatible), 48
   ease of use, 50
   and the enchantment of power, 47
   entry level, 50
   extending workday, 47
   graphics based, 51
   and greater independence, 47
   guru, 78, 82
   icons, 50
   inspiring dreams, 47
   installed base, 50

interface incompatibility, 50
the Mac family, 48
not magic, 47
"open architecture", 49
ports, parallel, 66
ports, RS-232, 66
ports, serial, 66
and putting together a small business, 47
software determines hardware, 49
speed, **54 - 55**
transportable, 7
the true home office computer, 48
unused slots, 66
users groups, 78, 82
watch out for true believers, 51
what makes a business computer, 48
See also DOS machines
See also fax boards
See also laptops
See also portables
Computree, 26
concentration, 4
disrupted, 6
spoiled, **223**
Conductor Software, 117
connections, laptop to desktop, 119
Brooklyn Bridge, 120
LapLink, 120
consultants, 214
context switching, 121
Software Carousel, 121
Switch-It, 121
conversions, 5, 12, 120
of data files, 119
DOS to Mac, 120
from one program to another, 120
LapLink Mac, 121
MacLink Plus, 120
Media Master, 120
Software Bridge, 120
success, 13
Word-for-Word, 120
XWord, 120
Cooper, James Fenimore, 173
copiers, personal, 181-183
cartridges for, 181
cordless telephones, 163-166
two-line, 166
corporate ladder
climbing from home, 220, 222
corporate library, none, 5
couch, 5

CP/M, 120
CPU
on edge in corner of work surface, **37, 39**
creativity, 18
curtains
blackout, 204
See also natural light
custodian, none, 3

D

daisywheel printers, 130-134
DAK, 168
data, moving to another machine, 119
See also connections
Data General, 71
Data Viz, 120
databases, 104-106
dBase, 105 - 106, 121
dBase II, 104 - 105
dBase IV, 84, 87, 105
FoxBase, 106
Paradox, 105
PC-File, 106
PFS:First Choice, 106
PowerBase, 106
Professional File, 106
Q&A, 106
Rbase for DOS, 105
VP-Info, 106
DataDesk, 68, 75
Datastorm Technologies, 108
Datavue, 71
Dell, 69
Delta Point, 95 - 96
designer, 18
to plan office for you, 202
working with, 17
designing a home office
as exercise in pleasing self, 185
basic designs, 190
best plan not always most obvious, 196
consider equipment, 187
consider work habits, 187
the galley, 194 - 195
the L, 190 - 194
list of personal priorities, 188
the most important thing, 202
program, developing, 186
self-analysis as vital, 188
standard heights, etc., 186

the strip, 190
the U, 195 - 196
See also clients
See also function
See also style
desk height, 36
desk lamps, 13
desk, roll-top, 6
desks, 13-14, 32-34
desktop publishing
 DTP Adviser, 114
 GEM Desktop Publisher, 114
 Newsroom Pro, 114
 Pagemaker, 112, 114
 PFS:First Publisher, 114
 Ventura Publisher, 112, 114
Dest, 149
Diconix, 136
Digital Research, 114
discipline, 213
 as less important than habits, 214
dishwasher, 207
disks, **125-126**
DisplayWrite 4, 76
distractions, 215
DOS machines, 52-70
 See also laptops
 See also portables
DOS shells
 Norton Commander, 122
 X-Tree, 122
dot matrix printers, 131-137*Dr. Halo*, 181
drafting board, 11
Dragonfly Software, 94
Dragoon, 178 - 179
drawings, scale, 200 - 201
dressing screen, 6
Dynamic Microprocessor Assoc., 110

E

easy chair, 5
EC20 Microcomputer Security Center, 32
Edwards, Paul, 163, 220, 224
Edwards, Sarah, 220, 224
efficiency, 229-231
Egghead, 127
elbowroom, **37**
electrical concerns, **205-210**
electronic equipment, 6
electronic mail, 110, 111, 112
elevations, drawing, 198

emergency power supplies, 151
Emerson Computer Power, 151
Endura workstations, 27
engagement calendar, pocket, 230
entertainment center, 6
envelopes
 manila, 4
 printer problems with, 134
EPA, 166
Epson, 69, 71, 129
equipment
 future upgrades, **205**
 rules for buying, 183
ergonomics, 19
Executive Systems, 122
expansion, 11

F

F-15 Strike Eagle, 78
farmers as home workers, 214
fastidious, pressure to be, 6
fax boards, 180-181
fax machines, 160, 173-180
 See also fax boards
fear, 217
 paralyzed by, 216
 See also panic
Federal Express, 4, 113, 180
Fifth Generation, 120, 124
file cabinets, 13, 40-43
file trays, 43-44
files
 active, 4
 dead, 4, 44, **197**
 legal-sized, 232
 loose, 36
 old, 12
 Pendaflex, 232
filing work material, 19
Final Word, 87
Finland, 156
firmness, **223**
fixed drives
 See hard drives
floor, concrete slab, 16
floorplan, drawing, 198
floppy disks, 62
Fluegelman, Andrew, **95**
 See also shareware
folders
 legal-sized, 40
 letter-sized, 42
Fontware, **142**

footcandles, 203
    See also lighting
The Forbin Project, 108
Foremost Computer Desk, Model 4530
    See desks
Fox Software, 106
Frank Eastern Co., 23
FreeSoft, 108
Frontline, 26
Fujitsu, 180
function, as key to successful home office, 188
    to soften utilitarianism, 188
    See also designing a home office
function and style, 188
functions, competing, 6
furniture
    add-on options, 30
    adjustable, 25
    adjustable legs, 29
    basics, 19
    build or buy, 6
    cable management, 45
    collecting over time, 45
    combinations and permutations, 26
    commercial, 25
    computer rack, 26
    considerations, 25
    designed for home offices, 25
    equipment protection, 32
    multi-level design, 29
    open cart, 28
    open rack, 28

    primary work surface comes second, 45
    start with your chair, 45
    storage comes third, 45
    the used market, 44
    three words and a short sentence, 46
    types, 25
    with built-in outlets, 27

G

garden house, 15
garrets, 15
Gazelle Systems, 124
GCC Technologies, 136, 140
GE, 158, 165
General Information, 116
Giants, New York, 189
Gibson Research, 123

glare, 11, 234
Glosbrenner, Alfred, 99
    See also shareware
good space, the key to, 15
graphic artist, 227
Grid, 71
GTE, 158
guitar, 13

H

hackers, 95
hammock, 163
hard disks
    See hard drives
hard drives, 64
    access times, 64
    in Mac, 75
    on cards, 64
    removable, 64
    as standard equipment, 64
Harmony Technology Assoc., 110
Hayes Microcomputer Products, 108
headsets, 167-168
health, 233
    hazard of overworking, 218
Hewlett-Packard, 71, 136, 149
high-tech look, 6
Hitachi, 180
holiday, psyche declares, 221
Home magazine, 166
home offices
    and barter, 233
    dealing with regulations concerning, 224
    and expense records, 225
    farming things out, 233
    first one as laboratory, 38
    keep track of all problems in, 38
    as percentage of house's space, 224
    as principle place of business, 224
    reasons for regulations concerning, 222
    regulations concerning, 222
    stay flexible, 38
    and tax deductions, 225
    unattached, 15
    See taxes
    See also health
    See also insurance
homes, funeral, 167
Hot Line, 153 - 154, 158, 160, 178
housewives as home workers, 214
housework, 215

Hubbard, 28 - 29
HyperCard, 49, 114, 117, **118-119**
Hyperpad, **119**

I

IBM, 68, 71, 87, 94, 136
IBM clone, 37
IBM-PC, **95**, 101
IBM-PC, **95**
ice cream, 234
image
    corporate, 172
    professional, 161, 174, 226
    style and substance, 226
    See also business cards
    See also stationery
    See also telephone manners
ImageWriter, 129, 136
    See also printers
Indy car, 104
Info World, 91
insurance, 225-226
integrated packages
    Framework, 85
    PFS:First Choice, 85 - 86
    Symphony, 85
    Works, 85
Intel, 62
Intersecting Concepts, 120
Irwin, 124
ITT, 158

J

Jackson Hole, **221**
Jade, 124
JC Penney, 26
junk, storing, 19

K

Kaypro, 69, 71
    as CP/M computer, 120
Key Tronic, 68
keyboard
    sliding tray, 13, 29, 34, 41
    surface for, 19
    rack on monitor arm, 37
Kirk, Captain, 165
Krueger, 35, 45
Krueger Databoard
    See tables

L

L.L. Bean, 77, 80
Lands' End, 77
LapLink, 72
laptops, 71-72
laser printers, 138-144
    toner cartridges, 144
layouts, inefficient, 12
Leading Edge, 69
Ledu, 211
library, 220
light, arrangement of
    to suggest limits of space, 4
lighting
    as angles, 204
    See also artificial light
    designers, 203
    and glare, 204
    See also natural light
limits, financial and spatial, 2
lofts
    See nooks
loneliness, 218, 220
    as a little depressing, 220
    how to avoid, 220
    usually not crippling, 220
Lotus, 62, 84 - 85, 87, 94, 101 - 103, 111 - 112, 115, 117
love, childlike, **225**
    transcendence of, 223
luggables
    See portables
luminescence, 203
    See also lighting
Luxor, 27
Lyben, 232

M

Mace Gold, 89
Mace Utilities
    See Utilities
Mace, Paul, 124, 127
Macintosh, 37, 74-75, 121
Mack truck, 135
MacUser, 91
MacWeek, 91
MacWorld, 91
mail, outgoing, 230
mailbox, 163
mailroom clerk, none, 3
mailroom, none, 5
maintenance staff, none, 5

"The Man in the Iron Mask", 173
"Management Station One", 32
marketing ideas, **223**
martinis, three, 220
Mastersoft, 120
Meridian Technology, 110
mess, purposeful, 230
Microlytics, 117
Microrim, 87
Microsoft, 62, 85, 87, 93 - 94, 104, 121
Microstuf, 108
MicroSync, 151
Mr. Big, 154
Mitsubishi, 180
modems, 146-148, 160, 162
monitors, 13, 37
    Amdek 310, 66
    articulating arm for, 39
    CGA, avoid for words and numbers, 67
    EGA, 67
    Hercules compatible, 66
    mesh diffusion screen for, 208
    monochrome, 66
    multi-scan, 67
    on shelf above work surface, 39
    VGA, 67
    video card, 66
moonlighters, 217
Morrow, as CP/M computer, 120
Mountain, 124
MS-DOS, 104
multitasking, 121
Murata, 180

N

The National Association for the Cottage Industry, 224
natural light 204-206
Natural Microsystems, 172
Nautilus, 20
NEC, 71, 134, 179 - 180
neighborhoods
    residential, 222
Ness, Eliot, **221**
New York, 173, 183
The New York Times, 183
newspaper clippings, ancient, 44
noise, white, 214
nook, 5
nooks and crannies, 9-11
Northgate, **58**, 68 - 69, 80

Northstar, as CP/M computer, 120
Peter Norton Computing, 122
notebook, 231

O

office, paperless, 129
Office Solutions, Inc., 94
office supplies, buying, 232
Okidata, 134
Omnium Corporation, 26
1-2-3, 84, 87, 101, 102 - 104
on-line services, 95, 107
    BRS After Dark, 113, 115
    BRS, 113
    CompuServe, 107, 109, 111
    Delphi, 107, 109
    Dialog, 113
    Dow Jones News/Retrieval, 109
    GEnie, 107, 109
    Infoline, 113
    Knowledge Index, 113
    Lexis, 113
    MCI Mail, 109
    NewsNet, 113
    Nexis, 113
    Orbit, 113
    Prodigy, 107, 109
    Vu/Text, 113
    Wilsonline, 113
    See also electronic mail
Osborne, as CP/M computer, 120
outlets, locating, 200
overworking, 217-218

P

Pacific, 163
Panasonic, 149, 158, 180
panic, 215
    remedy for, 216
paper
    advantages over electronics, 231
    computer, 4
    don't have to use fanfold, 135
    fanfold, 134
    graph, 200
    legal-sized, 182
    plain, 176
    printer problems with, 134
    thermal, 175
    watermarked, 227
paper clips, 232

paper handling, 134
Paperback Software, 103, 106
papers, spreading out, 19
Paris, 173
"The Pathfinder", 173
patterns for working at home, 214
Paul Mace Software, 122
PC Caddy, 26
PC Connection, 80
PC Designs, 69
PC Magazine, 58, 87, 91, 100, 146, 172
PC Network, 79
PC Paintbrush, 181
PC Week, 91
PC World, 91, 114
PC-File, 97, 99
PC-SIG, 99
PC-Talk, 95
PC-Write, 97
personal habits, 19
Personal Publishing, 114
pesticides, 166
integrated packages, 85
phone jacks, locating, 200
PhoneMate, 172
photocopiers, 4
   See copiers, personal
piecework, 222
PIMs, 117-119
   Act!, 117
   Agenda, 117
   C.A.T., 118 - 119
   Focal Point, 117
   Grandview, 117
   Hyperworks Organizer, 117
   Info-XL, 117
Pitney-Bowes, 180
plans, thumbnail, 198
plant, to suggest limits of space, 4
Plantronics, 167 - 168
Plus Development, 64
portables, 71-73
post office, 220
PostScript, 140, 141-143
Pournelle, Jerry, 29, 33
PowerBase Systems, 106
pressure, 223
   deadline, 217
Prime Solutions, 123
"The Principle of Obsolescent Technology", 184
printer, 4, 227

printers, 134-136, 146
   See daisywheel printers
   See dot matrix printers
   See laser printers
priorities, 12, 18, 45
privacy
   spatial and acoustic, 4, 12
   symbolic, 4
ProComm, 97
program
   for designing home office, 188
   See also designing a home office
Psion *Organizer II*, 230 - 231
public domain software
   See shareware
Publish!, 114
Publisher's Paintbrush, 181
pushiness, 223

Q

Q&A Write, 94
Q-Modem, 97
Quicksoft, 94
quiet, 6
Quill, 43, 232

R

Radio Shack, 69, 158, 165, 168
Rbase, 87
realism, 18
receptionist, none, 3
"The Red Badge of Courage", 173
refrigerator, 207, 215
rehabbers, 10
Relay Communications, 108
remodel, 16
remote computing
   Carbon Copy Plus, 110
   Co-Compute, 110
   Co/Session, 110
   In-Sync, 110
   PC-Anywhere, 110
   PC-MacTerm, 110
resolve, steely, 214
rhythms
   home and work, 214
   and stress, 217
Ricoh, 149, 180 - 181
Roland Gans Software, 120
Rolodex™, 32, 34, 211
roommate, 6
Royal, 29

Rubbermaid, 42 - 43
rudeness, 223
rug, to suggest limits of space, 4
ruthless
    about time, 219
    with others, 221

S

Sauder Woodworking Co., 33, 42
scale, architect's, 200 - 201
scale drawings, 198, 200 - 202
scanners, 5, 148-149
Sculley, John, 48
Sears, 26
secretary, 229
secretary, none, 3
Selectric, 33
self-starter, 215
shareware, 95, 97, 99
Sharp, 71, 180 - 181
Sharp *Wizard*, 231
shoes, uncomfortable, 15
sketch, rough, 198, 200
skylight, 163
snacks, 215
soft fonts, 142
SoftLogic Solutions, 121
software
    buying, 127
    choosing programs, 86
    concern over cost, 84
    copy protection, 102, 103
    don't learn all at once, 91
    How tp Get Free Software, 99
    ignorance about, 85
    the package you know, 84
    piracy, 102 - 103
    when choices are cut and dried, 84
Software Publishing Corp., 85, 114
Software Ventures, 108
solitude, 218
Sony, 165
space limitations, 19
space, finding more, 197 - 198
special needs, 19
spreadsheets, 101
    1-2-3, 84, 87, 101, 102 - 104
    Excel, 104
    PC-Calc, 104
    PFS:First Choice module, 104
    Quattro, 103
    SuperCalc, 101
    VisiCalc, 101

VP-Planner, 102 - 103
Works module, 104
Springboard Software, 114
St. Martin's, 99
stackware
    See *HyperCard*
standards, wood stove emissions, 166
Stanley Powerlock II, 199
staples, 232
stationery, 4, 227
Stengel, Casey, 189
stereo, 6
sternness, 223
stress
    and rhythms of work, 217
    as freelancer's constant companion, 223
stringers, 38
style, 188-189
suit, three-piece, 15
supplies, 12
supply closet, none, 5
surge suppressors, 150
    See also electrical
sweatshop, 222
Symantec, 94, 106, 117, 122
sysops, 88
System Compatibility, 120

T

T/Maker, 94
table
    changing, 163
table, low
    to suggest limits of space, 4
tables, 35-36, 45
TADs
    See answering machines
Talking Technologies, Inc., 172
Tallgrass, 124
Tandon, 64, 69
Tandy, 69 - 70
tape
    strapping, 4
    20-foot builder's, 199
task lighting, 210-211
taxes, 224-225
teamwork, 219 - 220
technology, necessary, 5
telecommuter, 220
telephone manners
    answering machine OGM, 228

282   Index

telephone book, computerized, 153
telephones, 152-162, **155, 157**, 159-160, 164-165
   See also answering machines
   See also cordless phones
   See also fax machines
   See also headsets
   See also voice mail
TENpoint0, 117
tension, **223**
386 machines, 59
Tiffany "Do-All Series"
   See desks
Tiffany Stand and Furniture Company, 32, 34, 44
tiles, cork, **198**
time, wasted, **223**
Tokyo, 173
Toshiba, 71, 173, 180
Toshiba 1351, 79
traffic flow, 7
transition, from rest to labor, 214
transportables
   See portables
Traveling Software, 120 - 121
Triton Technologies, 110
Trojan Horses
   See viruses
TSRs
   Express, 115
   Focal Point, 117
   Gofer, 117
   Hotline, 116
   POP, 123
   QuickDex, 117
   Sidekick, 115 - 116
   Sidekick Plus, 116
TV, 6, 10
typefaces
   Garamond, 140
   Univers, 140
typesetter, 227

U

Uniden, 158, 165
United Parcel Service, 163
utilities
   Disk Technician, 123
   Htest-Hformat, 123
   The Mace Utilities, 122
   Mace Gold, 123
   The Norton Utilities, 122
   PC Tools, 122

Spinrite, 123
Symantec Utilities, 122

V

vacation, 215
Valor Software, 117
ventilation
   none, 13
Versa Tec Corporation, 31
Viking, 232
viruses, **88 - 89**
Visa card, 183
voice mail
   BigmOuth, 172
   The Complete Answering Machine, 172
   Watson, 172
voice technology, 231
Volkswagen, 104
Volkswriter Deluxe, 87

W

walking through
   to check office layout, 202
Walkman
   to obscure other noise, 215
wall cleats, 38
wall offices, 5 - 6
Walltrak Shelving Systems, 28
washing machine, 163, 207
West Laryngitis, 169
wetsuit, 12
will, iron, 214
Winchester drives
   See hard drives
windows, none, 13
"The Winner", 28 - 29
Word, 87, 114, 121
word processing software, 93-100
   Display Writer system, 94
   DisplayWrite, 94
   FullWrite Professional, 95 - 96
   MacWrite II, 94
   MacWrite, 94
   Manuscript, 94
   MindWrite, 95 - 96
   MultiMate, 94
   Nota Bene, 94
   Office Writer, 94
   PC-Write, 94
   PFS:First Choice, 94
   PFS:Professional Write, 94

Q&A Write, 94
Sprint, 94
Word, 93 - 94
WordPerfect, 87, 89 - 91, 93 - 94, 114, 120
WordStar, 87, 93, 120
WriteNow, 94
XyWrite, 93 - 94
WordPerfect Corp., 87
WordStar International, 87
work, rhythm of, 214
Work At Home Special Interest Group, 224
work surface, 13
Workbench, 26, 45
working at home, as old tradition, 214
worms
   See viruses
writer's block, 36
writing by hand, 19

X

Xerox, 112, 180, 183
XT clones, 53-56
XWord, 99
XyQuest, 86
XyWrite, 49, 86 - 87, 89 - 90, 112, 120 - 121

Y

yardwork, 215

Z

Zenith, 70 - 72
zoning approval, 17

A Semi-Technical Note

I wrote *The Home Office Book* using *XyWrite III Plus* on a Northgate IBM-AT clone. And I thought that would be the end of it.

Then I had a serious disagreement with my publisher that left me with a torn-up contract and a manuscript with nowhere to go.

In a moment of bravado, and to avoid starting all over again with the long production cycle of another publishing house, I decided to publish the book myself. In the process, I learned a lot and proved some serious points about home offices. There's a whole separate volume in that experience, but here is the basic technical information.

I used Xerox *Ventura Publisher 1.1* for layout and design, the basics of which I borrowed from Colin Fletcher's *The Complete Walker III*, a book I particularly admire and one which, along with Peter McWilliams's works on computers and word processing, inspired this project in the first place.

The book is set in Bitstream *Fontware* Garamond, which was output to a Hewlett-Packard LaserJet II for proofing and—on special Hammermill Laser Plus paper—for camera-ready type. Vanna Prince and Mel Mathewson's line art was photographically reduced to the appropriate size and stripped in by Ripinsky & Co. Production Services. The cover was printed by New England Book Components. The book was printed and bound by Maple-Vale.

And boy, doesn't that synopsis make things sound misleadingly smooth and easy! The result, though, wasn't just *The Home Office Book*, but a book truly published—from concept through mechanicals—in a home office.

....And A Few Words Of Thanks

I'm grateful to Paul Mace for letting me use the quotation on page 124.

Technically, I couldn't have pulled any of this off without the generous help of Gary Mancini, a good friend and born teacher who also happens to reside very near the cutting edge of computerized publishing technology.

Editorially, I got perceptive criticism and valuable advice (much of which I actually took) from another close friend, my former colleague at *Fine Homebuilding* and *Home*, Paul Spring, whom I regard as the best in the business. My father, Dick Alvarez, supplied the proof-reading skills that I for some reason didn't inherit. Thanks also to Barbara Snyder, John Benjamin, Mary Jane McClay, Bob Travers, Paul Hadzima, Roger Holmes, Tom Long, Jill Smith, Jane Gallagher, Diane Okrent, Aaron Sheldon, Deborah Cannarella, Betsy Amster, Rollin Riggs, Eric Kampmann, Elane Feldman, John Lawrence and Leah Chatinover. Needless to say, any errors between the covers of this finished product are mine, not those of my kind friends and colleagues.

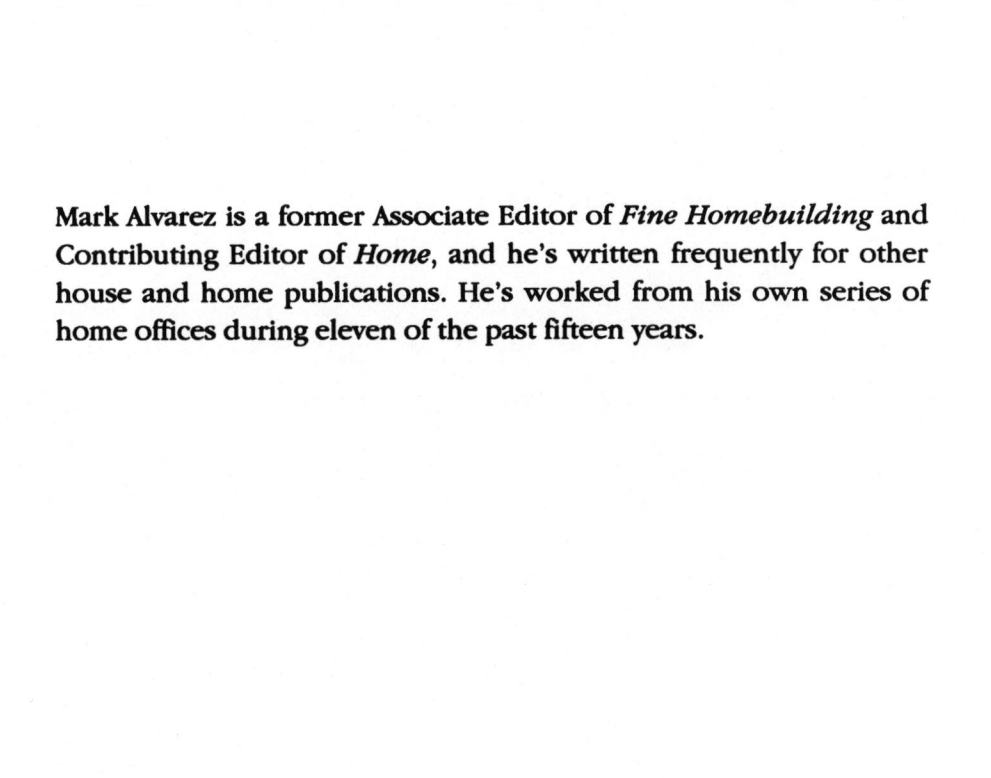

Mark Alvarez is a former Associate Editor of *Fine Homebuilding* and Contributing Editor of *Home*, and he's written frequently for other house and home publications. He's worked from his own series of home offices during eleven of the past fifteen years.

A-1